Adaptable Autocrats

Stanford Studies in Middle Eastern and Islamic Societies and Cultures

Adaptable Autocrats

REGIME POWER IN EGYPT AND SYRIA

Joshua Stacher

Stanford University Press
Stanford, California

Stanford University Press
Stanford, California

Printed in the United States of America on acid-free, archival-quality paper.

Library of Congress Cataloging-in-Publication Data

Stacher, Joshua, 1975- author.
  Adaptable autocrats : regime power in Egypt and Syria / Joshua Stacher.
    pages cm.--(Stanford studies in Middle Eastern and Islamic societies and cultures)
  Includes bibliographical references and index.
  ISBN 978-0-8047-8062-9 (cloth : alk. paper)--ISBN 978-0-8047-8063-6 (pbk. : alk. paper)
  1. Egypt--Politics and government--1981- 2. Syria--Politics and government--2000-
3. Dictatorship--Egypt. 4. Dictatorship--Syria. 5. Authoritarianism--Egypt. 6.
Authoritarianism--Syria. 7. Comparative government. I. Title. II. Series: Stanford studies in
Middle Eastern and Islamic societies and cultures.
  DT107.87.S73 2012
  956.7104'2--dc23   2012002768

Typeset by Bruce Lundquist in 10/14 Minion

To my parents, Kim and Marcia,
for giving me all the opportunities
anyone could ever have dreamed of

CONTENTS

ACKNOWLEDGMENTS

THIS BOOK IS THE PRODUCT of nearly a decade of research, writing, persistence, happiness, luck, and pain. Its completion would not have been possible without the generosity and love of so many friends and family members. While I am solely responsible for any errors that remain, I could not ask for a better set of friends and fellow journeyers. They not only helped me make a better book, they also made me a better person than had I been left to my own devices.

Firstly, I would like to thank Ray Hinnebusch for being a steady and thoughtful advisor while I was at the University of St. Andrews. His patience and care are impressive. I probably did not appreciate life in St. Andrews as much as I should have, but it was the perfect environment to design my research on Egypt and Syria.

My closest friends—academics and nonacademics—also taught me how to see the world from many different angles, which affected my research. Jason Brownlee and I have been close friends since first meeting in Cairo in 2002. In addition to sharing in each other's professional and personal milestones, Jason inspires me to keep pushing my intellectual boundaries. His sharp criticisms always make my work stronger. Samer Shehata also became a close friend in Cairo. He knows more about Egypt than I ever will. But, after each conversation, my research and ideas get more nuanced.

Story Monforte and I have literally traveled around the world together. He is my longest constant friend. His spontaneity and sense of humor have a way of breaking me out of my rigid routines. I am indebted to him and to the entire Monforte family for their generosity over the years. Ara Ayer is also a dear friend. A photographer by trade, Ara taught me how to capture the beauty of a moment and enjoy good jazz.

Of course, the debts to my many other friends and colleagues are as important. Unfortunately, there is not the space to detail their contributions. I will, however, make a point to tell them all how much their friendship, advice, and help over the years means to me. In alphabetical order: Abu Ala Madi, Adel Abd al-Moneim, Andrea Teti, Andrew Tabler, Anthony Shadid, Arang Keshavarzian, Ashraf Khalil, Bassam Haddad, Bill Noble, Bill Sullivan, Bob Dodge, Bob Springborg, Braulio Estrada, Bryan Spencer, Charles Antoine Allain, Charles Levinson, Chris Bruno, Chris Toensing, Chris Parker, Curt Ryan, Dan Murphy, Diane Singerman, Elijah Zarwan, Ellis Goldberg, Emad Shahin, Gasser Abd al-Razik, Greg Gause, Gwen Okruhlik, Haythem al-Malih, Hesham Sallam, Hossam al-Hamalawy, Hugh Roberts, Ibrahim Hamidi, Ihab Sakkout, Issandr El Amrani, Jailan Zayan, Jeannie Sowers, Jean-Marc Mojon, Jennifer Derr, Jillian Schwedler, Joe Evans, Joel and Mariam Beinin, Joel Gordon, Jonathan Noble, Kate Wahl, Khalid Fahmy, Lee Keath, Liam Stack, Lisa Anderson, Lisa Wedeen, Max Rodenbeck, Merhzad Boroujerdi, Michaelle Browers, Michele Angrist, Mohamad Habib, Mohamad Morsy, Nathan Brown, Nir Rosen, Paul Schemm, Pete and Jennie Moore, Raymond Baker, Sami Zemni, Sami Zubaida, Scott Bortot, Steve Lux, Steve Negus, Steven Heydemann, Sumita Pahwa, Tamir Moustafa, Tarek Masoud, Ted Swedenburg, Toby Jones, Tom Perry, Ursula Lindsey, Vickie Langohr, Yael Lempert, Yoav Di-Capua, and Zach Lockman. Some of my comrades have fallen during the time it took to write this book. In particular, I fondly remember Marsha Posusney and Mohamad al-Sayyid Said.

The colleagues in my department at Kent State have created a hospitable place to be productive and aim high. I feel very lucky to work with them all. In particular, Pat Coy and Mike Ensley deserve lots of credit. They are real confidents, and they educate me daily.

Life is most exciting because of the various roads we get to travel. With a few, I have actually covered some of this terrain with them on foot. I would like to thank my running buddies who have and continue to brave all types of weather, surfaces, and distances. In particular, Rob Lisy, Lloyd Thomas, Vince Rucci and the rest of my friends from Vertical Runner that routinely scale the hills, explore the trails, and pound the asphalt with me in the Cuyahoga Valley National Park. Running the Buckeye Trail and along the banks of the Burning Crooked River never gets old.

Last but certainly not least: if I have learned anything through my odyssey, it is the importance of family. In this respect, I have hit the jackpot. I'd like to thank my grandmother, June Stacher. Also, Audrey Foutz has always played the role of a stereotypical grandmother. She gives me nothing but support (and cookies) all the time. While I miss my late grandfather, I think about Larry

Foutz more than he would have ever imagined during his life. Their individual and combined influence has been nothing but positive on me.

My sister, Dex, and her husband, Josh, are always supportive of my exploits. I particularly thank Dex for friendship and honesty. Dex and Josh also have given me two wonderful nephews, August and Jonah, who will spend the rest of my life being corrupted by their uncle.

More than two years ago, Jasna Rados waltzed into my life and changed everything. I thank her for her love, enthusiasm, caring, and persistence. Living with a difficult academic who runs every day cannot be easy. But she manages with grace. Her encouragement over the last stretch when I was finishing this book was beyond commendable. Jasna always helps me realize my goals. Similarly, her family has taken me in as if I have been around forever. Thanks to Franjo, Janja, Sanja, and Anto Rados, as well as David, Sandra, Oksana, and Ekaterina Colombo. Sandra's editorial eye before this book went to the publisher was especially helpful.

Kimmy Stacher deserves thanks just for being the person she is. Although a great distance separates us most of the year, the thought of her lightens up my days. I live to spend time with her, and my heart breaks every time we part. I love watching her grow up even though it is intimidating to have someone that smart be able to stop me with her smile.

My mom and dad get the last word. Kim and Marcia Stacher have been the most influential and supportive forces in my life. They worked tirelessly and provided me with every opportunity I ever wanted. Their only request was to think bigger, be more creative, and pursue my dreams with greater passion. This book is the end of a long chapter of my life. Of all the people in my world, they are most responsible. I dedicate this to them. I love you both very much.

ABBREVIATIONS AND ACRONYMS

ASU	Arab Socialist Union
CIHRS	Cairo Institute for Human Rights Studies
CPA	Coalition Provisional Authority
CSF	Central Security Forces
EOHR	Egyptian Organization for Human Rights
FIRDOS	Fund for Integrated Rural Development of Syria
GONGO	Government Operated Nongovernmental Organization
HPC	Higher Policies Council
HRAS	Human Rights Association in Syria
ICG	International Crisis Group
IMF	International Monetary Fund
LE	Egyptian pound (currency)
MAWRED	Modernizing and Activating Women's Role in Economic Development
MB	Muslim Brothers
MEPI	Middle East Partnership Initiative
MP	Members of Parliament
NATO	North Atlantic Treaty Organization
NCHR	National Council for Human Rights
NDP	National Democratic Party
NGO	Nongovernmental Organization
NWC	National Women's Council
PLO	Palestinian Liberation Organization
PNF	Progressive National Front
PS	Policies Secretariat

RC	Regional Command
SCAF	Supreme Council of the Armed Forces
SCC	Supreme Constitutional Court
SCS	Syrian Computer Society
SYEA	Syrian Young Entrepreneurs Association
UAR	United Arab Republic
UNSC	United Nations Security Council
USAID	United States Agency for International Development

Adaptable Autocrats

INTRODUCTION
Changing to Stay the Same

AS POLITICAL REVOLUTION IMPERILED HIS ELITE STATUS, the Count in Giuseppi Tomasi di Lampedusa's *The Leopard* declared, "Unless we ourselves take a hand now, they'll [nationalists] foist a republic on us. If we want things to stay as they are, things will have to change."[1] One can envision many Arab elites in the various corridors of power uttering similar statements during the 2011 uprisings in the Middle East. Egged on by decades of unbridled repression, awash with crushing tsunami-like waves of neoliberal economic adjustments, and frustrated witnesses to unaccountable rulers, many citizens revolted in the largest regional *Intifada* (uprising) in the post–World War II period. Protests—in varying intensities and durations—began in December 2010 and took place throughout 2011 in Tunisia, Egypt, Bahrain, Algeria, Jordan, Libya, Yemen, Morocco, Palestine, Iraq, Oman, and Syria. Although the general conditions that ignited the revolts transcended the various countries' borders, the protesters lodged country-specific grievances at ruling elites, who had treated their citizens with disdain for years.

By mid-January 2011, a new era of popular politics seemed to be tearing down the older political order. Shortly after Tunisia's dictator of twenty-three years, Zayn al-Abidine Ben Ali, fled to Saudi Arabia on January 14, analysts debated whether Tunisia would be an isolated case or the start of a larger regional movement for change. Some regional specialists suggested no. As one predicted shortly after Ben Ali's fall, "Arab regimes have often been criticized as sclerotic and archaic; they are neither. Over the past two decades, they have confronted and overcome a wide range of challenges that have caused authoritarian governments to collapse in many other world regions. Arab regimes have demonstrated their resilience in the past, and they continue to do so in the wake of the Tunisian uprising."[2] People in the region interpreted Ben Ali's departure differently. Sensing a critical moment was underway, activists that had been—at times—comically unsuccessful at organizing against well-armed security apparatuses went on the

1

offensive. Networks of dissent multiplied. Street politics made dissenting voices heard as activists publicized their achievements on social-networking sites. These venues, of course, were literally the only refuges left to express dissent. The ruling elites—symbolized by the leaders of these states—had grown so effective at "authoritarian learning" that their decrees overrode many of the institutional attempts that had demanded political change for decades.[3] Yet, in doing so, these rulers had poured gasoline on their societies for a long time. The events in Tunisia lit the spark for people to take the initiative from their regimes. It was an instance of regional diffusion par excellence.[4]

Egypt erupted eleven days after Ben Ali left Tunisia. The protests, which lasted eighteen days, culminated in Egyptians physically defeating the Interior Ministry's coercive agents and occupying Tahrir Square before the Supreme Council of the Armed Forces forced Mubarak to cede the presidency on February 11.[5] Tunisia was essential. Without it, Egypt's half-revolution, half-military intercession would likely not have happened. But Egypt—given it's the region's most populated country, one of the most dependent on the United States, and a harbinger for the region's other states—transformed Tunisia's sizable tremor into a full-scale earthquake. With two "successful revolutions" on the books,[6] the region's autocrats were on notice. Protests began in Algeria and Jordan before fizzling out as Bahrain and Yemen became the epicenter of the region's uprisings. Libya and Syria soon followed down the path of protests.

While some scholars lamented the inability of Middle East scholars to predict these uprisings,[7] multiple debates emerged because of them. Yet, the outcomes quickly outpaced social science theories. While many scholars and analysts attempted to locate the underlying causes for the uprisings, they failed to produce many common linkages. For example, some focused on the US's differing policy approaches vis-à-vis in the countries experiencing protests.[8] Others focused on the socially unraveling character of neoliberal economic policies,[9] or whether a country's elites possess significant rents, such as oil, to offset political and economic grievances with material incentives.[10] Still others made the case that monarchies would fare better than republics.[11] Yet, the diversity of cases and unsettled outcomes defied a single explanation. Indeed, from the seemingly stalled transitions in Egypt and Tunisia, a stalemate in Yemen, brutal multinational repression in Bahrain, extensive military crackdowns in Syria, to a NATO-enabled war in Libya, the outcomes varied tremendously.

This is not to argue that the reasons mentioned above played no role. To make that case is to disregard the gross socioeconomic inequalities that exist in the region. It also discounts how practices of the ruling regimes and distorted legal documents advantage the incumbents. The ways in which the uprisings unfolded indicates that access to money to offset neoliberal social pain was important. Similarly, few could deny the American role in securitizing and militarizing the Middle East contributed to a failure to build democratic capacity since the 1970s.

Many prominent academics working in Middle East studies suggested that the larger commonality was one of dignity. Specifically, the origins of the uprisings were about the individual dignity of citizens trying to reclaim their countries from unaccountable ruling elites. The uprisings were also about dignity in the collective national and supranational identities of the Arab world.[12] While there is undoubtedly truth here, and ample anecdotal examples exist as evidence, it remains problematic as a concept of study.

Another way to study the uprisings relates to their outcomes. This also presents problems. By accepting that successful uprisings were ones that removed long-serving autocrats, then the protest movements that failed to achieve this arbitrary measure produced a mixed or failed result. The natural question to reflect on becomes why some of these uprisings succeeded and others failed. Yet, this makes complicated assumptions that are not truly reflective of success or failure. It also lessens what Syrians or Bahrainis, who braved military assaults and tank offensives, contested while overglorifying the effect of removing Ben Ali or Mubarak. After all, in examining the transitions, the social class structures in Tunisia and Egypt not only remain intact but also have been replicated with minimal disruption.[13] Changing the presidents in these states proved to be the easy part compared to revolutionizing the deeper social cleavages and structures. Also, because agents from the previous regime were responsible for ousting the presidents and shaving the ruling coalition, full regime changes did not actually transpire in Tunisia and Egypt. Hence, there was more continuity than change after the region's uprisings. Structural changes to the ruling coalition have undoubtedly occurred, but the problematic transitions reveal that the elites are trying to reconstitute themselves.[14]

If a large degree of continuity emerged out of the change in the "successful" cases, then the violence deployed to keep a regime in place more plainly reveals the lack of change in those cases. In addition to Bahrain and Libya, Syria's prolonged crackdown registers as one of the nastiest of the uprisings. Protests started in the southern border town of Dera'a. They spread sporadically around the country's cities. While there were moments of joint action, the protests never took a deep hold in either of the country's two largest cities. For its part, the regime barely balked. The tacit cross-sectarian political and economic agree-ment held throughout the uprising as President Bashar al-Asad made belated concessions such as lifting martial law. When such overtures failed to peel away dissent, the armed forces intervened against the protesters in order to protect the regime. Tanks advanced on Dera'a and shelled buildings in Homs. Soldiers conducted house-to-house searches to root out protest organizers, their fami-lies, and uninvolved bystanders as snipers took aim from the roofs of buildings. As the military's operations continued, more than five thousand were killed and thousands others imprisoned. The military ended up being the final arbitrator in Syria's uprising, just as the militaries resolved Tunisia and Egypt's crises. Yet, Syria's inability to avoid using lethal force in comparison to the other cases is suggestive. Why, then, did Egypt and Tunisia experience largely peaceful transi-tions compared to the violence unleashed in Syria?[15]

To develop this notion, this book compares Egypt and Syria to explain why Egypt was capable of achieving a quick and seemingly smooth transition of power in its ruling coalition while Syria experienced a more violent outcome. In both instances, the regimes survive albeit with different social power and outreach capacities. Egypt's state after Mubarak was qualitatively stronger de-spite its weaknesses compared to that of the Syrian state after the protests were crushed there. Yet, in the Egyptian case long-time leader Hosni Mubarak re-linquished the presidency and the ruling coalition was altered while Syria's al-Asad and his coalition remain in place for the time being. What explains the different paths that each political system traveled only to arrive at the similar outcome of regime continuity?

The argument of this book is that the variance of autocratic power deter-mines how Egypt and Syria experienced their uprisings. Specifically, by exam-ining how power is structured and operates, we better understand the seeming swiftness of Egypt's transition contrasted to Syria's more violent experience. Egyptian elites maintained centralized authority while Syrian power was de-centralized heading into and emerging out of their uprisings. To explain this difference, I examine the pre-2011 period because it reveals how executive elites in each political system structured and could use power. Because authority is centralized in Egypt, it could produce a swift transition of the ruling coalition. Syria's decentralized political system led to a protracted conflict between state elites and society as well as the regime's more violent response.

It should not be surprising that Egypt and Syria had vastly different experi-ences during their uprisings in 2011. Lisa Anderson penned a plausible rationale for the difference. Referencing Tunisia, Egypt, and Libya, she argued, "The revolutions . . . reflected divergent economic grievances and social dynamics—legacies of their diverse encounters with modern Europe and decades under unique regimes."[16] Much the same can be said of other cases that Anderson did not include such as Syria. Bassam Haddad underscored cogent points about Syria's experience.[17] Egypt and Syria should not have been expected to conduct similar swift transitions or similar violent responses by the state. Yet, accounting for how authority is structured and operates in each political system sheds light on the variance in the two states. This is expressly seen in how power operated prior to the uprisings. The next section's purpose is to provide representations of Egypt and Syria's uprisings as a unifying point of comparison before turning to a wider discussion of how power is structured and operates in the two countries.

THE UPRISING IN EGYPT

Since the 1952 revolution in Egypt, its senior military officers have not confined their activities exclusively to the barracks. The republic's first four presidents (r. 1953–2011) had a military pedigree. The institution served as the regime's spine.[18] Until the fall of Mubarak, generals accounted for a high majority of all of the president's appointments as Egypt's provincial governors.[19] The military is the largest landowner and has extensive business and commercial interests. The institution's members and former officers enjoy social privileges that include everything from access to private hotels and sporting clubs to discounted grocery stores. The armed services, which portray themselves to be the republic's stabilizing guardian, also garner much social popularity and respect. Despite such attributes, the institution had been in political and economic decline since the 1970s.

The trend is unmistakable. Gamal 'Abd al-Nasser (r. 1954–70) appointed nearly one-third of all of his ministerial positions from the military. Raymond Baker went so far as to say that the "army came to represent a personnel pool for far reaching extramilitary tasks."[20] This declined tremendously during Sadat's era (1970–81) when the military leadership was redisciplined and cowed under presidential authority. Sadat's realignment with the United States also ushered in a period of neoliberal economic policies. The creation and expansion of a dependent business class began gnawing at some of the military's business stakes around the country.

Hosni Mubarak (r. 1981–2011) adopted and developed his predecessor's model. Only 8 percent of Mubarak's ministerial appointments hailed from the military's ranks.[21] Increasing neoliberalism in the form of an IMF Structural Adjustment Program further eroded the military's political and economic positions. While still powerful, the armed forces were not what they had been when their leaders controlled the state's commanding heights during Nasser's presidency.

The military's relevance also declined because of the domestic situation. Mubarak waged a war against a militant Islamist insurgency during the 1990s.[22] Given the demands of the internal security threat, the Interior Ministry's prominence and budget grew disproportionately to the military during the 1990s. Ellis Goldberg remarked, "As the government became dependent on an expanded domestic police force, the army was reduced in size and importance. Over time, the police and the Ministry of the Interior supplanted the armed forces and Ministry of Defense as the keystone of the regime."[23] The final twist in the military's odyssey of decline coincided with the rise of President Mubarak's son, Gamal, who emerged as the seeming heir apparent.[24]

Despite the Mubaraks' frequent public denials that the son had presidential ambitions, the Gamal Mubarak succession project took place for more than a decade and became a source of resentment and embarrassment for many Egyptians. Gamal Mubarak's rise also accompanied an all-out assault of neoliberal economic adjustment that introduced Egyptians to unprecedented social hardship and economic dislocation. Seemingly with President Mubarak's approval, the advance of neoliberalism went unchecked beginning with the 2004 cabinet reshuffle. Ministers such as Ahmad Nazif, Yousif Botros-Ghali, Rachid Mohamad Rachid, and Mahmoud Mohy al-Din conditioned an environment where the state's business cronies thrived. Some, such as former steel-magnate Ahmad 'Ezz, merged their business empires with the ruling party by becoming parliamentarians. This deepening neoliberalism affected the military's business ventures because it introduced new competitors to its previously near-monopolistic ventures. Forcing the military to share its spoils was unpopular, and the threat of a Gamal Mubarak presidency proved highly contentious among the most senior generals as Mubarak aged and succession loomed.[25]

International financial institutions lauded Egypt's neoliberal economic program with its average growth topping out at near or over 7 percent between 2005–8.[26] Yet, beneath the international accolades lay a country weighed under by a deteriorating infrastructure, abject poverty, and a dwindling social safety net. Even the US Embassy recorded the widening economic disparities in dispatches back to Washington. As Ambassador Margaret Scobey argued, "Economic reform has been a success story, although Egypt still suffers from widespread and so far irremediable poverty affecting upwards of 35–40% of the population."[27] The rising inequalities increasingly marginalized the military because the internal security services and riot police (Central Security Forces) required even more resources in order to put down the political and economic collective action that Egypt witnessed during the 2000s.

The emergence of the Egyptian Movement for Change, or Kifaya,[28] along with the most intense period of industrial strikes in Egypt's history required domestic security forces to constantly suppress dissent (and keep it from spreading).[29] Given the number of strikes, this was difficult. Between 2004–8, when the Nazif government economic reforms project was at its apex, more than 1.7 million Egyptians participated in more than nineteen hundred strikes.[30] Dina Shehata noted that there were more than seven hundred strikes during 2010 alone.[31] Consequently, the security services experienced a boom period. By the late 2000s, Egypt's internal security services outnumbered the active military personnel by a factor of three-to-one with the security services reaching an astounding 1.5 million.[32] The Interior Ministry's tentacle-like reach for hegemony was insatiable as its budget increased each year.[33] Interior Minister Habib al-'Adly asked for additional resources just for crowd control and demonstrations.[34] Egypt began to look less like a "military state" and more like "state security state." Coupled with the smaller urban protests, which generally emphasized political rather than economic rights, Egypt was ripe for continued protests. As 2011 dawned, Egypt's military seemed poised for further decline as these existing trends continued unabated.

Meanwhile it was politics as usual. The parliamentary elections of late 2010 produced the most rigged contests of the Mubarak era. With a 93.3 percent majority in parliament, the ruling National Democratic Party seemed poised to govern forever. President Mubarak also seemed to believe in his own invincibility. The opposition attempted to organize a mock parliament so as to symbolically ignore the actual assembly after the elections. When discussing the opposition's initiative, Mubarak dismissively joked, "Let them have fun."[35] All the while the Gamal Mubarak succession plan seemed inevitable irrespective of the political and economic collective action.

With this scene set, no one foresaw what happened on January 25. While the opposition organized, the security prepared for demonstrations with meticulous care and vigilance.[36] Egyptians had been politicized, and they were not helpless recipients of a deteriorating standard of living and rising prices. Most

observers—including the Mubarak security apparatus and protest planners—
suspected that the demonstrations scheduled for "Police Day" would look like
the hundreds of protests that preceded it. Yet, with Tunisia in the rearview mir-
ror, Egyptians outsmarted, outflanked, out fought, and persistently poked holes
in the edifice of a seemingly unbeatable regime. As Mona El-Ghobashy elo-
quently put it, "In hindsight, it is simple to pick out the vulnerabilities of the
Mubarak regime and arrange them in a neat list as the ingredients of break-
down. But that retrospective temptation misses the essential point: Egyptians
overthrew a strong regime."[37] The arc, twists, and turns behind the eighteen
days it took for the uprising to remove its president was multilayered. Rather
than fixate on the details, it is perhaps more important to focus on some key
events in order to explain the uprising's larger structural effects.

The protesters succeeded initially because they outsmarted the security services on the initial day of protest. Orchestrating twenty-one separate and small
demonstrations across the capital, the plan was to converge on Cairo's central
nervous system—Tahrir Square.[38] For the first four days, the Interior Ministry detained organizers and protesters while the Central Security Forces (CSF)
fired innumerable tear-gas canisters, rubber bullets, and buckshot pellets into
crowds. As Cairenes rose up, their fellow citizens in Suez and Alexandria among
other locales around the country joined in the protests. The first day was a success, but it took an additional three days for the protesters to defeat the security forces. On Friday January 28, "The Day of Rage," protesters stormed the
Qasr al-Nil Bridge, overwhelmed the security personnel, and began occupying
Tahrir Square. After the police, state security, and riot police disappeared, the
military deployed armored vehicles, tanks, and soldiers around the capital. The
protesters had rocked Mubarak's regime to its core.

The NDP, which Gamal Mubarak spent ten years trying to transform into a
modern political party, also fell in those first four days. Although the party met
on January 26 to discuss the response to the protests, former party leader Mohamad Kamal said he did not hear from the party again for the remainder of the
uprising. As he stated, "No one from the party called me after those meetings.
I watched it [the protests] on TV."[39] The party simply disintegrated. The confusion was of epic proportions. 'Ali al-Din Hilal, another former party leader,
explained that relieving the membership secretary, Ahmad 'Ezz, from duty was
one of the most crucial mistakes. 'Ezz was one of the first sacrificial lambs that
Mubarak offered up to the crowds because of the population's disdain of him
as a leading crony capitalist. Yet, when 'Ezz left, he took more than four hun-

dred names and contacts of party organizers from across the country. Even had it wished to countermobilize, the party cut its own organizing arm off.[40]

Countermobilize or not, the damage was done because protesters broke in and razed the party's headquarters next to Tahrir Square. The building was torched, which symbolically killed it off. With the Interior Ministry no longer relevant, Gamal Mubarak's succession plans aborted, and the party's headquarters on fire, the president began a series of concessions. He first conducted a cabinet shuffle that changed the ruling coalition to placate the protesters. The cabinet's neoliberal economic team was fired, ending the Gamal Mubarak era formally. Mubarak elevated intelligence chief Omar Suleiman to the vice presidency, marking the first time he had appointed a VP in his twenty-nine-year tenure. While this appointment may have worked years ago, it proved to be too little, too late. Without a functioning security apparatus or ruling party, the only figures left to resolve the crisis were Mubarak, his inner circle, and the military. The protesters in Tahrir continued as demands coalesced around one that was nonnegotiable: the resignation of Hosni Mubarak.

By the night of February 1, Mubarak understood that the situation had worsened. He made his second appearance and smugly suggested that he never intended to remain president for the rest of his life. He pledged not to run for a seventh term in September's presidential election. He also promised to die on Egyptian soil as a private citizen. Many felt that Mubarak had outflanked his opposition. The silent majority of Egyptians, who spent the uprising in their homes, did not want to see the president, who they have known the longest, succumb to a humiliating end. Yet, as night turned to dawn, a troubling development occurred. Bands of armed thugs (*baltagaya*), who were probably Interior Ministry personnel and mercenaries paid by NDP supporters, gathered next to the entrances and exits of Tahrir. While the Mubarak clique made numerous mistakes during its last days in power, this proved to be the final dagger in its chest.

The following day produced some of the most deplorable images of the uprising. Men riding camels and horses stormed Tahrir and beat protesters with whips. In what has become known as "the Battle of the Camel," protesters—led by the Muslim Brothers—held off the thugs as vicious street battles lasted more than sixteen hours. The so-called neutral military stood by idly as witnesses to the violence. While the Muslim Brothers did not organizationally commit to the protests until January 28, they earned their mettle by teaching non-Brother protesters how to fight efficiently, treat the wounded, and keep a steady supply chain of rocks stocked and ready for defense. The regime's decision to, at least, not object to the use of force against protesters and journalists swung the momentum back toward the protesters. Everyone began to sense the end of Mubarak's reign might be near.

Omar Suleiman, the new vice president, ran the country for the rest of the Mubarak tenure. He fielded calls from foreign governments,[41] initiated an attempt to negotiate with the opposition, and promised reforms. Yet, he also displayed many of the traits that made Mubarak so supremely despised. Particularly, he called for the protesters to return home, or he would call their fathers and grandfathers to get them to go home. Fed up with patronizing statements, the protesters' ire had a new target.

Mubarak made one final case for prolonging his presidency. The problem was that his last address came after news media outlets and others indicated that he intended to step down. When the Supreme Council of the Armed Forces (SCAF) issued its first communiqué, many felt that it was a done deal. The crowd's elation turned to anger when Mubarak failed to resign during his speech on February 10. Protesters marched to the Radio and TV Building as well as the presidential palace before a sheepish-looking Suleiman, who had a military officer standing behind his left shoulder, announced that Mubarak had officially stepped down. The SCAF has run the country since February 11. They worked closely with the caretaker government headed by former NDP member Essam Sharaf, conducted a popular referendum, announced new constitutional changes, and set dates for parliamentary elections.

The importance of these events cannot be overstated. Egyptians grabbed the initiative from a regime that had controlled, repressed, and cowed them for far too long. The Nasser, Sadat, and Mubarak regimes promulgated laws and constitutional amendments that disempowered them. Sadat and Mubarak also upheld unpopular foreign policies that most Egyptians opposed vehemently. Their ability to prevent Gamal Mubarak's hereditary succession, force the state to drop its neoliberal economic team, sack the former spymaster after only thirteen days as vice president, and remove a dictator that governed them for nearly thirty years were not small feats. They deserve to be celebrated. Furthermore, the people have been able to maintain the initiative by overseeing the resignation of Ahmad Shafiq as prime minister, storming of the State Security Headquarters in Cairo's Nasr City, and forcing the detention and trial of the Mubaraks. Coupled with the Supreme Council's corruption campaign against former regime agents, Egypt appears to have been drastically changed. Most of the protesters, as well as observers, refer to the events as "a revolution," which suggests that a regime change has taken place. The military's choice to respect the demonstrators' will by ushering Mubarak toward retirement as well as its decision not to fire on protesters reaffirm the institution's popular place in the citizenry's collective imagination.

There is, however, an alternative understanding to what occurred in Egypt. The country's military played a major role during the uprising. Without an intervention that ousted one of its own, it would have been unlikely that Mubarak would have given up the presidency. Equally perplexing regarding the military's role is how they treated the protesters. In some instances there is evidence of soldiers fraternizing with the protesters as generals stood on tanks with megaphones to profess their solidarity. This led many pundits and the press to label the military's unwillingness to use violence as a sign of neutrality.[42] Yet, the soldiers stood idly by as thugs attacked the protesters, which led to injuries and deaths and which did not suggest neutrality. By doing little or nothing, the military sided with the incumbent. There are excellent reasons why they should not have fired their weapons. The military, by virtue of being in the streets, had outlasted the security services, so their competitor had vanished. Given its generals were close to the seat of power, the military was also in an advantageous position to unseat and remove the neoliberal economic team. By helping shave the ruling coalition of crony capitalists and redisciplining the Interior Ministry under their control, it was politically unwise to risk their reputation by using force given their all-or-nothing ability for crowd control. Similarly, with its opponents and competition removed, the military's economic stake was set to increase in a post-Mubarak Egypt. Since they would be the guardians of the transition, its leaders would be in a prime position to control the flow and direction of any subsequent corruption campaign. Hence, it created a situation where their old colleagues turned into golden chips that could be bargained and given away to counteract the protesters' resilience. Not only did this return the military to its former governing glory, but it also provided the appearance of the military nobly steering the country out of crisis.

While there are questions about the type of transition the Supreme Council wishes to impart as well as its real intentions, these are mute in comparison to the type of uprising Egypt experienced in 2011. Prior to the January 25 uprising, power was highly centralized in Egypt's political system. The presidency, which includes its key officials and the state institutions they oversee, exercised near monopolistic control over the ruling party, the security services, the bureaucracy, and the military. Because of Mubarak's power of appointment, Egypt's centralized system facilitated the control of (not dialogue between) the regime's constituent parts. While it is surprising that the regime's coercive elements were so roundly defeated as the party disintegrated into an abyss of disorganization, it was not shocking to discover that transfer of power came down to a handful of men. Without popular pressure, such an outcome would have been unnecessary. Yet, popular pressure without the actions of the generals would have likely produced a stalemate, as the world witnessed in Yemen.[43]

Since Nasser's presidency, centralized executive rule has been the norm in Egypt. Sadat strengthened this trend by creating a presidential office that shared little power with other state institutions. While Sadat did not govern alone, he made the presidency an office without peer. Mubarak inherited Sadat's engineered creation and doubled down by reinforcing the presidency's hierarchical command over the state's institutions. The bodies were hollowed out and existed to implement the presidential consensus in a top-down fashion. Egypt's state was strong and frequently weathered active contestation from a fragmented society below. Given that political power had a tradition of being centralized, which is buoyed by a homogeneous society and rigid class structure, Egypt's generals on the SCAF orchestrated the uprising's endgame by making the council the executive. While the protesters continued to maintain the initiative after Mubarak's forced departure, the centralized power that entered the crisis largely emerged from it. This feature of centralized authority can in large part explain why the country experienced a swift and relatively smooth changeover into the post-Mubarak period.

THE UPRISING IN SYRIA

Syria has rarely experienced the luxury of centralized rule. Syria's political elites have overseen one of the most volatile states in the region. Some academics claim that Syria experienced fifteen successful coups d'etat between 1949–70.[44] Historically, elites competed with internal and external threats during the Pan-Arab period,[45] and the country teetered on the brink of a civil war between 1976–84.[46] Hafiz al-Asad is credited with bringing a modicum of stability to Syria despite his regime's willingness to resort to violence to hold the weak state and heterogeneous polity together. In the words of Flynt Leverett, a senior fellow at the New America Foundation, Asad made a "semi-state into a veritable model of authoritarian stability."[47] However, rather than reduce politics to an individual president's personality, deeper structural relationships produced this stability. Hafiz al-Asad's durability as leader resulted from his lack of ideological rigidity and his decision not to construct a highly centralized system. Rather, he was pragmatic and built a regime on various pillars on which to help insulate the elites from further political fragmentation. Syrian political power empowered elites in state institutions giving the cross-sectarian benefactors a stake in the continuity of the regime. He took the mosaic parts of society and bound them together before expanding the regime outwardly into society, particularly into the rural areas. Asad's ability to make deals allowed the political system to rest on key pillars such as the military, ruling party, and security services. This imparted a degree of autonomy for elites in those institutions and gave them a say in the ruling coalition's policies. While a decentralized system suggests more participatory politics, it instead was a product of necessity. Such a design reveals the weakness of the state. Such weakness dictated Asad's style rather than him being able to craft a regime that asymmetrically favored his office above all others.

When Asad died after nearly thirty years in power, his son Bashar became the next president. Many academics, such as Eyal Zisser, felt this was the ultimate manifestation of centralized and personalized authoritarian rule.[48] Yet, the hereditary succession of Bashar al-Asad does not prove this point. In addition to contradictions in the predominant interpretations of Syria's hereditary transfer of leadership, ample evidence unmasks a decentralized authoritarian political system at work. This is because elites cooperating across institutional lines collectively decided and implemented their will—as opposed to the reported wishes of a dead autocrat.[49] Hence, the crucial difference between governance in Egypt and Syria can be understood in the varying way that state power operates. In this respect, a Syrian president, who operates in a decentralized system, simply could not imagine the executive autonomy that Egypt's centralized political atmosphere affords.

In addition to its decentralized political establishment, Syria is unique from Egypt in other ways. Syrian society is significantly less practiced at protesting and demonstrating. Civil society, and particularly organizations that focus on human and political rights, is not nearly as expansive, varied, or entrenched. This is mainly due to the severe restrictions and repression civil society organizers routinely experience as opposed to apathy of Syrians. By examining state-society relations after Bashar al-Asad became president, we gain the clarity of the context driving its 2011 uprising.

Many anticipated that Bashar al-Asad's education, cosmopolitan experiences abroad, and interest in information technology would usher in a period of political and economic liberalization after he assumed the presidency in 2000.[50] This was particularly heightened during his inauguration speech in which he spoke about democracy and impending reforms. He developed a social base almost immediately. Yet, these elevated hopes were dashed as time passed. Eager to test their freedoms in a "new" Syria, civil society activists initiated salons and increased activities that led to the "Damascus Spring" in 2000 and 2001. Encouraged by the regime's release of political prisoners and increased space, activists led by Jamal Al-Atassi, Riyad Saif, and Michel Kilo searched for the regime's red lines. By mid-2001, as Alan George has shown,[51] the activists found them.

The competing elites around Asad from the security services, military, and the ruling B'ath Party forced an abrupt end to the nascent experiment. The subsequent crackdown included the arrests of two elected parliamentarians, Riyad Saif and Ma'mun Homsi, as well as other activists such as Riad al-Turk, 'Aref Dalila, Walid al-Bunni, Kamal al-Labwani, and others. All were convicted in Supreme State Security Courts and given sentences between two and ten years in prison. As the experiment ended, it coincided with the reassertion of many of the elites cultivated and developed by Bashar's father.

Many of these so-called old-guard elites came to dominate the early years of Bashar al-Asad's presidency. Indeed, as will be discussed in later chapters, it was not uncommon for people to refer to politics during this period as having "centers of power."[52] This period underscored the structural weakness of the presidency as well as the flow of power among the elites. It was not simply a story of an unconsolidated leader. After all, Bashar al-Asad did not remain a puppet in the hands of his competing elites. Though attempts failed to outflank his opponents early in his presidency, the assassination of the former Lebanese prime minister, Rafiq al-Hariri, in February 2005 changed this dynamic. Despite unsubtle statements by intergovernmental agencies that suspect his clique of having connections to Hariri's murder,[53] Asad assumed full command of the political system in June 2005. He replaced or retired many of the heads of the country's various security services as well as longtime B'athist leaders. Some, including longtime vice president 'Abd al-Halim Khaddam, escaped into exile. All of the replacements were Bashar al-Asad's men.

Yet, despite the reconfiguration, Asad did not appear to become more greatly endowed with autonomous power. As the new appointees took over their positions, the political system still maintained its decentralized character. Regime consensus never resorted to the level of simply being executive fiat. The informal process of consultation and agreements before a policy is made between the regime's various corporatist wings remained intact.

On the eve of the revolt in Tunisia, Syria's ruling coalition resembled the one carefully constructed by Hafiz al-Asad to offset instability during the 1970s. Although the names and faces had changed, the coalition included a cross-sectarian mixture of selected 'Alawis, Sunnis, Shias, and Druze in the B'ath Party, security services, military, and bureaucracy. This was especially true in the two largest cities—Aleppo and Damascus—whose populations benefited disproportionately from the status quo. Irrespective of the limited political restrictions and repression, the country's heterogeneous population continued to view the current regime as vital for holding the state and society together. While one can presume that a Syrian president would prefer to accumulate more power vis-à-vis the other elites in the various state institutions, no drastic critical juncture permitted the chief executive to horde authority, as is the case in Egypt. Given these decentralized dynamics were at play in 2011, it becomes clearer that maintaining an option for a swift transition of the ruling coalition did not exist during its uprising, which began in March 2011.

There were opportunities for the president and regime to deescalate its conflict against the citizenry. Nevertheless, at each fork in the road, the collective decision was to respond with force. When routine repression proved futile, the regime responded with more lethal manifestations such as the use of military searches, tank shelling, and snipers to eliminate dissent and terrorize the population into acquiescence. The deployment of force merely underscores the inability to project power into society and resolve conflicts. Hence, Asad's conscious decisions led to his perilous position at the helm of an increasingly weak state.

The weak state and decentralized cross-sectarian ruling coalition explains why Syria entered and emerged from its uprising differently than Egypt. Between March and June 2011, state elites worked together to defeat the rebelling, but fragmented citizenry. This is not to suggest that all of the state's constituent parts equally participated. In many respects the B'ath Party and Asad disappeared as the military stepped forward to reinforce the state's authority. In Syria's uprising, the conflict between the state and society was uneven, protracted, and ruthlessly violent. In large part, this is a function of the decentralized character of authority in its political system. Yet, it primarily worked because the state's elites remained unified, and the dissenting and fragmented society never unified nationally during the insurrection.

Spurned on by the diffusive effects from Tunisia and Egypt, which was still undergoing its uprising, brave Syrians used social networking sites to call for a demonstration in Damascus in early February. No one showed up. As one activist, who asked for anonymity, said, "The culture of protesting is not present here. They oppressed it until they killed it."[54] Indeed, in the early phases of the region's uprisings, Syria looked as if its elites would be spared from a showdown with its society. Asad cited the absence of protests as a function of the legitimacy of the state's policies. As he said in an interview with the *Wall Street Journal*, "We have more difficult circumstances than most of the Arab countries but in spite of that Syria is stable. Why? Because you have to be very closely linked to the beliefs of the people. This is the core issue. When there is divergence between your policy and the people's beliefs and interests, you will have this vacuum that creates disturbance."[55] Yet, less than two months after this statement, state elites faced their most serious challenge since the 1976–82 uprising.

The protests started with an incident in the southern town of Dera'a. In mid-March, fifteen young boys—all under the age of seventeen—graffitied a wall with the iconic protest slogan of 2011: "The People Want the Fall of the System!" The local governor cracked down harshly. He ordered the boys thrown in jail, where they were tortured. The detentions galvanized the town's residents into action. On March 21, protesters tore down posters of Asad, destroyed a statue of his father, and set fire to the ruling party's headquarters. By the end of that evening, the protesters gathered at the 'Omari mosque and presented a list of demands: the abolition of the forty-eight-year-old martial law, more freedoms, and the release of all political prisoners. The army reinforced the police in Dera'a, but under the pretense it would not shoot protesters as Asad promised higher wages for state employees. He also promised more liberties while considering the repeal of emergency law. Four days later, military troops fired on protesters. Thousands took to the streets to reject this use of force. Asad countered by releasing some prisoners but was now forced to contain the protests, which spread to the coastal towns of Latakiya and Banyas. The cabinet resigned as a government committee formed to examine the grievances the protesters expressed. Still, the regime refused to capitulate to the protesters' demands. Asad addressed parliament and said that while some demonstrators had "good intentions," he suspected external elements were stirring up trouble. The demonstrations spread further to the cities of Homs as well as to the outskirts of Damascus in Domma but failed to take hold in either Damascus or Aleppo. As the casualties rose, the lack of alternatives beyond regime change started to factor into the elites' calculus. State gunfire killed thirty-seven on April 8 and more the following day as snipers shot at funeral mourners.

After demonstrations crept temporarily into Aleppo, Asad responded with a serious but belated concession on April 16. Speaking on state TV, he pledged to lift the emergency law within days as well as other new legal proposals. The new concessions failed to placate the protesters. Instead of peeling away protesters, the situation worsened as forty-three people died during Friday demonstrations on April 22. Without feeling there was more to give, the regime bound together and chose to fight its way out together. The state cut communications and Internet into restive areas and restricted movement and access into and out of rebellious towns. It also militarily invaded areas of dissent. Army soldiers and tanks launched mortars into buildings in Dera'a, Homs, and Domma while paramilitaries went house to house to eliminate organizers, terrify families, and force the population to submit.

The unity of state elites to use force as well as controlling movement and space allowed them to remain advantaged in the violent standoff. Yet, as the protests continued, they also failed to connect the disparate areas or unify those protesting for greater freedoms. Foreign governments and intergovernmental organizations, such as the United States and EU, leveled sanctions on leading regime figures and called for the violence to stop, but without a substantial effect. Without a good landing for the state elites, who seemed unable to conduct an Egypt-like transition, the options were reduced to the regime's survival or destruction. When placed in these stark terms, the elites doubled down in the hope that it would outlast and repress the dissent. Two Syrian human rights groups claim that more than three thousand civilians have died while tens of thousands have been arrested by late October. With no end in sight, these numbers continue to rise sharply as the demonstrations continue.

The decentralized way in which power flows in Syria's state determined the limited options for how the elites could respond. The Syrian regime did not have the same centralized options for a regime-saving transition as in Egypt. Firstly, the lack of a clear governing hierarchy made concessions a risky pursuit because they encouraged elite fragmentation, which threatened regime continuity. Secondly, the ruling coalition held. There were no key defections from coalition members in the Alawi community, Sunni business communities, or state's institutions.[56] Nir Rosen has shown that when defections occurred in institutions such as the military, the officers left unarmed and on an individual basis.[57] There was also minimal unrest in major cities such as Damascus. Given this was the case, there proved little motivation to jettison Asad. Third, and closely re-lated, Bashar al-Asad was revealed to be less of a penultimate leader and more a CEO responsible for facilitating consensus among his institutions.[58] In this sense, his authority never extended to areas that Sadat or Mubarak enjoyed. Ironically, centralization made it easier to remove the Egyptian president and re-place him with a transitory figure or institution like the SCAF. But, in the Syrian case, decentralized power made Asad indispensible during the uprising because his staying in power guaranteed an attempt to maintain the current regime. This signal helped placate the fears from the regime's various coalition members.

Whether Asad remains indispensible following the uprising as the state rec-ognizes its utter weakness remains a separate issue. Most analysts recognize that even if the regime survives it will emerge from the uprising isolated and unable to project power.[59] Asad could very well be deposed in the longer term if the elites within the military and other institutions make that decision. As one Damascene businessman remarked, "We're in for at least six months more of this. . . . After that we'll have a weakened Bashar limping along or the gen-erals will decide that the Assads are a liability."[60] Yet, it seems unlikely that he will be deposed during the actual uprising. Fourthly, and without intending to discredit the many brave protesters around the country, the protests never ma-terialized in the two largest cities in an enthusiastic or sustained way to cause fragmentation within the ruling coalition.

BEYOND TAHRIR AND DERA'A

While there are similarities for why Syrians and Egyptians revolted against their political elites, there seems to be one key difference in why the outcomes var-ied. In Egypt, power was centralized prior to the uprising. When the protests occurred, the homogeneous character of society helped protesters overcome their previous collective action problems as they put aside their political differ-ences. Their unified mobilizing pressure, combined with a rapid change in the balance of power between the coercive forces and the demonstrators, enabled a dynamic whereby members of the centralized ruling coalition could be and had to be dropped to save the regime. Then, when Mubarak became untenable at the helm, the SCAF could force his departure and slide into the centralized position of authority. While the SCAF was weak initially, it was in a better posi-tion to offset the continuous challenges from below.

Syria had no such luck. The heterogeneity of its society made centralized authority a difficult prospect in the early years of state formation. Hafiz al-Asad rectified this with his development of a cross-sectarian decentralized ruling co-alition that shares power and works together to keep the state intact. It is an imperfect system, but it has not provided much governing turnover. After the uprising started in Syria, options for a coalition transition did not exist. This reduced the crisis to a question of the regime's survival. The constituent parts of the regime would either hang together or collapse. In addition to forcing hands of the state elites to deploy repression, it revealed the decentralized and weak character of the state. When the population had to choose between a life in a weak state and no state and rising sectarianism in a diverse society, it chose the former. These factors doomed the prospects that society could overthrow their state without an external intervention.

In explaining how transitions unfold, there are—at least—three scenarios that structurally tip who comes to power, who remains in power, and the re-sulting relationship between the rulers and the governed. Generally, the three paths are as follows. Firstly, a relationship occurs where state elites and social opposition are both strong. This suggests minimal violence, positive exchanges between the state and society, and political outcomes where both the winners and losers have good places to land. This characterized many of the "pact tran-sitions" to democracy that emerged in states such as Spain.[61] Yet, even in cases where both state elites and social opposition are strong, who holds power and their worldviews are important for whether a state moves toward or away from democracy.[62] Secondly, on the opposite side of the spectrum, another possible outcome is when the state's elites are strong, but society is fragmented. In this scenario, the prospects that authoritarianism will continue are high. Even in a consolidated democracy, when this dynamic persists, the likelihood that dem-ocratic norms can be consistently violated becomes a possibility. With an im-balance of power favors the power holders, it structurally advantages the elites' continued dominance. Using force in such scenarios can happen, but there is a multiplicity of nonviolent ways that power can discipline and incorporate the population under the elites' authority. Lastly, there are political situations when ruling elites and social opposition find themselves both in fragmented states. If this becomes the case, a competition ensues around who can organize and unify first. If the social opposition does, the chances for a real revolution in-crease because there will be a break with the past. If the state elites prevail, it favors their ability to remake and order the polity.

Looking to other regional examples for comparative analogies proves help-ful for understanding Egypt and Syria's uprisings in 2011. With help from the universe of post-Soviet cases, the sharpest fissures with the past occurred when the opposition was strong and the authoritarians were either sidelined or cooperative. In the words of Valerie Bunce, "These transitions then produced a quick consolidation of both democracy and capitalism and, when accompanied by state disintegration, even the state."[63] As Bunce rightly notes, most of the transitions in the post-Soviet states did not travel this route. Rather, the new incumbents faced the unfavorable conditions, such as fragmented opposition vis-à-vis their fragmented authority. In the instances where democracy was thwarted and authoritarianism reemerged, the surviving authoritarian elites reconstituted themselves more quickly than society organized. Such situations where this structural imbalance unfolds favor a slide back into authoritarianism. Transferring this argument to the Arab states, we can somewhat anticipate where the postuprising political arrangements may head.

Given that Syrian society is a diverse mosaic and the state elites manipulated sectarian tensions during its uprising, many citizens opted not to invite political uncertainty through regime change. Without the option that popular pressure on state elites could alter the ruling coalition, many stayed home while the coercive apparatus crushed the rebellion. The longer the stalemate took place, the more sectarian it became, which did not help the situation.[64] Given that the state got increasingly more violent in its response reveals its weakness, but what explains the revolt's protracted character? The answer is found in fragmentation. Both the state and the opposition were weak. Syria's heterogeneous society produced conditions that did not favor the protesters' ability to overcome their collective action problems. This contributed to the lack of national connectivity among the protests and kept them fragmented. The state was also weak, but the elites remained unified. This favored the survival of the incumbent regime because it allowed the elites to reestablish control over its opposition. The decentralized character of state power—in part determined by this heterogeneity—helped regime elites hang together during the uprising. The state grew increasingly weak during the uprising as seen by the elites' use of force, but they never fragmented or produced ruling coalition defections. Given that the protesters fragmented and the elites did not, it structurally favored the regime's prospects to survive the challenge from below.

Egypt reveals another path. Prior to January 25, Egypt had a strong state, but a fragmented society. This relationship allowed the ruling coalition to manipulate, dominate, and repress society through the use of violent and nonviolent tactics. It was also this established relationship that changed in late January.

As Charles Tilly showed long ago, the prospects for revolution occur exponentially when this balance of power changes rapidly as it did during Egypt's eighteen-day battle to remove Mubarak.[65] Aided by the ability of Egyptian protesters to use their homogeneity to overcome their previous differences, the social forces bound together and reduced the security services' ability to repress. After the protesters defeated the Interior Ministry's personnel, the army interceded to lead a transition of the ruling coalition in order to perverse the regime. The option not to use violence in Egypt proved most preferable. The uprising had the option to end peacefully as the SCAF hived off former elites from the coalition and sacrificed symbolic figures to the crowds as evidence of change. In this instance, full regime change was not required to resolve the political challenge. The key factor for explaining this outcome is the centralized way that executive power operates in Egypt. As will be discussed in Chapter 2, the reason why elites interact in such a centralized fashion is in part derived from Egypt's strong homogeneous identity.

THE PAST EXPLAINS THE PRESENT

To understand how Egypt and Syria emerged from the 2011 uprisings, researchers need to identify and explain how power was configured prior to them. By doing so, we must recognize and analyze the differences of systems that are often grouped together. Although researchers working on the Middle East regularly distinguish between monarchies and republics,[66] scholars of comparative politics have not explored other differences within these categories in an explicit way.[67] Examining the staple textbooks on Middle East politics proves this point.[68] Yet, as the uprisings suggest, authority is structured and operates differently in these cases. This poses an important question: Which autocrats are most successful at adapting their political systems?

By exposing the differences in how autocrats adapt these systems, we gain new perspectives and understandings about regime power in the Middle East. Whether elites like it or not, political change is inescapable. Government officials have vested interests in apprehending and managing this process. As the Cairo bureau chief of the pan-Arab daily *al-Hayat* explains, "It is in a regime's interest to change so that it can stay in power. They reform to keep the [political] system going."[69] Such "reforms" help rulers avoid more radical changes in the future.

This book argues that Arab elites are not initiating reform processes, but rather are engaging in adaptation. Autocratic adaptation helps regime elites maintain their dominant position and hierarchical authority over society.[70]

Adaptation can be defined as political change that adjusts a state to changes in its environment (such as a more mobilized, complex society, weakening state economic capabilities, external pressures, and so on) without giving up power or sacrificing the cohesion of elites. Adaptation takes place through controlled openings. Specifically, researchers can see adaptation when new groups are incorporated into the ruling coalition or when previously privileged members are dropped. Co-optation, or the inclusion of new figures and groups, shifts the state's social base and allows ruling elites to pursue organizational innovations in state institutions.[71] However, adaptation does not mean that incumbent elites seek intentionally to transform or restructure existing relationships between the rulers and the ruled.

In examining adaptation, we journey behind the iron curtain to examine the microdynamics of co-optation in such political systems. I do this by showing how the degree of centralized or decentralized authority over organizations affects adaptive capabilities. Egypt and Syria provide two stunning and, at times, counterintuitive cases. For example, in a March 2004 interview, Egypt's then youth minister, 'Ali al-Din Hilal, remarked that despite Egypt's institutions, proposed governmental initiatives are "sometimes challenged by personalities."[72] Syria's "reform" process experienced different obstacles according to then Syrian expatriates minister, Bothaina Shab'an. She argued, "Change on the ground will happen. It is easy to change a person at anytime but institutions tend to stand in the way of larger reform."[73] While individuals supported by entrenched patronage networks complicate reform in Cairo, elites situated in organization bases block the process in Damascus. This variance becomes starker when examining the cases' centralized and decentralized political fields.

The difference between centralized or decentralized control over state organizations determines how and where ruling elites can include, reaffirm, and exclude lesser elites and nonelites. The political system's capacity to absorb and expel coalition members shapes the process of adaptation. Both the Egyptian and Syrian systems are capable of adapting. Yet, the findings complicate established conventions about authoritarian power in Egypt and Syria.

It is commonly assumed that political power in Syria is more centralized than in Egypt. My findings indicate this not to be the case. In Egypt, centralized authority over other state organizations provides ruling elites with greater governing flexibility. Conversely, in Syria, a decentralized political order forces elites in state organizations to compete for influence within the government. The process leaves no single organization to arbitrate control over the rest.

Elites in organizations including the presidency, ruling party, state-affiliated NGOs, and security services all incorporate new recruits. This not only decreases the possibility of channeling regime clients into a single venue, but also complicates the chief executive's ability to develop a consensus over such expansive terrain. Ensconced in decentralized organizations, autonomous agents protect their organization by obstructing initiatives from other elites from competing institutions. This also makes removing established elites or including newer ones a more arduous process. In addition to producing governance gridlock, it slows adaption.

Egypt's rulers operate in a more adaptable system because the centralized character of authority allows ruling elites to exercise authority over the state's organizations. The absence of organizational repositories of power means that the ruling coalition can be remolded more efficiently—enabling smoother transitions. This explains why the SCAF could alter the ruling coalition, depose Mubarak, and assume centralized authority over the country without resorting to mass violence. Dina Shehata agrees by arguing, "The regime's basic structure remains largely intact. . . . The military and the state bureaucracy are still in firm control of the country and in a position to dictate the course of the transition."[74] Conversely, in Syria, elites compete and may obstruct their rivals from other institutions. This complicates a Syrian ruler's ability to achieve a governing consensus across the bodies, which slows adaptation. It also restricts the regime's ability to remake its ruling coalition. This becomes further accentuated during moments of crisis. Indeed, transitions away from the ruling coalition become tantamount to a full-scale regime change. Since the elites do not maintain this option, opposition challenges become existential threats. Hence, without an ability to peacefully remake its coalition, it pushes the regime elites to employ violence to resolve political problems.

Authoritarianism is often presumed to signal personalism and weak institutions,[75] as rules give way to patrimonial leaders and prominent clientelist networks.[76] Egypt and Syria both exhibit weak institutional arenas dominated by political elites. This book illustrates why, even within these contexts, institutions yield different governing capabilities. The ways that elites use, interact, and influence other elites from different institutions determines the governing autocrats' adaptive capacity. The difference is not in the institutions. Rather, it is that Egypt's political elites have centralized control over its organizations while Syrian elites combat the effects of organizations that operate in a decentralized political arena.

This book joins a blossoming literature on authoritarian durability in the Middle East at a moment when we need to critically interpret how these important uprisings of 2011 affect our understanding of that phenomenon. Other works include Lisa Wedeen's work on Syria[77] and Yemen,[78] Marsha Pripstein Posusney and Michele Angrist's volume,[79] Oliver Schlumberger's edited work,[80] and Nicola Pratt's study.[81] Similarly, Jason Brownlee's book on authoritarianism,[82] as well as Steven Heydemann's work,[83] address issues of regime durability, upgrading, and leaning. Scholarship about authoritarianism (*istibdadayya*) in Arabic is becoming more prevalent. Since the fall of Ben Ali and Mubarak, we can anticipate this trend will increase. Yet, even before those events, social scientists and journalists in Arab countries broached the subject daily.[84] Yet, because it is emerging as a literature, it produces polarized written materials and exchanges. Regime-aligned analysts tend to write ideological and progovernment works on how elites are conducting incremental reform.[85] They did, however, also engage in soft criticism of the government.

Works that fail to toe the government's line stack bookstore shelves throughout cities in Arab states. Yet, opposition and independent figures often produce polemical books against government. Although lively, such publications are not always constructive when thinking about governing organizations in Arab states. Because these publications often focus on the president's personality, they fail to tackle questions of autocratic adaptation.[86] Rather than assuming that nondemocratic regimes are inherently unstable as some works have,[87] this project explores how such regimes adapt and change.

This study focuses on comparative origins of centralized and decentralized authoritarianism and their effects on co-optation practices in two republics in the Arab world. While the conventional alternative to political economy theory has been to ponder cultural attributes,[88] this book's approach combines the recent contributions from the literature on authoritarianism with how institutions structure elite consensus-building.

WHY COMPARE EGYPT AND SYRIA?

While studies of one country detail the analysis of a particular case's individual path, the question remains, "in comparison to what?" As Lichbach and Zuckerman argue, "Comparativists therefore insist that analysis requires explicit comparisons. Because events of global historical significance affect so many countries in so short a period of time, studies of single countries and abstract theorizing are woefully inadequate to capture epoch-shaping developments."[89]

Comparative studies invite a greater understanding and comprehension of the development processes.[90] Comparisons excavate similarities and spotlight differences. They assist in theory building, unmask contradictions, and expose larger trends.

By far, single-country[91] or regional[92] comparisons predominate in the robust tradition of studying of politics in Arab states. Nevertheless, comparisons between the politics in Egypt and Syria remain overlooked, undeveloped, and understudied in the field.[93] The two countries are both important regionally, enjoy a long shared history that includes a failed unification experiment between 1958–61, and are examples of postpopulist authoritarian regimes. There are a number of accounts that detail the inception and dissolution of the United Arab Republic (UAR),[94] but none that focus on contemporary comparisons. As a general rule, those working on Syria usually refer to Egypt. For example, in a chapter of *Contemporary Syria*, Hinnebusch makes five different references to the Egyptian experience. Similarly, Kienle's chapter in the same volume references Egypt four times.[95] Yet, the reverse seldom happens. This suggests that there is unexplored space for comparative work to be done.

Since 1966, there have been one journal article,[96] two chapters in books,[97] and a six-page comparison in a book about Syria that compare authoritarianism in the two cases.[98] In the 1960s, similarities in postindependence development strategies, expressions of pan-Arab ideologies, and the UAR experiment invited comparisons between Syria and Egypt. Then, in 1967, the Six-Day War changed the focus from direct comparative work to the effects of war and peace as the Israeli-Arab conflict gained primacy. The aftermath of the June War also produced a rupture in the states' trajectories. This transformation produced aftershocks that discouraged comparative academic work on the states.

By the late 1970s and early 1980s, Anwar al-Sadat drastically altered Egypt by eschewing Arab nationalism, implementing neoliberal economic policies, aligning with the United States, and signing peace with Israel. At the same time in Syria, Hafiz al-Asad designed a ruling coalition to enhance social and political stability while the country became embroiled in the Lebanese civil war. In addition to a continuing proxy war with Israel, the Syrian state contended with a violent domestic insurgency. Without peace and without a consolidated national identity, political elites continued to pay tribute to pan-Arabism as a means of holding their weak state and heterogeneous society together. Syria drifted toward the epicenter of "Arab politics," as Egypt disengaged from it. The differences that surfaced in the 1970s may have deterred scholars from comparing the two states. After all, they appeared to be heading in different developmental directions. One of this book's by-products is that the divide is not as great as was possibly perceived then. This transformative period is central to understanding why Egypt and Syria operate in the way they do today. The two regimes deploy power and manage society differently to achieve elite consensus. Through a direct comparative study, the similarities and differences in these systems provide new insights for understanding authoritarian durability.

A NOTE ON METHODS

The following chapters are the product of thirty-six months of fieldwork in Egypt and Syria. The methods that I employed consist primarily of formal and informal interviews in Arabic and English. Formal interviews were a structured process where I introduced a contact to the object of my project. They involved a strict, structured set of questions in a defined period of interaction. Informal interviews produced more penetrating information to explain inadequacies uncovered in formal interviews and the literature.

Relying on interviews requires gaining familiarity with participants in each of the two cases. The better researchers know the political geography of their cases, the better they can contextualize the data they collect. I conducted more than one hundred interviews with government decision-makers, political activists, journalists, academics, and dissidents in Egypt and Syria to complete the project. This included interviews with government ministers, people affiliated with the government, nongovernment organizations (NGO) and government-operated nongovernment organizations (GONGO) participants, members of political parties, members of parliaments, Islamists, writers, analysts, economists, academics, diplomats, and journalists in Egypt, Syria, Lebanon, Britain, and the United States.[99] By relying on the judgment of others and empowering local voices, the theories about how power operates in Egypt and Syria emerged from the cases. Over the months, I spider-webbed and outwardly expanded my research network to speak with and learn from new contacts. Substantial amounts of networking further enabled me to gain both trust and access to other individuals willing to share their insights, analysis, and experiences.

It is also crucial to reflect on how we come to think what we know. Asking questions about a political system's durability, elite personalities, and repressive apparatuses in nondemocratic contexts breeds obstacles and challenges. Unsurprisingly, hesitancy, suspicion, and distrust can trail any researcher raising these topics. To overcome this, I focused on gaining trust by carefully representing the material I collected. Building relationships to navigate these waters proved to be the easy part. The more demanding aspect revolved around the notion that the more sensitive the topic, the more cautiously the obtained information had to be handled. Being mindful of the various information channels and of an array of different individual perceptions of reality became crucial. The problem lies not only in interpreting what you are told, see, or read, but also in understanding the context in which people share and write about their experiences.

When dealing with oral data from formal and informal interviews, which are based on humans' memories and perceptions, I repeatedly rechecked anecdotes to ensure that respondents depicted them as accurately as possible. I triangulated this data by anonymously relaying one subject's account of a particular event to someone else's perceptions. For example, if one ruling-party member provided me with a narrative, I would cross-reference its accuracy with another party member to confirm intent and background, or to provide further elaboration. After adjusting the narrative to limit the chances that I engaged in misrepresentation, I would present it to a third party or a previous contact to get a reaction to the constructed narrative. By being vigilant and reflexive to the potential flaws of utilizing interviews (both formal and informal), these techniques of redundancy contributed to making my narratives fall within the confines of a "safe reality."

1 DEBATING AUTHORITARIANISM

THE NUMBER OF ELECTORAL DEMOCRACIES IN THE WORLD grew from 76 to 120 between 1990 and 2000.[1] During the decade that followed, democracies started to decline. In 2010, the fifth consecutive year of decline, the number dipped to 115.[2] Citizens in the political systems of the Arab world did not notice this expansion and contraction. Their systems have defied global democratizing trends for decades. Freedom House lists all Arab governments as "not free" with the exception of Morocco, Iraq, and Lebanon.[3] Yet, even these exceptions are suspect. Thoroughly authoritarian systems remain in the Arab world after democratization's "Third Wave,"[4] the Soviet Union's implosion, and decades of continuing failures by the US government's "democratization industry."[5] The region's exceptionalism left some academics perplexed despite protests from regional experts.[6] Some credited the region's predominately Islamic or Arab cultures as the obstacle for democracy in the region.[7] Yet, even those who do not resort to cultural arguments were seduced by the prospects of democracy.

Despite the recalcitrance of autocracy in the region, democratization frameworks and assumptions informed many of the research agendas during the 1990s.[8] So much so that, in 1999, Lisa Wedeen argued, "There are, oddly, few recent writings on authoritarianism in comparative politics and they tend to be concerned primarily with the transition from authoritarian to democratic forms of rule."[9] It is not that social scientists believed the region was experiencing democratization.[10] Irrespective of intentions or beliefs, the transitology framework became stitched into the work in the 1990s. While studies continue to vacillate between bottom-up and top-down approaches, research production shifted to explicitly explaining authoritarian durability in the 2000s. With the 2011 uprisings in the region, research agendas arrive at a fresh—if yet still unsettled—junction.[11] If those working on the Arab world follow the trail blazed by those who researched the post-Soviet transitions, then there will likely be more work on social groups than on elites in the coming period. Yet, given the convoluted transitions that emerged after 1989, democratization will likely be just as complicated as it has always been in the Arab world. There will not likely be a wholesale adoption or return to studying democratic transitions. Just because studying authoritarianism has been the dominant paradigm for the past decade does not mean that others were listening. For example, US policy circles have failed to move away from their liberalizing aims and rhetoric in the Arab world irrespective of the realities on the ground.

Successive American administrations also deployed foreign aid and other incentive programs to promote democracy in the Arab world.[12] Following the September 11 attacks, the US government viewed the lack of democracy as a national security question.[13] The Bush administration responded with the "Freedom Agenda."[14] Except for the military intervention into Iraq, Bush's agenda was just a repackaged attempt to democratize and "electionize" autocratic states. Yet, US democracy promotion efforts and aid has not directly impacted rulers' tenures in office. These efforts also have not improved educational standards, strengthened institutions, empowered women, or created middle classes in Arab states. The UN's Arab Human Development Reports record the lack of progress in these "deficit" areas regularly.[15]

Diplomatic exchanges between the United States and Arab governments dramatize this struggle over democratization. On one side of this reform struggle stand US political elites, who argue that Arab governments should reform by increasing freedoms and democracy. The Arab ruling elites respond by reconfiguring their ranks to appease international actors but continuing to block openings for greater inclusion. When American officials speak of reform, they seem to imply a change in the character of governance. When Arab leaders initiate reform, they have precluded such changes. This looks like a heated battle of wills between right and wrong, but it has traditionally been much ado about nothing.

This drama plays out every few years. The democratization industry amplifies the refrain that the American government has insufficiently or incorrectly promoted democracy. Congressional funding is channeled throughout the bureaucracy to sponsor various programs such as the Middle East Partnership Initiative (MEPI). Diplomatic exchanges occur whereby American officials ask for greater inclusive reform from their Arab counterparts. Secretaries of State visit and appeal for spectacles, such as elections, to demonstrate compliance. Arab elites, however, are not rendered defenseless in this performance. They respond. Leaders warn ominously of chaos if reforms are not managed responsibly. Government ministers and party apparatchiks claim that they are already democratizing. Newspaper editorials levy allegations of foreign meddling in their affairs. After bilateral relations are described as "tense," the incumbent regime reorders its hierarchy and produces measures that recalibrate their entrenchment.[16] Kienle has called this "political deliberalization";[17] and Pool notes the tendency for "a retreat to a stricter authoritarianism" when pursing reforms.[18] While US officials and policy centers claim victory over the superficial actions of Arab leaders, the outcome is cosmetic.[19]

Some analysts cite the importance of Washington's pressure as an impetus for Arab reform measures. This exuberance should be tempered. For example, Michele Dunne, a senior associate at the Carnegie Endowment for International Peace, argues that Washington positively nudged Egypt to establish multicandidacy presidential elections in 2005.[20] She fails, however, to disclose that the incumbent cruised to victory with nearly 90 percent of that contest's vote. It seems clear that no amount of incentives,[21] political will,[22] or strategic appointments within the State Department will reverse the barren fortunes of the US democracy promotion.[23] Regardless, the aid and democratization enterprises continue to double down on their failed efforts rather than change the assumptions or accept the projects' limitations.

Despite the ardency that these diplomatic face-offs produce in terms of impassioned exchanges and spilled ink by those across the transnational ideological spectrum, such maneuvers fail to correlate with their stated goals. Furthermore, irrespective of their vocal protests and superficial alterations, ruling elites in Arab states do not seem to worry much about American pressure to politically liberalize. This is because the political sound and fury overwhelmingly produce do-si-dos back to the status quo. Why, then, is this the case?

One answer is that such systems are buttressed from such external pressure. The elites exist in structures that can absorb and neutralize American pressure while favorably reordering the state's hierarchy. This serves the ruling elites by introducing changes to reinforce the current power relationships. But the actions of elites alone are not enough. They need vehicles. Hence, state institutions play a central role in the process. They help the ruling elites override, redirect, and funnel away foreign pressure as they channel domestic dissent. The institutions also benefit ruling elites by encouraging cohesion and making them agile when adjusting to pressure. The structures also preclude outcomes that may transfer or redistribute power to social forces. As Jason Brownlee showed, institutions are "the nerve center of authoritarianism" because they are "incisive for explaining regime change and stability."[24] In such systems, foreign diplomatic pressure has neither threatened nor challenged these regimes in existential ways.

Not all regimes, however, are created equal. The degree that an executive office has centralized authority over state institutions affects whether elites respond in a unified or disjointed manner.[25] Some systems possess centralized control over state institutions, which facilitate the ruling elites' cohesion and a regime's ability to respond in an efficient manner. Others do not. This complicates the emergence of consensus from across the political field's organizations. The origins of state institutions and the degree to which ruling elites exert authority over those arenas determine the range of possibility and shelter answers to durability.

Authoritarianism is not a stagnant governing approach. Political elites in Arab states constantly work to ensure that they remain in the regime and the system remains viable. They guide change to protect and replicate the status quo. All of the region's governments have undertaken or are pursuing legislative, constitutional, and institutional changes. Some of the states are confronting the aftermath of popular uprisings. While some may dispute the durability of authoritarian political systems in Arab states in the wake of the 2011 uprising, history shows that more likely than not authoritarianism—not democracy—emerges from moments of political transition. Nevertheless, this abstract concept requires some discussion given the intellectual history of studying such political systems.

STUDYING AUTOCRACY

Since Max Weber's identified traditional, charismatic, and legal-rational forms of authority,[26] social scientists have predominantly classified autocratic systems accordingly. This produces either overly generalized or specific definitions of authoritarianism. For example, Juan Linz provides a macrodefinition:

> Political systems with limited, not responsible, political pluralism, without elaborate or guiding ideology, but with distinctive mentalities, without extensive nor intensive political mobilization, except at some points in their development, and in which a leader and occasionally a small group exercises power within formally ill-defined limits but actually quite predictable ones.[27]

While this definition is accurate, it does not capture the intricacies or varieties of authoritarian rule. This is because the extensive diversity of such regimes makes defining authoritarianism difficult. Paul Brooker agrees when he argues, "The term 'authoritarian' is so widely applicable that it is difficult to develop a theory which can cover so many diverse cases without becoming either banal or incoherent."[28] Rather than ascribe or develop a single definition, social scientists have atomized the study of such systems by creating typologies to characterize regime types. Some of these typologies include dictatorships. Others include military, single-party, sultanistic, or hybrid regimes as well as personalized rule, semiauthoritarianism, pseudodemocracies, and liberalized autocracies. Others prefer to refer to such systems as electoral or competitive authoritarianism. None of these classifications are incorrect despite the pejorative biases that some imply. However, classifications can restrict comparability because a typology can get so specific that it applies only to a single case. Similarly, these imagined categories permit political systems to be incorrectly classified through deduction. Rather than allow theory building to emerge from the case, typologies are often mislaid on top of it. Beyond adding typologies, scholars have also enriched Weber's original theory on governing styles.[29]

The most widely used in contemporary debates is neo-patrimonialism, which descends from Weber's traditional type. In addition to the personalized attributes of a regime, the state's institutions also are argued to contribute to its ability to expand power. Bratton and van de Walle created the most established definition of neo-patrimonialism. It is

> hybrid political systems in which the customs and patterns of patrimonialism co-exist with, and suffuse, rational-legal institutions. As with classic patrimonialism, the right to rule in neopatrimonial regimes is ascribed to a person rather than to an office, despite the official existence of a written constitution. ... The chief executive and his inner circle undermine the effectiveness of the nominally modern state administration by using it for systematic patronage and clientelist practices in order to maintain political order. Moreover, parallel and unofficial structures may well hold more power and authority than the formal administration.[30]

Such regimes, therefore, combine traditional rule with "modern" (but not legal-rational) bureaucratic institutions of a state.[31] As a consequence, neither form of governance prevails in a pure form. But differences emerge. Some systems might be more legal-rational than traditional while other states exhibit opposing trends. When studying authoritarianism in Arab states, neo-patrimonialism is attractive because it reflects the mixed character of the region's regimes. Yet, just because the theory accounts for variance does not imply that theoretical blind spots have not surfaced in such analyses.

Some scholars working on the politics of Arab states have rightly considered neo-patrimonialism as an explanatory frame. "Neopatriarchy," as Hisham Sharabi calls it, reveals a process where a state blends its patrimonial inherited culture into its institutions. The remnants of tradition pollute the development process and reinforce dependency on the Western core.[32] As this relationship of unequal (capital versus dependent) states deepens, traditionalism flourishes.[33] The prevalence of such corrupted institutions hinders a state's ability to encourage economic development because elites pursue a distorted development strategy. While Sharabi's work focuses on Arab societies' poisonous effect on the economy, other academics consider neo-patrimonialism's effects on political development.

Halim Barakat uses neo-patrimonialism to explain the impotence of civil society in the Arab world. As Barakat argues, the potential for opposition to rise organically to challenge the state is unlikely because neo-patrimonialism discourages political contestation. In his words, "The conditions described above—dependency, underdevelopment, patriarchal and authoritarian relationships, social and political fragmentation, class distinctions, successive historical defeats, and a generalized state of repression—have rendered the Arab people and society powerless."[34] Barakat argues that Arab elites have so successfully channeled wealth and resources to serve their own benefits that their polities became apathetic, demobilized, and depoliticized. This depravity has reached such a degree that the "Arab world does not seem to have a society that functions well."[35] As he sees it, this eliminates the possibility that a political opposition can contest the ruling class.

In addition to being empirically wrong, using the theory in this way is corrosive. It fails to distinguish between authoritarian states or the historical context of their institutions. Sharabi and Barakat do not draw out distinctions between various authoritarian regimes as they focus on the "Arab World." Similarly, neo-patrimonialism is primarily a social phenomenon that impedes political and economic development. Yet, social and cultural explanations fail to illuminate the wider causal chain because they exclude alternative theories. For example, the lack of political development in individual Arab states stems from other institutional, historical, economic, and transnational geopolitical geneses—not cultural or social causes.

This also reveals a common misstep when employing neo-patrimonialism. While many scholars mention institutions when discussing such hybrid regimes, the organizations merely serve as exploitable façades without vested political power. While there are some notable exceptions where scholars cite venues of contestation,[36] many scholars do not bring theoretical clarity to the concept of a regime. For example, many simply reduce "a regime" to the chief executive and his cronies. This, in turn, excludes a state's elaborate bureaucratic structure or quotidian practices, which also discipline and condition the lives of citizens. By only exposing the weakness of these structures, it undervalues how the state apparatuses contribute to governing. Similarly, the historical origins of such institutions are rarely considered (perhaps given their perceived weakness). This permits for greater focus on unconstrained agency, which invariably drifts analysis back to the omnipotence of an individual ruler over society. As such, a leader remains the narrative's crucial factor. Institutions remain subordinate to elite agency as opposed to being able to condition elite behavior. A neo-patrimonial institution, therefore, is not well positioned to defend itself against a power-hungry leader wishing to appropriate the appearance of an organization's structural autonomy.

By identifying how neo-patrimonialism manifests itself through different structural formats and by transferring weight to the power that institutions have, the concept gains new analytical clarity. Examining the degree that an executive office has centralized control over state institutions as well as analyzing how this impacts elite and nonelite inclusion into the ruling coalition explains the ability of autocratic elites to adapt. It also uncovers new lessons that we previously did not appreciate. While elites and agents drive developments and seek to keep power relationships as predictable as possible, it is their structural environment that determines the scope of the agency. This stands in opposition to other readings of authoritarianism in Arab states that focus on the primacy of agency and preferences.[37]

Academic research that explains authoritarian durability from an institutional or elite power-sharing perspective is gaining prominence.[38] In these publications, the structural framework constrains the options of leading elites.[39] Hence, weak institutions become central to explaining the durability of authoritarian political systems. State organizations and institutions, such as a presidential office, ruling party, or the military, maintain nonpersonalized attributes that encourage and facilitate elite cooperation. Brownlee's work has shown this in respect to a ruling party's ability to mediate elite conflict.[40] Dan Slater agrees and observes that institutions facilitate collective decision making and restrict a leader's authority.[41] This represents a shift in thinking about autocratic political systems.

Scholars previously viewed authoritarian institutions as weak because they were personalized. Yet, "unlike democracies, authoritarian regimes can be highly personalized and highly institutionalized at the same time."[42] Analyzing an authoritarian system's institutions leads to reexamining how senior elites adapt their systems. Conceptualizing institutions as such makes them vehicles that support but also condition the actions of the system's agents. As Jennifer Gandhi argues, "By now, it should be evident that dictators do not rule alone. They govern with institutions that are particular to their type."[43] While many of these scholars have included cases from the Arab world, extended comparisons of Arab-only cases have yet to be conducted. Theoretical debates about institutions, co-optation, and coercion follow because they are the central constituent parts of autocratic rule.

INSTRUMENTS OF DOMINATION

Weber's scholarship not only informs debates about authoritarianism, it also supplies a barometer for when institutions reach political modernity. Weber notes that traditional governance accommodates the least amount of participation from social forces. In these settings, institutions are unable to incorporate and channel social demands. Because the institutions are weak, politics descends to the ruling elites' will. The second of his typologies is also based on personal politics and is dubbed charismatic rule. This occurs when a leader drives radical change and mobilizes mass support behind a development project. The third designation is legal-rational, which is characterized by the development of state institutions and impersonal interactions. Weber's institutions are visible through the creation of a meritocratic bureaucracy. As he argues, "By virtue of its depersonalization, the bureaucratic state . . . is less accessible to substantive moralization than were the patriarchal orders of the past."[44] By developing a bureaucratic state, characterized by institutions, personal rule decreases and a state operates in a professional way. The reference to "the past" adds a temporal distinction to the spatial presentation of modernity. Modernity's linear aspects are similarly implied.[45] This sketch of bureaucratic institutions remains a central theory in the contemporary social sciences.

Institutions are the building blocks of a political system or state.[46] They organize power relationships in ways that do not require sustained interventions by individuals. In fact, the structures are self-sustaining beyond the choices of their participants. Institutions discipline and distribute power though written laws, quotidian practices, and public spectacles. Samuel Huntington argued, they, and particularly the single-party, were essential for political order in developing contexts. He argued traditional societies are more likely governed by organizations, which are distinct from bureaucratic structures. According to Huntington, organizations represent traditional groupings such as ethnic, religious, or occupational sectors of society.[47] Organizations can maintain order, mediate conflicts between rivals, elect leaders, and contribute to solidifying a particular interest group. Yet, because they are interest-specific, organizations are unable to incorporate other competing interest-specific groups. Hence, "The more complex and heterogeneous the society . . . the more the achievement and maintenance of political community become dependent upon the workings of political institutions."[48] Much like Weber, Huntington connected political development to the presence of impersonal institutions. Institutions are argued to contribute to social stability because of their ability to incorporate disparate social forces. In his words, "A strong party system thus provides the institutional organizations and procedures for the assimilation of new groups into the system. The development of such party institutions is the prerequisite for political stability in modernizing countries."[49] This notion of using a single party to drive institutionalization of the political field continues to be relevant in social science literature.[50] Indeed, Francis Fukuyama has revived the idea in the wake of the 2011 Arab uprisings to prove that Huntington was right all along.[51]

In recent years, theories about institutions have gotten more sophisticated for explaining autocratic durability as opposed to transitions to democracy. Brownlee argues that a single-party system contributes to the authoritarian maintenance because it provides a platform to mediate elite conflict and prevent defections from the regime. In his words, "A ruling party's capacity for intra-elite mediation is particularly important. . . . [P]arty institutions sustain those preferences while providing a site, the party organization, to pursue them."[52] This argument shows that institutions structure and enable elite cohesion, thereby precluding a potential democratic transition. Consequently, ruling elites deploy the "single party" to buttress a system of political hierarchy. While this sounds like personalized politics, the institutions take on a life of their own and extend beyond the ruling elites' control. State institutions— even weak ones—demarcate, restrict, and influence an elites' range of choices through their creation and habitualization. For ruling elites, institutions can add governing cohesion without inevitably drifting toward inclusive rotations of power. But they also erect the governing cages from which their preferences are structured.

For some, including David Waldner and Steven Heydemann, an institution's past helps reveal its present. The origins of institutions both condition and determine which elites are included and how elite consensus is reached. Origins explain why a political system's institutions function the way they do.[53] As a consequence, the degree and level of elite conflict determines the size of a government's ruling coalition. Where conflict is high, ruling coalitions tend to be larger and incorporate more societal actors. This facilitates stability but decentralizes power relationships between coalition members. In turn, it also encourages higher levels of clientelism, bureaucratic politicization, and precarious forms of state economic interventions.[54] Alternatively, in scenarios where elite conflict is lower, power is more centralized and coalitions tend to be smaller. Such scenarios are likely to empower the agents that comprise the executive office. These insights demonstrate that institutions in different political systems vary depending on their inherited dynamics. It also suggests that when institutions become path-dependent, they are difficult to divorce from inherited constraints.

THE EFFECTS OF CENTRALIZED AUTHORITY OVER INSTITUTIONS

Many institutions, regardless of their constraining attributes, still become tools in the hands of power-holders. How these organizations come to be and how they are disciplined to participate are central concerns. It is helpful to be reminded of ideal types.

The structure of authority determines who and how elites can participate in developing a regime's policies. Decentralized institutional arenas occur when apolitical professional state organizations (security agencies, civil service) are autonomous and have elites that can compete with elites situated in the state's political arms: the presidency, parties, and the legislature. Professional state institutions are *supposed* to exist to help leaders execute the duties of their office. Yet, ensconced in institutions in a decentralized field, agents have power bases and seek to protect their bases from elites in competing institutions. Hence, elites possess greater autonomy from the president. Elite rivalries emerge because everyone prioritizes their individual institution's interests over other elites' institutional interests. This allows elites from multiple organizations to affect and slow down autocratic adaptation by turf guarding. In this respect, elites in depoliticized arenas are able to use their structural base as a repository of power against elites from competing institutions. Too much decentralization complicates the ruler's ability to cohesively confront systemic challenges or change the regime's direction. In such systems, rulers find themselves competing against elites over policy control and implementation. Elites in state institutions become repositories of power that can obstruct governance. Thus equipped, these actors are unable to reach consensus. This wide competition between elites in various institutions then impedes the ability to adapt. A president can appoint ministers and initiate programs, but other elites can disrupt these efforts, costing the government time and resources.

Institutions in centralized political fields, conversely, are not captured and manipulated by midlevel or senior elites. Rather, the office of the president or another executive body that practices centralized control over these state organizations dominates this political landscape. These elites manipulate the state's institutions so that agents in these institutions must rely on the presidency or central authority. Elites in these types of organizations, including unambiguous political institutions such as parties and parliament, do not openly compete with other institutionally supported elites. Such elites rarely oppose the upper elites' expressed decision. Rather, these agents serve the interests of the central authority at the expense of their organizational homes. In short, centralized political fields do not allow state organizations to be sources of autonomous influence. While ruling elites may be affiliated with institutions, their power derives from their proximity to the central authority or chief executive rather than their official positions. Because the arena is more centralized, it makes achieving consensus a more straightforward affair. While ranking elites may debate among themselves, the organizations—whether professional arms of the state or its supposedly political branches—will not help them promote their goals over the upper elites/state's interests. Indeed, when a powerful elite dissents, he or she will be unable to take cover in an institution of a centralized organizational field.

The Egyptian political arena entered its uprising in 2011 comprised of organizations in a centralized order. One only needs consider the apolitical character of the security services or the weakness of the ruling National Democratic Party (NDP) vis-à-vis the presidency to observe the contrast with Syria. In Egypt, the executive branch, formerly the presidency, dominates the political order given its centralized authority over state organizations. The individuals that used to run the NDP and the security services depended upon the presidential elites' will. No other institutions had the autonomy to compete with the presidency. The executive cultivated this authority and this produced networks that accelerated consensus building. As a result, Egypt's institutions are more flexible than Syria's. Egyptian ruling elites can incorporate new politicians and shed established figures with relative ease as the aftermath of the 2011 uprising revealed. Consequently, because of this ability, the system is more adaptable. Arguably, the only drawback to such a centralized order is that its participants are isolated from societal demands because there are few venues for outside actors to articulate their interests. While this likely factored in the forced departure of Mubarak and his cronies, the regime nevertheless survived the popular uprising because of its centralized character and ability to remake itself in the midst of an existential challenge.

By contrast in Syria, conventionally political institutions as well as theoretically apolitical organizations all command the ability to intervene because the executive lacks centralized control. Civil society activists such as Michel Kilo highlighted the presidency, B'ath Party, and the security services all acting as "centers of power" in Bashar al-Asad's Syria.[55] The army could easily be included as well. Central elites, with their own patronage networks, control these distinct institutions. As rival networks jockey for position, they reduce the chance of striking a specific consensus for the regime. Thus, the parts of the Syrian political system can only agree on fundamentally broad arrangements. As internal conflict escalates, the presidency, the ruling B'ath Party, and the security services all become embroiled in an internecine struggle for influence. Absent a superior authority able to adjudicate disagreements, consensus proves elusive. When confronted with a political challenge, decentralized authority slows the ruling elites' ability to respond. It also forecloses the abrupt inclusion or exclusion of coalition members such as in Egypt. As Syria's 2011 uprising revealed, the existential threat allowed the elites from the various institutions to band together in a unified manner and unleash lethal force instead of excluding key regime constituents. Yet, it took an existential threat to reduce the elites to uniformity. Outside of extreme examples such as this, Syria's elites experience more power sharing but also more gridlock—and thus are less adaptable—than their Egyptian counterparts.

These differences establish an intriguing comparison between Egypt and Syria. This is, in part, surprising because it contradicts traditional convention about authority in Syria and Egypt. Most would assume that Syria is more centralized than Egypt. In Syria, the party is more institutionalized and more politicized than in Egypt. While the theoretically apolitical security services were less institutionalized in Syria, they were more politicized than was the case in Egypt. Egypt's presidency may have been more institutionalized than Syria's

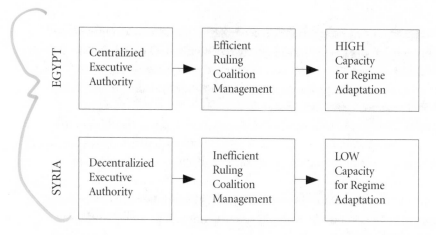

Figure 1 Explaining Autocratic Adaptation

because it is so strong relative to the state's other institutions. Consequently, there is less centralization and more power sharing in Syria than in Egypt. It is, in essence, the difference between oligarchy and autocracy. For the remainder of this book Egypt is described as having centralized institutions while Syria maintains decentralized institutions.

COLONIZING OUTSIDERS

This book describes Egypt and Syria's clientelist and corporatist practices before the 2011 uprising to demonstrate the difference between how executive power operates in each system.[56] It is, therefore, necessary to examine the concepts. Co-optation is a process of mobilizing and incorporating individuals into state organizations. It operates on informal patron-client and corporatist relationships. Patron-client relations, or clientelism, are

> an exchange between roles—may be defined as a special case of dyadic (two-person) ties involving a largely instrumental friendship in which an individual of higher socioeconomic status (patron) uses his own influence and resources to provide protection of benefits, or both, for a person of lower status (client) who, for his part, reciprocates by offering general support and assistance, including personal services, to a patron.[57]

Co-option is important because it expands the ruling elites' authority over the governed. Ruling elites are better positioned to divide and dominate society by including new actors into their service. The elites use state organizations to wed individuals or segments of society to the political system. Once people are brought in, their activities are effectively colonized. Once new agents are included, their affiliation compromises their previous independent status. Co-optation also strengthens the state because institutions define politically acceptable behavior.

There are many reasons why individuals might join an unpopular political system. People seek to be co-opted because it increases their social status. By accepting to be integrated into the government's institutions, a public role brings social prestige and recognition. Elements of personal security may also factor in one's decision. In systems where the rule of law is arbitrary and redesigned routinely, being co-opted increases the chances one will be protected from the legal changes. Co-optation into a state's institutions also reveals a material aspect where one's submission to the hierarchy produces benefits and favors the newly co-opted clients. While pay scales may lag behind rising costs of living, a government can offer an array of other benefits such as subsidies, low-interest bank loans, and job perks that keep people incorporated into its structures and respectful of the hierarchy. By supporting a regime's elites and their policies, one acquires security, benefits, and greater social status, but also a promise for greater upward social mobility. Tacitly or actively supporting the elite's constituted power hierarchy while privately acknowledging the existence of exclusive political contradictions becomes a crucial compromise for understanding co-optation.

Eisenstadt and Lemarchand argue that "patron-client ties involve dyadic bonds between individuals of unequal power and socioeconomic status; they exhibit a diffuse, particularistic, face-to-face quality strongly reminiscent of ascriptive solidarities; unlike ascriptive ties, however, they are voluntarily entered into and derive their legitimacy from expectations of mutual benefits."[58] More often than not, this translates into access for acquiescence. Participation in the system increases a person's access while opponents and individuals unknown to the regime remain excluded. For instance, a candidate's primary motivation for competing in authoritarian elections is access to resources in exchange for supporting the ruling elites' policies. By winning a parliamentary seat, an MP gains access to information relating to discounted land and real estate speculation, business monopolies, construction projects, or import licenses. Also, there is the informal notion of *wasta*, or connections, which are the informal networking webs that underwrite being a part of the national elite. Lastly, by being included, one enjoys the required networks to expedite or circumvent bureaucratic procedures. While the above describes the motivations that drive co-optation, merit-based prerequisites factor into the process. This reveals the elites' intentional design of the process rather than it being a haphazard occurrence.

There is a tendency when studying the co-optation process in authoritarian systems to view integrated individuals as negative rent-seekers.[59] Such agents attach themselves to the government in order to exploit and withdraw as many material benefits as possible. Consequently, their participation has wider deleterious effects. This construction is only partially accurate. People that wish to be co-opted also need to be *worthy*. This is an immeasurable but real quality. Ruling elites focus on a prospect's social capital and ability to positively contribute to the regime's social base. Similar conditions have been observed in other contexts. As Fernando Cardoso argued in reference to Latin American cases:

> Those who control the state apparatus select various people to participate in the decision-making system, a selection process that will be extended to include even the most powerful of social forces, and even sectors of the lower classes. But they will never subscribe to the idea of representation. The delegation of authority from below is not encouraged. On the contrary, the decision regarding who will be called to collaborate, and for how long, is made at the apex of the pyramid of power.[60]

A completely compliant and flexible person is likely to be co-opted at the lowest levels. Clients that bring value added with their inclusion are more attractive for the elites. For instance, a person who holds an advanced degree from a Western university or possesses technical expertise is a better catch for regime integration than an unqualified "yes man." Also, potential clients with expansive networks are more attractive to the government than those without such links. In Egypt's former ruling party, "candidates are nominated not on the basis of dedication to the party, hard work, political capability or the like, but on whether a person, because of his personal influence and social networks within the community, merits co-optation into the system."[61] Selective co-optation extends authoritarian control by including promising clients, but it also preempts dissent. Indeed, little incentive to challenge the regime emerges if one belongs to a party, think-tank, parliament, advisory council, trade union, bureaucracy, military, or academy. Co-opted individuals, therefore, become part of the status quo. Ruling elites may be concerned that excluding too many talented people could prompt their convergence as opposition. Making the talented shareholders in the regime invigorates the political system and promotes durability.

Co-optation provides an additional safety valve for dealing with potential dissent. While there may be some attempt to attract opposition figures, co-optation is designed primarily for those who are neither aligned nor opposed to a regime. By including unaligned individuals, a regime ties its clients' personal and rational interests to the system's continuity. While co-opted members could band together and take over an organization, more prominent actors with established networks within the institution can respond punitively to challengers by expelling them. Alternatively, if a co-opted person defects from the regime for altruistic reasons or on principle, this leaves the excluded agent open to political attack. The ruling elites can discredit them by levying accusations of impropriety, political opportunism, or being unpatriotic. The ruling elites possess considerable means and instruments for ensuring acquiescence once a person becomes a part of its structures.

The process of co-optation reinforces informality, which authoritarian elites use to maintain the norms of a particular institution. In this regard, co-optation is a continuous process of negotiation and interaction that induces competition, as each client seeks to demonstrate their utility and move up the chain. Authoritarian systems thrive on the cohesion and mutual dependence that co-optation produces. For example, a president tries to make a ruling elite dependent on his rule so as to remain less challengeable. Powerful elite figures try to make a president and other elites dependent on their usefulness. The president and ruling elites make agents in their institutions, organizations, and society dependent on them. With everyone trying to ensure the dependency of others, it produces and replicates an inherent logic of cohesion among the actors within a system's hierarchy.

Co-optation allows authoritarian elites to extend power into society and garner social support. Unlike democracies, authoritarian regimes rely on the distribution of patronage to form a clientelist system that secures some form of stability. The above discussion of co-optation does not imply that the process operates uniformly in authoritarian systems. Co-optation works differently in similarly designed states. How co-optation operates depends on the degree of the executive's centralization over the organizational arena, which is a product of the institutional formation period.

CONCENTRATING POWER

Coercion is the most widely reported aspect of authoritarian rule. This is because it is the most repressive characteristic of authoritarian governance.

Coercion can be described as a regime's ability to use force or the threat of force against dissenting individuals or groups. Coercion, although the most distinguishable strategy for maintaining authoritarianism, is also the least used. As Hannah Arendt reminded us long ago, "Power and violence are opposites; where the one rules absolutely, the other is absent. Violence appears where power is in jeopardy, but left to its own course it ends in power's disappearance."[62] The problem is that coercion has few flexible properties. Intelligence services, police, and militaries in authoritarian states maintain the country's sovereignty, defend it from external aggression, and keep day-to-day order. In addition, they protect the ruling regime. It is because of this role that they develop a political logic. The security services in such states are a final bulwark for maintaining authoritarian rule.

While a regime can use force to resolve its political problems, the threat of force is more productive. As the uprisings in Syria, Bahrain, Yemen, and Libya reveal, using force has limitations and does not definitely resolve challenges. In fact, it can spurn more dissent as societies rally around fallen victims. Yet, if segments of society perceive the possibility of the security services using coercion, it changes people's behavior. Myths are often spread about the depth and efficiency of security services as a warning. In this way, the threat of force is more of a deterrent than force itself. The presence of plain-clothed informers on the streets, who may be informally on the service's payroll, operates as a daily reminder that the state is always watching. Furthermore, the overlapping notions of co-optation and patron-client relationships dominate the security services and link them to the ruling elite. The ruling elites disburse vast amounts of patronage to keep their soldiers loyal and willing to support their rule in the face of dissent. As Eva Bellin has written, "Patrimonial linkages between the regime and coervice apparatus . . . enmesh the two."[63]

Whether the security services and repressive apparatus possess an autonomous ability to participate in forming the governing consensus remains central for explaining autocratic adaption. The security services differ in Egypt and Syria. In the former, the services acted as depoliticized enforcers of executive power while in the latter they behave as overt political actors competing with official policy organizations. This variance between the two services is attributable more to the degree to which the respective institutions are politicized rather than the degree of coercion utilized by either regime. Coercion works differently in each system. This is seen in the varying degrees that a president exercises centralized authority over the organizational field.

CONCLUSION

Debates about authoritarianism, institutions, co-optation, and coercion all make critical contributions for understanding autocratic adaptation. Rather than view authoritarian systems as possessing only traditional instruments of domination, executive centralization proves insightful for explaining an autocratic system's durability. Three factors explain the process of adaption. The degree of executive centralization determines *the degree of institutional politicization*. Whether a system's institutions are politicized or not conditions *the location of elite and nonelite co-optation*. How co-optation transpires influences how the ruling elites *develop a ruling consensus*.

Egypt and Syria demonstrate the significance of "weak" institutions in authoritarian political systems. While the Egyptian elites have cultivated depoliticized, professional, apolitical state instruments appropriately, the supposed political institutions—such as parliament and the party—are also depoliticized. This left the presidency before and the Supreme Council of the Armed Forces (SCAF) after the 2011 uprising as the most powerful repository of power for developing a regime consensus. In Syria, a different trend is visible. The political arms of the state, such as the party and the presidency, are rightly politicized, but so are the state's apolitical instruments such as the security services and the military. While both states are postpopulist authoritarian regimes, the more adaptable system maintains a strong executive engine and depoliticized institutions. This is because it facilitates regime consensus more rapidly than a system where there is less institutionalization, less centralization, and more politicization among the state's institutions.

Neither Egypt nor Syria possesses strong institutions per se. The cases, therefore, advance three main conclusions. First, institutions tend to be weaker—more politicized and more personalized—in authoritarian states. Nevertheless, institutions exist and are central for explaining how elites are structured to interact. Secondly, bureaucratic institutions tend to be stronger than political ones (as in Egypt), but this is not uniform where the party is relatively stronger (as in Syria). Thirdly, institutional configurations vary in similar-looking authoritarian states. When the presidency is consolidated and has command over professional apolitical bureaucratic arms and a weak patrimonial party, the upper elites have greater freedom to co-opt and shed members from the ruling coalition. Conversely, where the bureaucratic arms are not reliable instruments of central authority—and, therefore, are politicized—and where the party is strong and able to check the president's central authority, makes it harder to direct co-optation into specified organizations. Hence, this restrains this system's adaptive capacity and allows societal (vested) interests better representation to defend the status quo in the policy process. Because the process of adaptation depends on a regime's ability to remake itself, the relationship of institutions and co-optation becomes the important basis of this study. This degree of executive centralization or decentralization shapes the ability of ruling elites to co-opt and micromanage outside forces. However, before this relationship can be explored fully, we must first turn to the origins of executive centralization and decentralization in Egypt and Syria.

2 THE ORIGINS OF EXECUTIVE AUTHORITY

SCHOLARS OF MIDDLE EAST POLITICS tend to view Egypt as the harbinger for developments in the republics throughout the Arab world.[1] They have company when imagining this analogy. Syrians also cite Egypt's experience as instructive when thinking about their country.[2] As the now-exiled dissident 'Ammar 'Abd al-Hamid argues, "Syria is Egypt just ten years behind. The regime [here] has not made an attempt to reverse land reform or cut the public sector workforce, but it is inevitable."[3] This not only implies a linear development process, but also that populist authoritarian states eventually adopt a neoliberal economic strategy. At a minimum, it also implies that they are governed similarly.

While this convention has not been explored in a focused comparison, there are good reasons to reject it. For example, Volker Perthes cites key differences in each state's economic policies. He observes, "In contrast to countries like Egypt . . . Syria has never, to date, allowed bilateral donors or international financial institutions to interfere in any substantial way with its economic policies, nor negotiated aid for economic reform programmes."[4] This suggests Syria is on a more inward-looking economic journey than Egypt. However, this qualification is not the only distinguishing feature.

Other historical and political contingencies also make the "Syria is Egypt" generalization untenable. For example, Egypt has been ruled centrally from Cairo while Syria lacked such control from Damascus. Yehya Sadowski (1963) notes that pre-B'athist Syria

> was more diverse and fractionalized regionally than Egypt. Syria's state structures never penetrated society and regional cities the way they did in Egypt. The public sector does not and never intended to dominate the commanding heights of the economy like in Egypt. Aleppo's industry was unlike any Egyptian city in 1952. Lastly, Cairo has always cut its political deals through the state while in Syria political arrangements were conducted through local government.[5]

The degrees of regionalism and centralization are important, and this story about comparative governance has not been sufficiently told. The differences between Egypt and Syria stretch deeper into how people within those countries identify with their states. Citizens' ideas of what "Egypt" and "Syria" are, as nations, helped determine which state-builder constructed a system with centralized executive authority while the other settled for decentralized executive authority. National identity, therefore, contributed to the establishment of Egypt and Syria's varying political orders by granting or precluding the leader's autonomy from the state's institutions.

Egypt and Syria's presidents made critical decisions during the 1970s that cemented these distinctions into reality. While identity factored in the adoption of differing political arenas, it was not the lone cause. Two other factors accelerated the diverging institution-formation processes: the states' differing treatment by the international hegemon and the severity of opposition challenges at that time. These factors made the existing identity differences irreconcilable. This chapter traces the origins of executive authority in Egypt and Syria to reveal how elites structured state institutions, which determines the ability of elites in each political system to co-opt elites and nonelites. While the political systems in Egypt and Syria both stand to change in the wake of the 2011 uprisings, this review provides an insight into the type of systems that existed prior to them. The differences between centralized authority in Egypt and decentralized authority in Syria also help explain why the uprisings unfolded in the ways that they did.

Egypt's Anwar al-Sadat (r. 1970–81) and Syria's Hafiz al-Asad (r. 1970–2000) are shown to build similar state organizations that differ in their degrees of executive centralization. This ultimately affects the amount of authority each executive has over the political arena. While the leaders made hard choices regarding executive authority, Sadat and Asad selected from different pools of available options. The reason for choosing the paths they did is not a product of free will. Rather, it results from constraints imposed in varying social identities, treatment by the international hegemon, and opposition challenges during this formation period. Historical developments, then, inform the discussion of the present. This is not a novel approach. As Brownlee reminds us, "Historical accounts . . . are integral to a full understanding of how the legacies of the past are imbricated with the politics of the present."[6] Centralized executive authority in Egypt and decentralized authority in Syria are the outcome of what each leader had to work with during the 1970s. Once the leading elites placed their state's structures on top of society to discipline politics, the varying institutional types shaped elite and nonelite co-optation differently.

DOMESTIC IDENTITY CONSTRAINTS

After independence in 1946, Syrian elites confronted the challenge of organizing a heterogeneous society into an artificial state without a political or administrative center. Syria had no tradition of being a self-contained state entity or having well-defined geographic boarders. Hence, it proved impossible for elites to stitch Syrian nationalism into society. As noted scholar on Syria Raymond Hinnebusch argues, "Syria had no history of prior statehood that might underlay a distinct (non-Arab) Syrian identity. Situated at a crossroads of the movement of peoples and religions, it is very religiously heterogeneous but also overwhelmingly Arabic speaking. As such, secular Arab nationalism was its most plausible and potentially integrating identity."[7] The country's diversity made Arabism the best available option for tying citizens to the state.

This was easier said than done. The lack of an established national identity helped produce rancorous political turmoil between independence and Hafiz Asad's assumption of power in 1970. Fifteen coups d'etat brought different regimes to Damascus between 1946–70.[8] The coups and countercoups reduced politics to a competition among the diverse groups and heightened sectarian awareness.[9] Social heterogeneity and regional fragmentation never allowed the elites to create state institutions that penetrated society or produced citizens with an integrated national identity. The connections between the various urban centers and regions were weak unless trade and commercial linkages previously existed. Not until Hafiz al-Asad expanded the pan-Arab B'ath Party did a Syrian leader link the country's regions in a way that crossed sectarian lines. Syria's artificial character, a legacy of colonial incompetence, informed Asad's efforts at centralizing authority.

Egypt did not have to address a Syrian-like dynamic. Egypt's rulers enjoyed centralized rule over the Nile Valley and the Delta because of the country's defined borders, distinct dialect, and homogeneous population. Egypt's geography made it an isolated island compared to the more religiously and ethnically cosmopolitan countries of the region. Plus, given the homogeneity, it facilitated the development of Egyptian nationalism during the colonial period.[10] This social homogeneity and Egyptian nationalism meant that after 1952 its leaders did not have to focus their energies on building an "imagined community" between different sectarian groups.[11] Consequently, ideas of what it meant to be "Egyptian" coexisted and overlaid with concepts of what it meant to be "Arab."[12] Although the main ideology of Gamal 'Abd al-Nasser (r. 1954–70) was Arab nationalism, Arabism never consumed Egyptian identity.[13] Arab nationalism merely supplemented an already operational Egyptian identity.

As a consequence of these favorable attributes, Egypt's Free Officers had a number of state-building options after taking power in 1952. These options included establishing a strong executive, which they did.[14] Because centralized authority and bureaucratic state penetration existed prior to 1952, pan-Arab institutions that attached Egyptians to state authority were not a necessity. In effect, Nasser established a presidential authoritarian system before deciding on a pan-Arab hue. Then he used and frequently changed the state's single-party vehicle and other state institutions to oversee the political arena during his tenure.[15] Many elites in other Arab states reproduced these types of ruling parties. However, differences in social composition and interregional dynamics produced distinct variations of this system. Because Egypt's ruling elites inherited a homogeneous society, an operational national identity, and an established tradition of centralized rule, they had less work to do than Syrian politicians when constructing their state.

Despite the differences, the political systems in Egypt and Syria appeared to be similar in the late 1960s. Both had single-party Arab nationalist regimes led by military officers that had broken from the earlier colonial era. Elites in both states flirted with radical populism following the failed United Arab Republic experiment between 1958–61.[16] Both states suffered devastating military defeats to Israel in 1967. Coincidentally, both Egypt and Syria experienced leadership changes in late 1970. As populism began to exhaust, both Sadat and Asad wanted to pursue economic liberalization. The presidents planned and jointly confronted Israel in the October 1973 war. The war's outcome granted them popular legitimacy and facilitated the prospect of peace negotiations with Israel under America's auspices. Nevertheless, despite these similarities, post-1970 Egypt and Syria went in different directions when it came to the executive's authority.

The different inherited identity constraints furnished each leader with a different set of options as they built or reconfigured state institutions during the 1970s. The leaders' pursuit of separate strategies produced political orders with varying degrees of executive centralization. How did the identity differences underwriting the Egyptian and Syrian experiences contribute to the diverging strategies?

The central difference is that Egypt's elites divorce their system from Arab nationalism while Syria's elites imbricate theirs with it. Sadat jettisoned pan-Arabism in favor of state nationalism.[17] Yet, identity constraints prevented Asad from moving in a similar direction. Syrianism was not an available option at that time. Instead, he was forced to use Arabism to keep the society from fragmenting as he built a consolidated state. Asad's ideological preferences were not the driving impetus behind his choices. Rather, necessity for stabilizing the state made resting the political system on Arabism the best available option.

COMPARATIVE PARTY DEVELOPMENT
The Egypt of Sadat

Creating a political arena where the leading executive office has centralized authority over the state's institutions requires sapping those organizations of the ability to autonomously participate. This process of emasculating Egypt's ruling party started soon after Sadat assumed the presidency. Before 1970, populism, Arab nationalism, and Nasser's charisma formed the core of political legitimacy in Egypt. While the 1967 military defeat to Israel called into question the viability of Arab nationalism, established ruling elites in Nasser's Egypt showed political resilience in their mobilizing capabilities.

Sadat was permitted to succeed Nasser because he was a Free Officer, which fostered a sense of continuity with the Nasser era. More importantly, Sadat ascended because powerful politicians and military officers perceived him as unlikely to upset the political hierarchy.[18] Sadat inherited Nasser's political institutions but changed their ability to participate so they would be forced to obey his directives. This, in effect, centralized the amount of authority that an Egyptian president exercises over the political arena. Because of minimal social and ideological constraints, the Egyptian polity could be kept unified and cohesive without a strong party that could compete for influence with the president. Obviously, some institution had to regulate politics, but Sadat ensured that the ruling party did not have autonomous power to challenge the presidency's power.

Egypt's formal political arena became drastically more depoliticized during Sadat's presidency. This did not transpire by accident and in no place was this more apparent than in the ruling party. Sadat reorganized Nasser's single party, which initially served as a repository of power for Nasserist politicians against him. Between 1971–76, Sadat repeatedly disciplined the Arab Socialist Union (ASU) until he hemmed it out of existence. The president penetrated, hollowed out, and dismantled the ASU in favor of a more impotent ruling party—the National Democratic Party (NDP). Sadat did not merely rename Egypt's single-party organization, he created a toothless version. Hence, the NDP cannot be portrayed as a descendent or extension of Nasser's Arab Socialist Union, as some claim.[19] Although Nasser's presidential powers dwarfed the ASU's strength, the Union was more organized, ideological, and coherent than the NDP. As 'Abd al-Gaffar Shukar, a former head of political education in the ASU, recalled:

> The political organization and ideology was stronger in the ASU. The Union was more internally organized and politically active than the National Party. To date, it is impossible to understand the NDP's internal structure because of how personalized and unorganized it is. Additionally, the Party has no ideology and all the positions are personal appointments, driven by individual interests. There is no comparison between NDP and the ASU. The Union was harder for one person to control.[20]

Sadat acted aggressively to become president in authority as well as in name. He realized that Nasserist politicians and networks strove to limit his control over the political establishment. He was in a weak position vis-à-vis the existing power centers with "no institutional base of power and no organized clientele."[21] Elites in the ASU structured politics by determining appointments in the state bureaucracy and dominating the various corporatist organizations such as the labor unions. By 1964, there were more than four million members in the ASU. It was nearly a necessity. As John Waterbury points out, "One had to be a member of the ASU to be eligible for appointment or election to any cooperative board, local, regional, or national assembly, or board of any union or professional association. In some instances the right to exercise a profession (viz. journalists) was dependent upon ASU membership."[22] Viewing a future where he would be beholden to oligarchic political struggles over Egypt's future, Sadat opted to attack elites from competing institutions that actively governed.

Sadat perceived Nasser's system to rest on institutions that could *potentially* counterbalance the presidency. He began depoliticizing the ASU by purging figures that maintained strong institutional support like 'Ali Sabri (the vice president) and Sh'arawi Gum'a (the minister of interior). Other figures he perceived to be constraining him were Nasser's director of personal security, Sami Sharif, and Defense Minister Mohamad Fawzi. The impending confrontation became a question of not who had to go, but when and how.

Following the annual May Day rally in 1971, where Sadat was forced to publicly defend himself against Nasser's legacy, the unconsolidated president retaliated in anger. He ordered Sabri to be placed under house arrest on May 2, 1971. Nasserist politicians chose not to mobilize on behalf of Sabri, which further encouraged the president. On the weekend of May 12, Sadat had Gum'a arrested. In a show of solidarity with Gum'a and Sabri, Nasserist politicians and military leaders resigned their posts. They wanted to expose Sadat's autocratic behavior and, thereby, galvanize the Nasserist base against him. No such protests materialized. Sadat ordered his security director to arrest the remaining leaders on May 14 while famously responding, "They should be arrested for political stupidity," when asked what the charges were.[23] The following day, Sadat proposed a new constitution, which extended the presidency's powers. The new president labeled it "the Corrective Revolution." By December 1971, ninety-one Nasserist politicians and senior officers, who were arrested in May, had been sentenced to various prison terms.[24] Sadat had rid himself of Egypt's entrenched ruling elites.

The president, then, transformed the political arena with a combination of interrelated tactics to further defang the ruling party. Since the structures housed elites that could be autonomous of the president's reach, he focused his centralizing ambitions there. Sadat decided to deconstruct and replace the state's institutions with weaker ones. This produced a political field where the president's office was the only active politicized institution. All other governing structures and the elites within them became subject to the presidency's encroaching authority. This allowed the holder of the presidency in Egypt the ability to divide and rule supporters and opposition. Waterbury noticed this long ago and argued:

> It is a testimony to the space that Sadat created around himself that Mubarak had no institution satraps to fear. . . . Sadat's National Democratic party had no leaders of the caliber nor with the organizational power of 'Ali Sabri. The party secretariats were more ward heelers than political infighters. They lacked all semblance of the organizational power or public image that would have allowed them to make a bid for power. Indeed, they could not even aspire to be power brokers. . . . Mubarak thus reaped the benefits of the process of continuous decapitation that Sadat began in May 1971.[25]

Sadat hollowed out the ASU, weakening it incrementally, before dismembering the structure. He eventually turned it into three forums in December 1976.

The forums became Egypt's initial political parties—the Liberal (Ahrar) Party, the National Progressive Socialist (Tugam'u) Party, and the president's Arab Socialist Misr Party (which became the NDP in 1978). Then, parliamentary elections were held. After winning a supermajority in parliamentary elections, Sadat announced that new parties could be formed while ordering the abolition of any organizations under the ASU's sponsorship. With that, Nasser's civilian vehicle was history. As Waterbury recounts, "Sadat, having destroyed the centers of power, now established the power of the center. . . . All that remained of the superstructure was a Central Committee in suspended animation."[26] This led to ramifications that are still felt today in Egypt. Namely, as political analyst Wahid 'Abd al-Magid argues, "The regime is designed to have one party, and suddenly political parties were introduced. The existing political structure, with its constitution, laws and political mentality, did not have this concept [of pluralism]."[27]

A strong ruling party, in theory, serves to center political power as much as incorporate different social groups. Nevertheless, what Sadat sought to do was different. He stripped the ruling party of any potency to resist his office. He dismantled an ASU that was not wholly pliant by hiving off opposition elements into powerless and disparate opposition parties so the rump NDP would be purely loyalist in character. In the process, the NDP became a toothless, disorganized party where elites serve at the executive's pleasure. This affected the political arena by making it more fluid and susceptible to the manipulation by the president's elites. Sadat's centralization project also increased the ability of the president's elites to co-opt supporters and adapt the political system. Depoliticizing the ruling party effectively made its autonomous activity impossible.

While Sadat centralized power at the expense of the ruling party, Hosni Mubarak reinforced this legacy. Mubarak, much less an exhibitionist than Sadat, cautiously deepened his predecessor's experiment. The NDP remained less structurally ingrained or necessary to the political establishment than the ASU. However, the NDP was never conceived to be a power center from which elites structurally competed in developing a consensus. Egypt's party of state remained a recipient, rather than a repository, of power until it was disbanded in April 2011. Perhaps the most astonishing aspect is the degree by which the NDP operated without even the slightest pretense of independence from the president. It made the party docile to alter, strengthen, or weaken depending on the presidential elites' will and a situation's demands. As one scholar argued years before the 2011 uprising, "Should Mubarak's successor decide, for one reason or another to disband the NDP and create his own party, or indeed, to suspend elections in-definitely, the NDP, regardless of its current status, would hardly be in a position to oppose him."[28]

Between 1978–2011, Egypt did not have a legal political party capable of con-tributing autonomously in politics. Instead, the president and the small elite surrounding him remained the only ones capable of initiating a policy direc-tion. The centralized presidency among depoliticized institutions produced a higher capacity for co-optation as well as autocratic adaptation. Such a design granted these elites tremendous range to co-opt and shed participants from the ruling coaliton because of the lack of alternative political repositories. Central-ized executive authority also served Egypt's system well during the 2011 uprising. It allowed for the Supreme Council of the Armed Forces (SCAF) to intercede to eliminate former key constituents of the regime and remove powerful per-sonalities without requiring extensive force to save the regime. By allowing the system to easily change ruling coalition members, it kept a full regime change from taking place.

The Syria of Asad

The trend that emerges from the Egyptian experience is not present in Syria during the 1970s. Faced with different dynamics, Syrian elites pursued different governing options, which produced a different type of authoritarian state. Un-like the Egyptian political arena, Syria's field became crowded with repositories of power. This includes, among other organizations, the ruling party in Syria.

After the Egyptian-Syrian United Arab Republic (UAR) collapsed in 1961, Syrian politics entered a two-year period of political struggle. After attempting to reestablish the political arrangements of 1954, elite conflict between vying capitalists, socialists, and large landowners led to the B'athist military coup of March 8, 1963. Between 1963–65, the government, led by Hafiz al-Amin, made significant populist promises to attract members to its tenuous base. While the party tried to keep stability after assuming power, its small internal ranks di-vided into competing factions due to a lack of leadership and direction. This culminated in Salah al-Jadid's faction conducting a coup in 1966 and initiating a radical populist political program.

The ideologues decided not to purge the party's more pragmatic wing be-cause of a lack of members. But failing to close the diametrical gap between the party's wings compounded the problem. Led by Hafiz al-Asad, the pragmatists inserted like-minded colleagues into the military's command and control positions. These appointments in the military accelerated after the 1967 war. The factions' dissimilarity widened into the "duality of power" that was officially recognized at the 1968 party congress.[29] Two years later, following the military's refusal to attack the Jordanian regime during the Palestinian's Black September uprising, Asad launched a coup against the radical populists. When Asad became president, the B'ath Party was neither an autonomous institutional power center nor as institutionalized as Egypt's ASU. Asad focused on strengthening and integrating the party in order to stabilize the state.

After launching a corrective movement against the B'ath Party's ideological wing in November 1970, President Asad faced numerous challenges. Syria remained fragmented regionally and was without a cohesive national identity. Most importantly, the president had to build an institutional order that was wide enough to withstand another coup. These inherited constraints dictated his course. To keep the country stable, he emphasized Syria's Arab identity. By using the existing governing party that championed pan-Arabism, it became necessary to broaden it to become a pillar for the system. The B'ath Party became crucial to regime stability because it absorbed a cross-sectarian coalition under a common Arab identity. Given Syria's history of elite conflict, introducing an inclusive political center was a necessity.[30] It presented an immediate, and short-term, solution for resolving the predicament of sectarian heterogeneity. Yet, by building a strong party, it contributed to a decentralized executive order. Although there are indications that Asad wished to follow a more pragmatic path vis-à-vis Israel and to liberalize the economy, he was not in a position to issue such centralized directives.

When Asad took over the presidency, the B'ath was a small but ideological party. It had been in power for seven years when he took control. Neither large in membership nor a vehicle for political organization, the B'ath Party had a long history out of power, with real ideological and procedural traditions that Asad relied on to construct a political system.[31] The party produced committed members that believed in Arab unity. Asad's strengthening of the party expanded regime power. This allowed Asad to build a durable system but at a cost. While his presidency became synonymous with Syria's domestic political stability, its source came through implanting the party. How did Asad achieve this?

With the military's blessing, Asad moderated the party's populist ideology. By retaining a high percentage of the party's members and expanding recruitment, the party's social base broadened. Asad initiated a limited economic liberalization program by easing restrictions on state control over foreign trade and imports.[32] This attracted support from the previously well-established private sector in Damascus. Additional bodies included other interested groups.[33] Asad protected the fragile system by maintaining strong lines of communication with the military and developing the intelligence services. Without a civilian party to channel political activity, Asad's system arguably would have been susceptible to external and internal disruptions.

The party's increasing numbers during Asad's first fifteen years in power reflect a strategy of encouraging stability through a party. Party membership under Jadid (between 1966–70) totaled thirty-five thousand members. By 1977–78, the party had at least two hundred thousand full and candidate members. By 1980, although members were declining in "quality," nearly 375,000 members had joined the B'ath. Four years later, membership accounted for 8.36 percent of the age-eligible population and numbered 537,864.[34] This spike is not coincidental. The membership increases coincide with the moments of greatest political turmoil of his presidency. The more Asad poured resources and bodies into the party to protect the state against collapse, the more it became a politicized repository.

Building a ruling party based on pan-Arabism in Syria had consequences. The party's ideology became enmeshed in the state. Once the party digested pan-Arabism, it became inextricably linked to any future diplomacy and conflicts. Whether this was a conscious choice is immaterial. The party connected and better integrated the fragmented regions by attaching citizens to the state's corporatist organizations. As such, the ruling party became the "essential instrument in mobilizing large parts of society."[35] Although inherited, the ruling party was largely Asad's creation because he transformed it into a pillar the state rested on.[36] It remains the state's central vehicle for social patronage. While the party's pan-Arab ideology helped resolve the lack of a national identity and regional fragmentation by penetrating society, it introduced new limitations.

One limitation is that elites within the ruling party maintained some autonomy. Once the party became a base as a politicized actor, the only way to change its character was to destroy it. Yet, Asad could neither destroy nor dismantle the party as Sadat had done with the ASU. Attacking the B'ath was the equivalent to attacking the political system itself. Without a viable replacement, the political establishment would lose one of its anchoring foundations. Given that the party's politicized character promoted stability, it is difficult to imagine that it could be eliminated without inviting a return to instability in Syria.

Evidence is scattered throughout the secondary literature that suggests the B'ath has lost influence but cannot be eliminated. One major problem is by penetrating society and tying people to the state, the bulk of party's members remain dependent on the state—whether they are educators, public sector employees, workers, or farmers. Citing that only 2 percent of its members is upper-middle class, Hinnebusch concluded that the "party cannot be readily transformed into a party of business such as Egypt's National Democratic party."[37] Despite this, some analysts argue, the B'ath Party looked increasingly irrelevant by the mid-1990s. For example, Nabil Sukkar notes that economic planning policy was taken away from the B'ath's control after the 1985 regional congress, and this stunted its role in policy making.[38] Indeed, the party has not been an economic or social-planning force since the liberalization experiments of 1986 and 1991. Others point to the party's declining role because of its failure to convene congresses between 1985–2000.[39]

Rather than signaling the end of the B'ath, these shifts could as equally be attributed to the fact that no space existed for any unsanctioned political activity after Rif'at al-Asad's failed presidential bid in 1984. In this respect, all institutions witnessed their political activities reduced, not merely the B'ath Party. Accounts of how Syrian politics were demobilized in the late 1980s and early 1990s complement this interpretation.[40] The B'ath's fortunes changed again as leading elites from the party reasserted themselves in the lead-up to Asad's death in 2000.

The B'ath Party experienced a revival as Bashar al-Asad got close to assuming the presidency. Although the party was rendered dormant during his father's long presidency, its potential to unleash elites supported by this institutional pillar reemerged as succession neared. The previous institutional autonomy during the critical period of its formation allowed for its reassertion. After all, the B'ath's role was always a key "support of the regime or even . . . one of its seats of power."[41] This enables its elites to obstruct and slow system adaptation because the organization is autonomous within an arena where the executive execises decentralized authority. Yet, the party is also merely one of a handful of autonomous politicized organizations that competes for influence. The intelligence services, military, and office of the presidency can also be considered participants in Syria's decentralized political arena.

The party's experience in the 1970s and early 1980s transformed it into a political force throughout Asad's presidency. While the party experienced periods when it was less potent, its role as a regime pillar permitted it to remobilize. As Eberhard Kienle argued, the party "in spite of its marginalization in the decision-making process, remains the only large-scale political organization with a viable infrastructure and branches all over the country."[42] While Hafiz al-Asad maintained an ability to dominate his elites in the B'ath, the dynamic changed as his health declined. The party has proven far more structurally autonomous than is generally credited.

Presently, B'ath Party membership rolls claim nearly two million, but the character of membership has changed. While many opportunists now join for better opportunities, advancement within the party is more managed as it can take decades to become a full member. Yet, as Scott Wilson reports, "the party has grown into a parallel government, monitoring education, political and economic policy through a network of committees from the national to the village level."[43] Syria's ruling party remains an autonomous repository of power because of its origins.

The necessity of constructung a stable state shaped the type of institution-building strategy that Syria's elites chose. At that time, Syrianism was not a viable ideological current that could attach the population to the state. However, a vehicle with a pan-Arab ideology offered a path away from instability. The B'ath became integral for unifying the different sects and regions. Rather than existing as a top-down elite patronage machine only, the party fulfilled an integrating role that made it a regime pillar. This politicized it and meant that Asad had to share, at least, some power with it. The party needed Asad as he needed the party for the state's continuity. This lent itself to the emergence of a political arena where executive centralization was not an option.

A politicized ruling party is not fundamentally a detriment if the goal is political development. The role of a party is precisely to channel mobilization and political contestation. But the other institutions Asad nurtured—including the military and security services—also were developed as pillars for the system's continuity. Hence, all these pillars acquired some autonomy and required extensive interactions for agreement on regime policies to be achieved. Asad ably became the chief arbitrator in managing this parthenon-shaped political system.[44] Toward the end of his presidency and after his son inherited power, elites in these organizations reasserted themselves. This decentralized design—unlike Egypt's where the leading executive body exercises centralized authority—contributes to Syria's occasional governing gridlock as well as its inability to rapidly alter its ruling coalition. As the 2011 uprisings show, an inability to efficiently adapt prolongs political crises and increases the proclivity to use violence against one's citizens.

COMPARATIVE MILITARY DEVELOPMENT

Sadat's Puppets

As with the civilian political institutions, Anwar Sadat depoliticized Egypt's military in order to extend executive control over the political landscape. The military holds a place of pride in Egyptians' collective imaginations as a stabilizing force. Following the 1952 revolution, the Free Officers promised to develop the country and provide true independence. Yet, as military officers, their plans were largely uninformed. Nevertheless, the regime received a legitimacy windfall after Nasser nationalized the Suez Canal and withstood the tripartite aggression in 1956. That, and the use of pan-Arabism, produced large dividends as it placed the Egyptian elites at the forefront of the nonaligned movement in the Arab world.

Rather than establish a professionalized military, Nasser blended the military into the political wing of the state. Many of the leading cabinet positions went to military officers after 1952.[45] One study reports that military officers accounted for nearly 34 percent of ministerial appointments during Nasser's sixteen-year presidency.[46] Raymond Baker perhaps said it best when he noted, "These military figures undoubtedly stabilized Nasser's regime and guaranteed the political survival of Free Officer rule."[47] This cross-fertilization was so extensive that the military became a "state within a state" under 'Abd al-Hakim Amir's command. Amir, Nasser's closest confidant, was careful not to directly challenge Nasser, but the military emerged as an autonomous power center by the late 1960s. As Said Aburish pointed out, "Nasser's assumption of the position of commander-in-chief was a strictly decorative measure, and Amer continued to run the army unencumbered. . . . This confirmed the existence of 'two states,' the one led by Nasser and the shadowy one headed by Amer."[48] Even if Nasser had informal control over the military, the institution was highly politicized. The popular myth of the army's strength flourished as the elites portrayed the military as the country's savior. The Israeli rout of the Egyptian, Jordanian, and Syrian militaries in a mere six days shattered these perceptions in June 1967. The debacle necessitated that the elites deemphasize Egypt's Arab identity. The fact that Egypt had its own national identity anesthetized this transition. The moment of vulnerability also allowed for the role of the military to be changed.

When they could no longer claim Egypt's military was the vanguard of the Arab world, ruling elites seized the opportunity to reorganize the military. Nasser initiated the process of hallowing out the military. The defeat in the 1967 June War gave Nasser a justification to eliminate powerful figures in the military. He removed Amir and his base of support as well as most of the air force's officers.[49] Nonpolitical senior officers were promoted to expand and professionalize its ranks. By the time Sadat assumed the presidency, he was in prime position to deepen the project. Given this previous momentum, and perhaps his personality, Sadat moved to establish full control over the military. He created a military complex built on professional merit within the rank and file, while making senior officers utterly dependent on the president. This reconfiguration, which he conducted incrementally, assured that the military would be a loyal auxiliary of state rather than a repository of autonomous power.

From the beginning of his presidency, Sadat employed divide-and-rule tactics among the military elite in order to domesticate them. The frequent turnover of military leaders, whose tenure in office was linked to unconditionally supporting Sadat's controversial policies, produced a depoliticized military establishment. His tactics produced elite behavior loyal to the office of the presidency, rather than to the institution to which they belonged. The president maintained their allegiance by playing off intermilitary rivals so that his appointees could not amass networks of support within the institution. There was, however, occasional disagreement between Sadat and his appointees that encouraged the president to constantly rotate appointments. For example, Mohamad Ahmad Sadik was elevated to minister of war after Mohamad Fawzi's demotion for his Nasserist affinities during the 1971 Sabri affair. Sadat used Ahmad Isma'il 'Ali, who had personal links to the president, to remove Sadik.

The president also struggled with Chief of Staff Sa'ad al-Shazli over his decision to cooperate with the United States after the 1973 War. He was replaced by a more loyal 'Abd al-Ghani Gamasi, which effectively ended open resistance to Sadat within the military. Gamasi later became minister of defense. As Hinnebusch illustrates, "Gamasi, the very model of the respected non-political professional prepared to defer to the authority of the President, became the key figure in further consolidating the principle of military non-intervention in political matters."[50] Nevertheless, even Gamasi was replaced along with Chief of Staff Mohamad 'Ali Fahmi over their opposition to the Camp David Accords. Stepping forward, a new crop of presidential loyalists emerged, including Vice President Hosni Mubarak and Minister of Defense 'Abd al-Halim Abu Ghazala. Generals like Mubarak and Abu Ghazala, who were completely prostrate to the president, became the model for how high-ranking officers retained their positions in Sadat's military.[51]

No one military officer—much less a bloc of opposition within the military—acquired autonomy to participate in politics. If someone differed on a policy decision, the president chopped his legs out from under him. Hence, political survival became dependent on allegiance to the president. This affected the military as an institution, which did not independently participate in politics after Sadat took power in 1970. Sadat emasculated the military's leadership man by man as he centralized power over the political arena, which fundamentally changed from Nasser's time.

Reducing the military's political role did not just involve the institution as an autonomous actor, but it also extended to military officers appointed in the government. Sadat reduced their representation with only 20 percent of all ministerial appointments going to military officers.[52] While this remained a sizable portion, it was a considerable decline compared to Nasser's appointments. Sadat's successor, Mubarak, continued this trend. During his nearly thirty years as president, military officers held less than 10 percent of all ministerial positions.[53] Yet the expansion of the executive's centralized authority changed the character of the military and the political system. This transformation in the Egyptian military between the Nasser and Sadat eras is of great importance. Hinnebusch captures this change by arguing:

> At the beginning of his [Sadat] rule, the military constituted a privileged ruling group dominating top elite posts. By the end, it had been reduced to a much smaller, weaker component of the elite. Its claims for a decisive role or veto even in its field of special responsibility had been repeatedly defeated. Indeed, every major foreign or defense policy decision under Sadat was a purely Presidential initiative, often taken without consultation or even against the wishes of top generals. . . . The military still had some input, informally or through the consultations of the National Security Council, into defense policy, but its role had been reduced to that of simply giving political advice.[54]

The military and top generals still mattered in the Egypt of Sadat and Mubarak. However, the military and security services were agents involved in preserving the executive's interests—often at the expense of their own institutions—until the 2011 uprisings.

The military and security organizations served the Egyptian president until January 2011. Their depoliticization between 1970–2011 is generally viewed favorably. A more professionalized, apolitical security apparatus and military is a sign of political maturity.[55] However, in tandem with depoliticizing the system's civilian parts, it left the presidency to centralize a disproportionate amount of power. When an individual or group occupies the office, they inherit favorable conditions from which to exercise centralized authority over elites in the institutions of state. This combination of high degrees of presidential centralization and institutional depoliticization gives the Egyptian political system a greater capacity to remake its ruling coalition as well as adapt during a crisis.

Asad's Other Monster

Unlike Sadat, who saw Nasser cede Egypt's Arab nationalist credentials and begin to tinker with the political establishment, Asad confronted altogether different obstacles. Out of necessity, and similar to the ruling party, the new president expanded the coercive apparatuses to serve as stabilizing pillars for the political system. While the military and security establishments should be the state's apolitical arms, this was not a practical option at the time. The military and security services reflected the unresolved identity and regional divisions that plagued Syria. Not only was Asad forced to construct a cohesive single party to center civilian politics, but he also needed to develop the coercive apparatuses to buttress the country's precarious stability. In the process, it produced apparatuses that became inherently politicized and further contributed to a lack of executive centralization in the political arena.

Asad did not have the option to reorient a consolidated political system toward executive centralization. Rather, he enlarged institutions on which to anchor the regime in order to offset existential crises. The new president pursued an institution-building strategy that rallied behind the idea of Arab nationalism as it cultivated a cross-sectarian military. The binding ideology attempted to integrate Syria's sectarian mosaic. Yet, Arabism lent itself to an overtly politicized role for the military and security establishment in Syrian politics in the years that followed. It also constrained future policy decisions particularly in relation to Palestine.

The roots of the army's disorganization under the B'ath Party state can be traced to Jadid's presidency (1966–70). During that time, the military and party overlapped indistinguishably. Jadid led the radically populist faction while Asad led the more pragmatic wing. As minister of defense, Asad witnessed from close quarters the crushing defeat of the Syrian and Arab armies at the hands of the Israelis in 1967. The defeat was a political earthquake that eventually cleared Asad's path to the presidency. The following year at the B'ath Party Congress Asad and Jadid agreed to disagree as a "duality of power" became formalized between the party's factions. However, this recognition exposed the party leadership's inability to effectively control the military. Asad benefited from the party's withdrawal from military affairs. As defense minister, Asad used the power of appointment to create a network that superseded the B'ath Party's reach. It was not long before the diverging factions collided.

At the November 1970 party congress, Jadid stripped Asad and his closest confidant, Mostapha Tlas, of their party membership because of their "indiscipline." Their dismissals were, however, a moot point. Asad had the military surround the conference hall, and the bloodless coup was complete. The military had overpowered the ideologues in undramatic fashion. As one former civilian party member, Munif al-Razzaz, remarked, "Jadid's fatal mistake was to attempt to govern the army though the party. It was a mistake with which we were familiar."[56]

Having witnessed the B'ath Party's inability to control the military, Asad separated the two and invested in each institution. He used a two-pronged strategy for expanding the military: he decided that the parts closest to the regime would be disproportionately comprised of his fellow 'Alawis; whereas in the wider military apparatus, professional qualifications would be the more important criterion. In work on the Syrian military, scholars have discussed three distinct circles. First, there was Asad's personal 'Alawi kin and clients, who were the closest to the regime's center.[57] The second circle consisted of senior non-'Alawi B'athist officers that had long been close allies of Asad.[58] Their primary task was to serve as conduits between the party and the military. However, Asad transformed the role of the military by allowing it a wider hand in security and defense issues while civilian politicians in the B'ath were responsible for all domestic and non-security related foreign policy. The third circle was the officer corps that operated at the outer ring of the military establishment.[59] The circle's primary role was to serve as a corporatist interest group to lobby the state on behalf of the military's special interests. The three circles acquired a deeply politicized role in Syria.

Yet, the military was never the sole source of authority as Asad sought to establish a more widely supported state. It is also not, as some have written, a minority institution or military regime.[60] Rather, there is a relationship between the military and civilian party apparatus that crosses sectarian lines and reveals decision making to have a shared quality. Hinnebusch supported this characterization by arguing, "While the army is certainly first among equals, army, party apparatus, and state bureaucracy are each mutually dependent, none capable of ruling alone. And while there certainly is overlap, especially of senior

personnel at the very top, the three are functionally specialized and partly autonomous partners with real power in their domains."[61] Because of a lack of options, Asad used the military—like the party—to integrate society and stabilize
the political system because it helped overcome the challenges of regionalism
and sectarian diversity.

The military became an integral instrument of penetrating and integrating society. Through the adoption of Arabism, various sects—particularly
Sunnis and 'Alawis—became united behind a common purpose. The Syrian
military, together with related security services, proved crucial to safeguarding
the regime. They came to be institutions with which Asad shared power and
around which he designed his policies. The military developed a strong contributing role in policy and an autonomous politicized character. As an organization, Asad could not reconfigure or depoliticize it at will. The military, although
a repository of power, shares power, giving Syria a more oligarchic and decentralized political system than in Egypt.[62]

As Asad's health declined and succession appeared on the horizon in the
late 1990s, Syria's politicized institutions reasserted themselves in governance.
By the time Bashar al-Asad assumed the presidency, the established and powerful institutional centers were in a position to block his initiatives and check his
presidential authority. Bashar al-Asad's challenge was loosely analogous to that
of Sadat in 1970. Unlike Sadat, the younger Asad was comparatively weaker in
terms of being able to change his decentralized political establishment. In addition to the ruling party, a politicized military and security establishment did
not want to readily cede power.[63] This undercuts a president's ability to exercise
authority over elites in state organizations and the political system's ability to
co-opt elites and nonelites in a centralized fashion. This makes drastically altering the ruling coalition or adapting during crisis a more difficult task, which
reveals the brutal levels to which the regime stooped during the 2011 uprising.

EXTERNAL PATRONS AND DOMESTIC CHALLENGES

The differences in Anwar al-Sadat and Hafiz al-Asad's inherited constraints led
one leader to construct a political arena where he exercised centralized authority while the other settled for decentralized control and power sharing. As these
differences began to take hold, Egypt and Syria launched a joint attack against
Israel on October 6, 1973. Although not a military victory, the war's outcome
provided Sadat and Asad with the possibility to pursue peace with Israel. Yet,
just as Egypt and Syria exhibited different state-building trajectories, so too

the presidents traveled different paths during peace negotiations. In particular, each country's relationship to and treatment by the region's chief hegemon, the United States, as they pursued peace is exemplary. This is another contributing—albeit supporting—factor that helped consolidate a centralized or decentralized political order.

As the chief mediator in the peace talks, the United States favored working with Egypt. The United States wanted able partners and was willing to diplomatically isolate resistance. For Sadat, realigning with the Americans enhanced his centralization project; for Asad, peace with Israel would betray the Palestinian cause, which would undermine the state. Confronted with the self-destruction of his state-in-progress, Asad chose not to pursue American support or peace with Israel. This led to a situation of US patronage for one state and an Israeli security threat for the other. The external patron's support or lack thereof, therefore, accentuated these differences in centralization and decentralization at a critical and formative phase.

Domestic challenges to the state are a final supporting element that exacerbates differences in Egypt's and Syria's political field. Particularly important, during the critical junctures of the 1970s, the degree and severity of these challenges affected the two processes. Opposition manifestations encouraged leaders to accelerate and deepen their existing strategies. Severe opposition challenges to the system led Asad to deepen decentralization so that party and military pillars could help counter the opposition. In Egypt, Sadat faced limited domestic challenges as he took centralized authority over state institutions. The lack of a sustained oppositional response allowed for him to nurture an over-developed executive body relative to other institutions. As with the external patron factor, the domestic challenges enabled—rather than caused—the executive's centralized or decentralized control of institutions in Syria and Egypt.

AMERICAN FRIENDS AND FRAGMENTED DOMESTIC CHALLENGES

To supplement the executive's incremental centralization over the ASU and the military, Sadat launched an "Egypt First" campaign to extricate political elites from having to appeal to Arab nationalism. Baker observed this transformation by recalling how Sadat described himself as an "Egyptian nationalist" who was "solving Egypt's problems." Moreover, billboards sprung up around the country praising "Mother Egypt" or other "Egypt First" doctrines.[64] Yet, the real blow to Egypt's participation in the politics of Arab unity occurred when Sadat pursued a diplomatic alliance with the United States and peace with Israel.

The American-led peace diplomacy after the hostilities in 1973 helped Sadat transform Egypt's political system. Specifically, Sadat began pursuing neoliberal economic policies (*Infitah*) as he inched toward the American sphere of influence. These postpopulist maneuvers incorporated the interests of the business class into the ruling coalition while incrementally excluding the populist elements from the previous era. Hence, Sadat revealed the successes of centralization with the ease by which he transformed Egypt's ruling coalition. The Americans cannot be held responsible for Sadat reconfiguring Egypt's coalition or his reliance on a neoliberal business class. Nevertheless, the superpower's treatment of Sadat helped the process along as well as encouraged him further to sign a peace agreement with Israel. This has netted Egypt more than $60 billion dollars in US military and economic aid since 1979.[65] One byproduct of this budding relationship was that it increased Sadat's political and economic capital to intensify his centralization of presidential power.

Indications that Sadat felt he needed American patronage to transform Egypt's political landscape appeared early during his tenure. After a Nixon-Brezhnev summit in May 1972, Sadat understood that the superpowers would discourage further wars in the Middle East. Consequently, he feared a permanent freezing of the post-1967 situation. Reactively, 7,800 Soviet consultants, advisors, and military experts were expelled from Egypt in July 1972 to signal to the United States that the country was open to American influence.[66] In addition to this public gesture, Heikel details that the Saudi intelligence chief, Kamal Adham, conducted extensive, secret connections between Sadat and the American government in the year prior to the Soviets' repatriation.[67]

When the Americans failed to respond to the Soviet's expulsion, Sadat felt that only a war could change the dynamic. The 1973 October War helped Sadat reorder regional power relationships by forcing open a diplomatic route between the United States, Arab states, and Israel. The war's aftermath afforded an entry point for the United States to be the chief arbitrator in peace negotiations. Secretary of State Henry Kissinger epitomized the shift in American policy to reflect the region's emerging political reality. As Avi Shlaim argues, "Once the status quo had been shaken up . . . Kissinger moved with remarkable speed to develop an Arab dimension to American foreign policy. His aim was to use the fluid situation created by the war in order to move the parties, step by step, towards a political settlement."[68] Initially, the United States appeared surprised with Sadat's eagerness to share information and declare his intentions. As Kissinger famously noted about the pre-1973 period, "Sadat boldly told us what he was going to do, but we did not believe him."⁶⁹ However, Kissinger rapidly realized that Sadat could be a vital ally for the United States in addition to presenting an opportunity for an Egyptian-Israeli peace settlement.

All of the sides benefited from the peace agreement. The United States benefited from Sadat's centralization, which allowed for swift and unilateral decisions, while its aid helped to encourage a US-friendly business class. Egypt gained access to American aid and had its occupied land returned in exchange for peace. Consequently, Sadat could pursue limited capitalist development and integration with world markets. While the United States may not have been essential for the Sadat-led transformation, it did allow the liberalization project to go further than it might have without such favorable treatment. But, the United States also won a big and important ally in the region. What had once been the vanguard state for nonalignment, Egypt had now become the symbol of America's increasing political and economic penetration into the Middle East. While these transnational political elites benefited, the Egyptian population lost.

Economically, Sadat's Egypt and the relationship with the United States introduced a number of changes. The influx of new resources reactivated the private sector, which increased investment, primarily in the service sector. The industrial base weakened as a result of the state's retraction. Sadat was initially unconvinced the local capitalists could come through with expected investment. So the Egyptian president appealed for a stronger commitment from the Americans, who were willing to provide aid and loans to replace the public sector's input. This produced a rent boom but also increased national debt. As a result of lost state investment, many of the goods that had been produced locally were imported. This, coupled with the availability of new goods, encouraged a consumption-based economy. Sadat's postpopulist turn increased inequalities as public sector middle-class salaries depreciated. In addition, the populist social coalition that included agricultural workers and labor was jettisoned in favor of the emerging capitalist class. Despite, or perhaps because of, the dislocations, new economic and social changes produced domestic opposition against Sadat's policies. These, however, were sporadic and scattered. The opposition also focused intently on the president rather than the wider political system.

Sadat confronted major challenges to the peace and liberalizing projects only twice between 1973–81. Neither campaign affected the process of incrementally expanding the authority of the presidency over the state's other institutions. The first challenge was the "Bread Riots" of January 1977, which were some of the first anti-International Monetary Fund riots in the world. Sadat, in keeping with his neoliberal economic policies, repealed subsidies on bread and other food staples. The following day, protests erupted at Cairo University before spreading throughout Cairo. By the second day, the protests consumed Egypt from Alexandria to Aswan leaving seventy-nine people dead, approximately one thousand injured, and fifteen hundred under arrest. The riots ended when the subsidies were reinstated. Although these riots were the most visible expression of the population's discontent with Sadat's economic policies, the regime did not appear in danger of collapse. Since 1977, no Egyptian government attempted a radical cut of subsidies, opting instead for a selective approach. While this event affected the manner in which the regime pursued economic liberalization, the riots failed to alter or disrupt how authority is exercised among the state's organizations or between the state and society. Opposition groups recognized that the economic liberalization project marginalized the middle and lower classes at a time when Sadat's increasingly unaccountable authoritarian hand coincided with his increasing ties to the United States. Although he navigated the riots, the president was less successful in convincing the citizenry of his policies toward Israel or dependency on the Americans.

The Camp David Accords proved to be Sadat's second challenge. Sadat replaced key military and political personnel in favor of dependent and loyal figures. While these regular political decapitations undercut dissent within elite circles, societal opposition mobilized against Sadat's unilateral push to sign the agreement. Sadat focused his attention on domestic opponents and potential sites that opposition might mobilize. Parliament was dismissed and rigged elections ensured that no opposition figures won. The journalists' syndicate was shut down because of "irresponsible criticism" while Sadat initiated a "code of ethics" that "outlawed transgressions against traditional family values such as disrespect for the head of the big Egyptian family, that is, the President."[70] As dissent increased, Sadat encouraged the Islamists to act as a counterbalancing force.[71] Nevertheless, Sadat galvanized networks of dissent by signing the peace agreement during an Israeli attack on southern Lebanon in 1978.

By early 1980, Sadat had overstepped the bounds of what Egyptians perceived to be politically acceptable. His support continued to fray at the edges. In May 1980, Sadat assumed the post of prime minister, as well as president, in the hope of maintaining strict control over his political establishment. He promised the second post would help eliminate corruption and cronyism. Pledging to reform his *Infitah* program, Sadat tried to sooth discontent by reverting to populism as price controls increased and popular goods were subsidized. However, it was too late. By the end of his tenure, Sadat continuously battled oppositional challenges. While Sadat outwardly appeared in control, other portraits tell another story. Mohamad Hassanien Heikal's account, which is biased, describes a man out of touch, isolated, and resentful of his alienation. As he argued, "He [Sadat] now lived almost entirely in a world of his own creation, in which he was the continuing star and from which all the hostile forces or rivals were effectively excluded."[72] Sadat's last infamous attempt to stop the opposition to his policies happened on September 3, 1981, when he ordered the arrests of approximately fifteen hundred people from all political trends and professions. In prison, Islamists mixed with Nasserists as journalists met engineers. They all unified against Sadat. A month later, on October 6, Khalid Islambouli assassinated Sadat during a military parade commemorating the eighth anniversary of the 1973 War. An assassin, who happened to be a soldier as well as a member of al-Jihad and the brother of one of the imprisoned, ended Sadat's insatiable project for unlimited presidential centralization.

While Sadat paid with his life for depoliticizing state organizations and expanding presidential authority, Egypt's political system and the relationship to the United States survived him. Hosni Mubarak (r. 1981–2011) deepened the Egyptian-American relationship. He kept the depoliticized institutional order impotent while the ruling coalition's links to the business class multiplied incessantly. The demands of the rural farmers and labor sectors were increasingly marginalized and underrepresented.[73] Yet, as a consequence of the Egyptian-Israeli peace treaty, more than goods and services have been exchanged. The Americans effectively controlled the most powerful military (Israel) and the most influential and populated Arab state (Egypt) in the Middle East. In exchange, the Egyptian president was awarded a political system where the chief executive body wielded expansive authority among a host of hapless state institutions. While this centralized system and neoliberal environment were precisely what most Egyptians protested against during the 2011 uprising, the ongoing transition is a consequence of this process. Indeed, the forced departure of Mubarak, the expulsion of the neoliberal economic team, and the reemergence of the military back in front of the curtain of power suggest that while a structural change to the ruling coalition has occurred, the regime was only partially changed. The fact that the military could swiftly change the ruling coalition while allowing the regime—in some form—to endure emphasizes the adaptive power that centralized political systems possess.

AMERICAN ADVERSARIES AND STRONG DOMESTIC CHALLENGES

Hafiz al-Asad engineered a decentralized ruling coalition replete with institutional repositories of power to remedy Syria's regional fragmentation and lack of a Syrian national identity. Constructing a political system to overcome these challenges affected the president's authority over domestic and foreign policy choices. In this order, the political elites struggled with the discursive and ideological commitments to Arab nationalism and Palestine. Pan-Arabism limited Asad's options and interactions with US patronage. While Sadat's alliance with the United States expanded the authority of Egypt's executive, Asad's inability to realign with the Americans helped to deepen Syria's decentralizing path. The lack of American political support also meant that Syria could not opt for peace with Israel. Had the United States treated Syria favorably in the post-1973 period, Asad still could not have broken away from his ruling coalition as Sadat did. Elites in Syria effectively built an inescapable prison for their ruling coalition in exchange for a lasting system. These attributes also affected domestic considerations. The decentralized authority Asad had also restricted the options for economic liberalization and strained the social cleavages he sought to bridge.

Sadat's ability to realign with the Americans is juxtaposed with Asad's inelasticity. With Arab nationalism stitched into the political system and a decentralized coalition, the president deepened Syria's alliance with the Soviet Union because he did not have the option of siding with the United States. While it may have been optimal for Kissinger to have Syria and Egypt to sign agreements with Israel, Asad's inherited constraints precluded such a possibility. Confronted with the reality that Egypt could but Syria could not sign an agreement, the secretary of state made the Egypt-Israeli peace agreement the primary goal. A settlement with Syria could be left for later according to such thinking. In a memorandum to Nixon, Kissinger describes Syria's self-imposed exclusion as "very satisfactory for us—a blessing in disguise . . . we should let Asad stew in his own juice for a while."[74] Kissinger also rightly blamed Syria's ruling party for its president's rigidity. Yet as Asad seems to have known—if the political system was to be durable, he could not tread toward peace with Israel or an American alliance.

Without Sadat's options, Asad relied on the state's institutional pillars more than ever. He continued strengthening the B'ath and military establishments while expanding the bureaucracy, the security services, and the public sector. This necessitated enhancing the relationship with the USSR. Unable to provide the same level of economic rent or political assistance that the United States offered Egypt, the Soviets transferred arms and trained military officers. How-ever, the arms served as a deterrent against Israel rather than a sufficient stock-pile for recovering the Golan. This dynamic relegated Syria into the frozen "no-war, no-peace" situation Sadat publicly feared.

Coupled with being unable to use military assistance to aid the economy, Asad tried to introduce economic liberalizing measures. Yet, the ongoing state of war with Israel made Syria's investment climate unattractive. Exclusion from Western markets precluded the development of a business class with links to the international capital that may invest in the country. Facing diminishing op-tions, Asad used Syria's "front-line" status against Israel to extract funds from oil-rich Arab states. While this buoyed the public sector, it failed to produce in-vestment opportunities. Building autonomy into the institutions represented in the ruling coalition empowered important veto players that were unwilling to compete with the private sector.[75]

Constrained by these structural dynamics and the lack of US support, elites in politicized institutions stunted movement toward economic liberalization. While the B'ath and military both restricted the president's peace option, the military proved particularly active in preventing the emergence of a viable busi-ness class. This, again, stemmed from Syria's existential identity crisis. The la-tent social cleavage between the military's senior 'Alawi leadership and Sunni Damascene-based capitalists checked the leader's rapprochement with the pri-vate sector. Politicized 'Alawi officers "turned into a major obstacle and a burden on development" because they were "wary of economic or political liberaliza-tion, for the Sunni bourgeoisie [were] better situated to benefit."[76] The officers were also responsible for rampant levels of corruption and deterred both private investment and making the public sector more efficient. Without a willing ex-ternal patron or political cover, Asad could not create a large pro-Western busi-ness community prepared to invest in the country.

If the above factors helped create a decentralized coalition with elites backed by politicized institutions, opposition challenges crystallized the process. Unlike Egypt, Syria confronted sustained and severe challenges that endangered the po-litical system during the 1970s. These not only required Asad and top elites to rely on the military and the party but also contributed to the institutions' overly polit-icized characters. As the challenges increased, this encouraged its coalition mem-bers to hang together rather than attempt to exclude one another from governing.

Major internal and regional challenges nearly overtook Syria's stabilizing state. One instance was the Lebanese civil war, which began in April 1975 and

lasted for fourteen years. During the war, the establishment of numerous sectarian and intrasectarian militias that different regional states supported at different times became commonplace. This instability attracted the attention of
Lebanon's southern neighbor. Consequently, during the civil war, Syrian forces
periodically engaged the Israeli military in Lebanon. Hence, while Egypt ex-
tracted itself from the Arab-Israeli conflict, Syria became more embroiled in it.

Considering Lebanon to be a part of greater Syria, political elites in Damascus became involved in the civil war and its continuously changing dynamics.
Yet, multiple political constraints informed Syria's involvement. The regional environment initially led Asad to support the Maronite Christians. Syrian elites calculated that relocated revolutionary Palestinian groups, such as the PLO, would
prolong the conflict because it would attract unrelenting Israeli military attention.[77] They also feared the Palestinians would establish a radical state in Lebanon. Not wanting the Israelis to open a front on its flank or the PLO to establish
a vanguard state, the government adopted an anti-Palestinian posture. Syrian
politicians effectively gambled on Lebanon's existing confessional arrangements.
All this related to Asad's inability to sign a peace agreement. The unwillingness of
the US to intervene on Syria's behalf with the Israelis forced Asad's hand against
the Palestinians. Further, the Israeli, Palestinian, Iraqi, Saudi, and Iranian involvement in Lebanon effectively reshaped regional political relationships in ways that
isolated Syria. Unable to sign a peace agreement or join with other forces in managing the Lebanese conflict, Syria was forced to muddle through on its own. Yet,
its regional problems paled in comparison to what the regime combated at home.

Elites in Syria were concerned that a prolonged conflict in Lebanon might
seep into Syria and destabilize the country's delicate political balance.[78] Yet,
the policy of not supporting the PLO galvanized Syria's domestic opposition.
Siding against the Palestinians cost the regime national legitimacy as well as
much of its limited support. The policy spurred the rise of the Syrian Society
of Muslim Brothers (al-Ikhwan al-Muslimin) into action. Faced with this challenge, a legacy of instability, and unable to reconfigure his decentralized coalition, Asad pursued repressive strategies to stop the Islamist advances. Rather
than Asad battling his elites, the regime unified against a society that sympathized with the Islamist sentiment. The structure of the situation coalesced into
a sustained and violent internal rebellion.

While Asad and the 'Alawi sect became an increasing target for criticism,
the future of the Syrian state lay at stake. Islamists had frequently challenged
the B'ath Party since it came to power in 1963. In 1964, the Muslim Brothers

had protested against its monopoly of power. In 1973, they challenged the new constitution because it initially did not designate a state religion. The regime made conciliatory gestures to defuse these episodes. However, after Asad decided to intervene against Palestinians in Lebanon, the Brothers launched offensives against their rulers. For all intents and purposes, society was at war with the state between 1977–82.

The Brothers intended to discredit the regime as a minority-run government that opposed the majority Sunni population's interpretation of Islam. They exposed the state as weak while presenting themselves as the stable and righteous alternative. The confrontations escalated when the group began attacking government buildings, politicians, and parts of the military. The Brothers succeeded in polarizing sectarian lines by killing more than fifty 'Alawi officers at an Aleppo military school in August 1979. By separating the Sunnis from the 'Alawis, the Brotherhood sent a firm message that they intended to eradicate 'Alawi favoritism from the political system. It was a sentiment that society shared. As one scholar noted, "The broader, urban public, far from showing any inclination to assist in curbing anti-regime terrorism, tacitly sympathized with the Brotherhood."[79] Faced with this dynamic, the president and senior elites contemplated their next moves.

Initially, the government responded with a mixture of repression and concessions. State elites reverted to populist measures such as increasing public sector wages and price controls to combat inflation. Simultaneously, the state executed Islamists for their antigovernment violence. Regional developments, however, such as the success of Iran's Islamic revolution, and money channeled by Iraq and Jordan to weaken the Asad government, bolstered the insurgency. Aleppo emerged as the seat of the Islamist resistance against the Damascene political center. The state and Islamists exchanged blows. The scope and activities of the Defense Companies (Saraya al-Dif'a), Syria's most advanced paramilitary units, expanded as state repression widened. Led by the president's brother Rif'at, the Defense Companies sent troops into Aleppo that launched mortar attacks against mosques and arrested more than five thousand people in house-to-house searches in early 1980.[80] The dispute turned personal as Islamists tried to assassinate the president outside of Damascus's Guest Palace on June 26, 1980. Within twelve hours, two units of the Defense Companies mobilized and were turned loose on detainees in Tadmor's desert prison. More than five hundred inmates were killed. By July 8, 1980, it became a capital offense to be a member of the Muslim Brothers.

The escalation forced state elites into an increasingly desperate confrontation for survival. Yet, rather than fragment, the decentralized coalition held together, dug in, and pursued greater repression. Unable to modify the coalition or drop constituents to assuage the opposition's ire, the situation got more violent. With no external state to appeal to for assistance, and despite getting military help from the USSR, Asad saw Syria as standing alone. Asad's biographer, Patrick Seale, sums up the view from Damascus at that time:

> He [Asad] saw himself as the victim of a "terrible alliance" of external and internal enemies. . . . Asad's fears were not paranoiac. He was indeed surrounded by enemies. He had exasperated Washington by his attacks on the Egyptian-Israeli peace treaty. He had broken with Iraq and after the emergence of Ayatollah Khomayni had sided with revolutionary Iran. He was on the worst possible terms with King Husayn of Jordan. He had tangled dangerously with Israel in Lebanon. Another center of hostility was the Syrian expatriate community in Saudi Arabia and the Gulf . . . many of them members of the former landowning or political families. They had no love for Islamic fundamentalism but saw guerrillas as a battering ram which might bring Asad down.[81]

Pressed into a corner, Asad and the Brothers turned state-society relations into a zero-sum game that neither could afford to lose. The conflict reached its apex in February 1982 when clashes occurred in Hama, a conservative town 150 km south of Aleppo. As the government frequently targeted Islamist-sympathetic Aleppo, more and more of the insurgents migrated southward to Hama. The town transformed into a base of antiregime activity and became home to many of the underground movement's leadership such as 'Omar Jawad.

Following an ambush of army units patroling Hama in early February, the government unleashed its fury. Rif'at al-Asad led the Defense Companies and twelve thousand other soldiers into Hama, which ended with the death of at least ten thousand guerillas and civilians. As Seale writes, "In Damascus, there was a moment of something like panic when Hama rose. The regime itself shook. After battling for five long years it had failed to stamp out an underground that had killed the flower of the 'Alawi professional class and had tarred Asad's presidency with the charge of illegitimacy. Fear, loathing and a river of spilt blood ruled out any thought of truce."[82] Hama produced lasting effects on the Syrian state. Some argue that "the failed Islamic revolution arrested the development of the B'athist state."[83] Seale poignantly states, "The iron-fist methods he put into practice probably saved the regime, but also changed its character."[84] Basic political liberties were all but suspended and civil society was decimated after Hama. The president's office, however, never attempted to actively depoliticize the state's institutions.

The key instrument that protected the state during its near civil war was its decentralized ruling coalition that consisted of a politicized presidency, ruling party, and military. These events and the lack of a reliable external patron reinforced the decentralizing course Asad adopted in 1970. While they cannot be seen as important as the regional fragmentation and lack of a national identity, they do help more fully explain the origins of state institutions in Syria. As the situation worsened, the president leaned more heavily on the state's pillars. When institutions are politicized and operate in a decentralized political arena, they acquire an ability to participate autonomously whether political life is active or hibernating. They remain politicized until they are reconfigured or depoliticized. Hafiz al-Asad never actively depoliticized the system's institutions or made an attempt to centralize authority of his coalition partners. As such, they remained the ruling pillars throughout his presidency. While the elites in these institutions remained dormant, they proved capable of reasserting themselves at the soonest available opportunity. As Bashar al-Asad prepared to become president, elites began using their institution's politicized character to expand their influence in a post-Hafiz al-Asad era. Syria's decentralized arena outlived its creator, just as Sadat's centralized political arena outlived his presidency. However, elites backed by politicized institutions that operate in a decentralized arena produce oligarchic competition as the executive is forced to share power.

COMPARING CENTRALIZED AND DECENTRALIZED POLITICAL ORDERS

Anwar al-Sadat overcame fewer identity and state-building constraints, enjoyed American largess, confronted less sustained challenges, and is seen as the great transformer of Middle East politics. Meanwhile, Hafiz al-Asad resolved Syria's identity and regional issues while constructing a lasting state, only to be forced to balance against system-threatening opposition, meddling neighbors, and a lack of US support. Nevertheless, he is upheld as the archetypical authoritarian leader in a region dominated by such creatures. The irony that traipses through the details is that the narrative's hero left behind a highly centralized political system that is in some ways more efficiently autocratic and durable. The executive's exercise of authority in such a political system is highly concentrated, discourages institutional debate, and witnesses elites rotating in and out of state organizations that are unable to defend themselves. The story's villain oversaw the construction of an executive that maintains decentralized authority over elites in an arena where nearly all the governing and security institutions compete with one another. In terms of how authority operates, Egypt is more autocratic while Syria is more oligarchic.

The absence of a functional state and regional cleavages left Arab nationalism as the only unifying identity to bind and organize Syria's then fractious polity. Asad not only built pillars on which to stabilize the political system but also created autonomous organizations. Asad consciously built social support through politicized institutional bases—namely, the B'ath Party and the military/security services. The ruling party and the military apparatus were essential to political stability because they helped overcome Syria's sectarian heterogeneity. Conversely, Egypt did not require such unifying political institutions because social homogeneity is high, identity consolidated, and the state's social penetration has a long tradition. Given Egypt's ready-made national identity and developed state, Sadat could pursue the depoliticization of state organizations when the opportunity presented itself. In doing so, he uprooted any institutional obstacles to the presidency as he reconfigured the political order. Yet, he never replaced or inserted similarly politicized structures after reorganizing the military and dismantling the ASU. He developed an executive body with tremendous centralized authority. Mubarak inherited this arrangement and unoriginally continued along the path Sadat blazed until he was removed from power in 2011.

The multiple challenges that each leader confronted after taking power placed constraints on Asad and created opportunities for Sadat. Just as Sadat could easily break away to pursue his opportunities, Asad found stability by outwardly building decentralized executive authority into the state. Although the two leaders were pulled in different directions regarding their strategies, the leaders were both one-dimensional in their ruling styles. Sadat seemed to have an inclination to depoliticize every institution he could, so as to centrally dominate the state's institutions. Without such options at his disposal, Asad politicized each of the state's pillars for the sake of political durability, which left a decentralized ruling coalition. Neither of these systems lends itself to having an easy trajectory for more balanced political development.

This points to significant conclusions. Once an institution has achieved a certain degree of autonomy, its potential to participate in politics remains unless completely redisciplined and depoliticized. Alternatively, if institutions are created but never endowed with political potency, then their ability to organize politically or grow stronger on their own is unlikely. Hence, the B'ath Party and military/security services apparatus can be described as politicized institutions and the NDP and Egyptian military as depoliticized institutions. If given a choice between ruling a politicized or depoliticized institutional order, the latter shows a higher capacity for system adaptation. This implies that, should a political crisis arise, Egypt will be more likely to adapt by changing the ruling coalition while Syria will be unlikely to make such alterations. Given this is the case, we can anticipate Syria to resort to using violence to save the regime and its ruling coalition.

The differences in Egypt and Syria's adaptive capacity are a product of the origins of executive authority. Since 1970, Syria has been more of an oligarchic system where elites from competing organizations share power and protect their interests. This type of political system requires a president to be more actively involved in reaching governing compromises and consensus with other elites. It constrains the president's ability to dramatically break away from the system's existing course or horde power. Hence, changing the ruling coalition during a crisis is an unlikely alternative because it risks the entire regime's survival. Egypt, by contrast, is an executive-heavy political system where other state organizations do not maintain the ability to act independently outside an executive body's purview. Hence, an institutional oligarchy does not exist in the Egyptian system. Whoever occupies the position at the system's apex is structurally advantaged in determining the composition of the flexible ruling coalition.

The varying origins of executive authority led to a divergence in the character of politics that developed in Egypt and Syria. In Syria, the politicized institutions that emerged were capable of political participation outside of the executive while Egypt's depoliticized institutions proved incapable of defending themselves, much less independently participating in politics beyond the centralized executive. This, in turn, produced different styles of co-optation of elites and nonelites, which is a fundamental aspect that influences an authoritarian political system's capacity to adapt. As we will see, politics based on individuals is easier to alter than that of institutions.

3 ADAPTATION AND ELITE CO-OPTATION

THE RULING COALITION'S SENIOR ELITES are the central agents for maintaining a political system. The more centralized executive authority over the ruling coalition, the more senior elites connected to the executive can affect change. These elites possess the greatest ability to induce change or maintain the status quo because they are structurally positioned near the epicenter of the governing process—regardless of the weaknesses of the institutions to which they belong.[1] These elites emanate power by holding sensitive government positions, such as being ranking party members, government ministers, or presidential advisors. Not every included member of the ruling coalition, however, is an elite with direct ties to the executive. A ruling coalition can also include middle elites, which include pro-government intellectuals, editors-in-chief of official and semiofficial newspapers, and leading members of government operated nongovernmental organizations (GONGOs).[2] Yet, the higher one is, the more powerful one is in terms of elite politics. How does someone become an elite? Under what circumstances does someone become a senior elite with an ability to implement or obstruct the work of the ruling coalition?

The ability to network and attach oneself to a patron permits entry into the elite circle. It appears to require an unquantifiable mixture of informality, social capital, and effort. Individual power, nonetheless, varies. Whether one cracks the ceiling of being an elite depends on extensive patronage networks, how useful someone is to the executive elites, and a proven commitment to the system's cohesion. Proximity—be it the presidency, another executive body, or a power center—determines an elite's impact or vulnerability. This process of going from being an outsider to being incorporated into supporting the system's services, or co-optation, unveils the nexus for explaining autocratic adaptability.

The varying origins of Egypt and Syria's executive authority affect elite co-optation. Where the executive commands centralized control over state organizations, the executive elites can introduce new members with greater ease.

They can also remove elites without producing blowback from the institutions they belong to. In arenas where the executive competes with other state organizations, elite co-optation is more diffuse. There, elites are co-opted into various organizations across the ruling coalition. Powerful elites are harder to introduce and established ones tend to be more resilient as institutions provide more cover in a less centralized, oligarchic system. This chapter comparatively evaluates the politics of elite co-optation in these two cases.

Elite co-optation focuses on the changes among the highest elites and on the management of the ruling coalition. Building on the argument of levels of executive centralization, the differences between Egypt's centralized system and Syria's oligarchic political field are exposed. While demonstrating that elite competition produces cohesion and encourages durability in both instances, we also see how levels of executive centralization structure elite co-optation differently in these similar-looking political systems.

THE PRESIDENCIES

The political systems in Egypt and Syria possessed different types of presidencies prior to the 2011 uprisings. This can be seen in the amount of authority that each executive maintained over his political field, which helps explain why each country experienced different outcomes to those uprisings. This section explores these differences prior to 2011. This is partially a consequence of presidential consolidation. Yet, consolidation is not the sole factor for determining the relationships between executive autonomy and the ruling coalition's elites. Rather, the degree that the executive exercises centralized authority over the state's ruling coalition contributes to the amount of power an executive body can eventually wield. Executive centralization conditions a president's ability to efficiently overcome a rival or institutional challenge. Such a design determines who governs, how many, and how. Part of being in power is remaining relevant to those alongside whom you govern. Authoritarian political systems are fluid and demand a leader's constant attention and adjustments to maintain control over the elites. All presidents continuously wrestle with and redefine their ruling coalitions to maintain or attempt to increase autonomy vis-à-vis other agents, institutions, and social forces. When analyzing presidents, each chief executive navigates the particular arrangements and legacies that they inherit.

While a lack of institutionalization emphasizes personalized attributes, politics in such systems is not reducible to one-person rule. Presidents need elites for developing a consensus and for outwardly implementing policy decisions. To say that elites have no influence is erroneous. A decentralized ruling coalition with elites in politicized institutions is more difficult to manipulate or manage, which makes it less adaptable. This is because such decentralized characteristics contain elites from more than one institution, or repository of power, contributing to coalition change, policy implementation, and cohesion. Hierarchy and authority exist, but they are not stitched into routine or predictable outcomes. The absence of a centralized executive makes resolving differences among the elites across the institutions a time-consuming process filled with obstructions. On occasion, it even produces gridlocked governance.

Decentralized political fields encourage turf guarding. Elites supported by individual institutions possess the ability to defend themselves (and their institution) against other agents from competing institutions. This characteristic perpetuates itself and makes developing a governing consensus an arduous endeavor. Failure to protect their institution from other repositories leads to a situation where elites confront the possibility that their influence is marginalized or eliminated. Elites engage in a competition that aims to make other elites and their institutional homes dependent. Elites also realize that reaching outside of the governing circle to appeal for more populist support jeopardizes balance. A decentralized field with competitive institutional interests does not inevitably produce elite conflict. While such politicized institutions are more prone to such conflict, competing senior elites recognize they risk the system's viability if politics deflate to all-out elite conflict. For elites, the system's stability takes precedence over one institution's complete dominance over others. Hence, as the Syrian uprising has shown, elites in decentralized political orders will band together and employ all repressive measures necessary rather than threaten the regime's survival by altering the ruling coalition. In this respect, elites in autocratic systems unite against the mobilization of large social blocs that threaten their incumbency.

In systems where the executive possesses centralized authority, the president's position is stronger. A president, who is endowed with extensive constitutional powers and is capable of using them, becomes the arbitrator over top elites housed in the state's governing organizations. In such a position, the executive becomes the source for the system's policy changes. This makes the system highly adaptable, which means that even the chief executive becomes dispensable because its adaptive qualities are so efficient. As Egypt showed prior to the 2011 uprising, the executive and his elites managed and changed the ruling coalition with great ease. Yet, when the regime was threatened, SCAF could insert itself into the position of the chief executive and trim the ruling coalition by eliminating the neoliberal economic team, redisciplining the internal security services, and even deposing the president himself. Through the system's centralized design, it allowed SCAF the ability to introduce a structural change to the ruling coalition rather than experience a full regime change.

Sadat depoliticized the state's institutions and the ruling coalition. This blocked the emergence of structurally supported, autonomous elite power centers. Sadat emasculated Nasser's ASU before replacing it with the impotent NDP. Similarly, he depoliticized the military by incrementally removing high-ranking and powerful officers from having participatory roles.[3] Mubarak continued the processes Sadat initiated throughout his presidency. Egypt exhibited an executive-dominated system. Syria's experience evidences a differing trend. Executive authority is decentralized. This is because Hafiz al-Asad nurtured politicized institutions to stabilize the system during the 1970s. As his death approached, elites in these regime pillars reasserted their autonomy. Therefore, elites in organizational power centers and the president compete for influence. This difference affects each state's capacity to co-opt and shed elites into and from the ruling coalition. Within this context, the specificities of Egypt and Syria's contemporary presidencies are examined.

HOSNI MUBARAK'S EGYPT

Egypt's last president, Hosni Mubarak, assumed the office after Sadat's assassination in October 1981. He ruled until a half-popular revolt, half-military intervention deposed him on February 11, 2011. During this nearly thirty-year period, Mubarak refused to appoint a vice president until his final days in office. He used a host of approaches that mixed degrees of coercion and concession to domesticate allies and opposition. The only public accountability that Mubarak ever faced was a vote every six years, although his nomination was closely controlled before 2005.[4] The former president was constitutionally entitled to unlimited terms.[5] Mubarak's insatiable pursuit of political power at the expense of the ruling coalition's autonomy adversely affected Egypt's political culture.[6] The 1971 constitution, which remains in effect, grants the president far-reaching powers. Mubarak's ability to use such powers allowed for his keeping the presidency dominant throughout his tenure.

Generally, analysts view the early 1980s as a period of relative tolerance and accommodation[7] while political deliberalization characterized the 1990s.[8] Mubarak not only maintained control over the system's elites, he also expanded executive authority. His governing philosophy was best reflected through his perception of being the father of all Egyptians (his children), who pine for stability at all costs. Nowhere was this more prominent than in his interview with a media mogul 'Imad al-Din Adib, entitled, "My Word on History" in April 2005.[9] Over the course of six hours, Mubarak explained his leadership qualities and experiences as unique. He portrayed himself as the only person capable of governing Egypt. Since Mubarak sat at the structural apex of this classic political pyramid, it should not have been surprising that his political perceptions were highly patrimonial.

Mubarak was capable of checking the development of autonomous elites and institutions. The institutions that formally governed Egypt in the pre-2011 period were not capable of defending themselves against the president, much less independently participating in the formation or execution of a governing consensus. This is attributable to design as much as action. Mubarak did not seem content with his position of authority vis-à-vis formal institutions. Rather, he continuously reached deeper into individual areas of governance to keep elites and institutions enfeebled. He penetrated governmental portfolios and jurisdictions and violated the autonomy of state institutions, so as to constantly fortify his unchallengeable position in the system. As publisher Hisham Kassem argues:

Whenever Mubarak sees any organization or anyone *potentially* capable of challenging his rule—be it a prime minister or a NGO—he not only moves to remove the person, he annexes their office ensuring its future submission to his rule. One only needs to compare Fu'ad Mohy al-Din with 'Atif 'Obayd to see the Prime Minister's declining role. Egyptian politics under his rule has been about the complete destruction of the legislation, judicial, and executive branches save his powers.[10]

Even the appearance of being independent from the presidency was unacceptable in Mubarak's Egypt. Mubarak was initially constrained when he inherited Sadat's liberalizing doctrine with commitments to the rule of law. As such, he never disregarded a Supreme Constitution Court ruling.[11] Yet, by selectively applying the court's decisions, manipulating a ruling's implementation, or promulgating parliamentary legislation to counter laws, Mubarak managed to project a shallow guise of respecting judicial independence.[12]

Mubarak confronted various domestic crises such as the 1986 Central Security Forces (CSF) riots over salaries. A military and political challenge emerged when he was forced to compete with a popular Minister of Defense 'Abd al-Hamid Abu Ghazala in 1987–88. Mubarak eventually outflanked and excluded him in 1988. Military officers did not support Abu Ghazala's house arrest, but Mubarak weathered the backlash of the key constituency and strengthened his position by further restructuring their ranks.[13] In the 1990s, economic challenges such as an increasing external debt, deflating currency value (L.E.), and price inflation forced the president to steer the country away from economic stagnation, by selectively implementing an IMF-sponsored Structural Adjustment Program. The regime also battled a radical Islamist insurgency in the 1990s that targeted government officials and tourism—Egypt's second-largest revenue earner.

Similarly, regional political developments, such as the Palestinian Intifadas, forced Mubarak to defend his unpopular foreign policy positions. Despite only visiting Israel once for the funeral of Yitzhak Rabin in 1995, Mubarak honored the Camp David Accords and was responsible for overseeing the return of full Egyptian control of the Sinai. Indeed, Egyptian-Israeli cooperation accelerated as Egyptian security became more involved in securitizing and blockading Gaza in the final years of his rule. Also, the close alliance with the United States caused frequent criticism from Egyptian society. Mubarak was criticized for Egypt's direct and overt military participation in Operation Desert Shield against Iraq in January 1991. His position before America invaded Iraq in March 2003 helped encourage the local protest movement that eventually became known as the Kifaya, or Enough, movement.[14] Regardless of the unpopularity of his foreign policy, Mubarak survived and incrementally strengthened his position at Egypt's helm until January 2011.

His ability to overcome political challenges was made easier because he operated in an environment where the office of the executive exercised centralized authority over state institutions. Elites without institutional support that challenged Mubarak were removed with little difficulty. Decades of ministers, technocrats, parliamentarians, and a robust military-security complex failed to produce a power base autonomous of the presidency. The now-disbanded NDP remains the most apt example. It was institutionally unable to defend itself and consisted of individual personalities instead of being an organization. Even if the NDP achieved a milestone, credit stemmed from the party's relationship with the incumbent rather than the fruits of its labor. The repressive apparatus, based in the Interior Ministry, was left to mop up the party's shortcomings and failures to politically resolve matters. In practice, the state, ruling party, and coercive forces were indistinguishable. Hence, when the protesters took down the coercive apparatus, the party and state were paralyzed to respond until the military made its move against Mubarak.

Until that point, the Egyptian military had served as presidential appendages. As one scholar argues, "It [military] remains the president's private preserve."[15] This type of relationship had its origins in the Sadat presidency but was also a hallmark of the Mubarak era. As Harb states, "Mubarak has allowed for the economic independence of the military while assuring himself complete domination of it."[16] Mubarak's wide-reaching powers of appointment reinforced loyalty to the president and kept the military docile.[17] As a professional organization, the military remained unable to act until the regime's survival was threatened. It was only then that SCAF inserted itself into the centralized position of the executive and altered the ruling coalition. The ability to do this, and in the process save the regime without resorting to mass violence to quell popular protests, reveals the adaptable character of Egypt's centralized executive.

Mubarak's rule demonstrated the extent to which the executive remained the only politicized institution in Egypt. The chief means of Mubarak's success consisted of incrementally eroding any organizational, personal, or institutional resiliency that surfaced. As a result, Mubarak's twenty-nine-year tenure made him the longest ruling leader since Mohamad Ali (1805–48). While this discussion of Egypt's presidency suggests that Mubarak was an omnipotent figure, this is an inaccurate depiction. The president needed elites to perpetuate the prevailing system of hierarchy. Mubarak was, after all, unable to rule by himself. Power may have been concentrated in his office, but he had to expand it outwardly through elites' networks to remain unchallengeable and to command authority. This, in turn, placed constraints on him although they were not institutionally based. Thus, even in a system blatantly unbalanced in the executive's favor, the president's office had to maintain consensus among the elites in his ruling coalition. While he was capable of influencing his establishment by introducing new elites or removing older ones, compliant followers still had to perform their duties and incorporate their patronage networks to perpetuate the system in the absence of an institutional-based environment. Mubarak never dreamed popular protests could end his reign. Nevertheless, the Egyptian president used to have to maintain constant engagement and work to discipline and rediscipline the political elites. The Syrian presidency functioned in a markedly different fashion before its uprising began in March 2011.

BASHAR AL-ASAD'S SYRIA

Prior to Hafiz al-Asad's death, the Syrian presidency looked similar to other regional examples. Indeed, a brief examination of the constitutions of Egypt and Syria does not show much difference in the executive's formal powers. Like Mubarak, Asad was a former commander of the armed forces, head of state, and apparent arbitrator in all high policy matters. During Hafiz al-Asad's tenure, he presided over an "authoritarian-presidential system with distinct neopatrimonial traits."[18] Divide-and-rule tactics, corporatism, and repression protected a system previously rot with destabilizing elite conflict.

One central difference, however, distinguished Syria from Egypt's leader. Asad balanced several institutions headed by security "Barons," senior ministers, and veteran party apparatchiki. Rather than remain above the top elites and state organizations, he consulted with those figures from these institutions to construct consensus on policy. Thus, Asad anchored his regime in the pillars of a ruling party and its corporatist subsidiaries, the state bureaucracy, and the security forces.[19] Governing institutions, and particularly the B'ath Party, do matter in Syria. The institutions, which Hafiz al-Asad manipulated, became centers of power in his absence. While Hafiz al-Asad developed institutions to insulate the state, he never depoliticized them. Hence, when institutions become politicized, their potential to act as independent power centers existed because of the elites' capacity to organize politics in the organizations. The ability of politicized institutions to assert themselves can be seen as not only elites protecting their positions but as an obstacle to adaptation.

Syria's political system may have appeared to transform after Hafiz al-Asad died on June 10, 2000, but in fact, it had not. Decentralized executive authority, which occurred when the state was constructed during the 1970s, just became more evident. As such, the younger Asad has neither consolidated the presidency nor appeared capable of doing so without a dramatic alteration of the political arrangements he inherited. Indeed, not only did the B'ath Party and security services acquire policy influence and the ability to obstruct one another, they were able to constrain the president's power. Syria's succession was elite guided,[20] and it demonstrated the tense relationship of decentralized executive authority and politicized state organizations. The elites would have been powerless to constrain the new president for long without politicized institutions capable of independent interventions. Within their various institutions, the elites were capable of rallying their power centers to slow the pace of change and check presidential power. As Perthes emphasizes, "Bashar al-Asad owed his position to the very regime at the top of which he had been placed. At the outset, therefore, it seemed that some sort of collective leadership would emerge whereby the President would have to share his power with other members of the leadership, particularly those who had been brought into their posts by his father."[21] It seems that new presidents always must decipher existing power relations and interests as they consolidate their positions. However, in the case of Syria, Bashar al-Asad's inability to outmuscle a politicized ruling party and security establishment made consensus building fractiously inefficient. Yet, this is structurally based rather than an instance of personality or leadership traits.

Some analysts question Asad's real power and paint him as a figurehead beholden to entrenched elites that play puppet-master.[22] Without question, he is a key figure in Syria's oligarchic system. Yet, the presidency in Bashar al-Asad's Syria is a power center competing for influence as much as the B'ath Party or the redundant security services are. As Patrick Seale argues, "We cannot say the president has no power. While other interests exist, he effectively has all the extensive services and powers of the presidency. He sets the tone for the country."[23] While Syria's current president may not be able to utilize the extensive constitutional powers his father possessed, he still has the most cohesive of competing institutions at his disposal. As Syrian opposition politician, Samir al-Taqi, suggests, "The office of the presidency is the most developed institution in the country. For instance, his office has the best-trained and armed military squads defending it, the constitution's legal powers, and popular legitimacy that the party does not have. Regardless of the centers of power, the system was created to point to the presidency. It is not his arena to win, it's his to lose."[24] Rather than argue that this is purely a matter of consolidation, this dynamic originates in the institutional differences between the Egyptian and Syrian presidential systems.

According to observers of Syrian politics, the president does not have the power to counter the ruling party. He often makes pronouncements but is unable to implement reforms because he lacks the will to do so.[25] Many point to al-Asad's inaugural speech in July 2000 when he argued for reform based on "accountability," "transparency," and "the rule of law," and "democratic thinking."[26] Despite these statements, other analysts note the president failed to create a plan of action. An International Crisis Group's (ICG) report bears this out when arguing, "There is little doubt that he remains dependent on the regime he inherited and of which he is a quintessential product. . . . He has yet to devise or implement a coherent project or strategy of his own, domestic or foreign."[27]

Instances where elites supported by the B'ath Party, military, 'Alawi community, and intelligence services constrain the president are abundant. This largely entails two broad tactics. Firstly, ruling-party elites circumscribe the president's initiatives by disregarding them. They do this by bureaucratically obstructing them or simply ignoring them. An example of Asad's lack of control over the ruling party is Executive Decision 408 of June 2003. According to one participant, al-Asad battled the party's Regional Command (RC) for months to get the body to accept a decision that separated executive policy creation from the party's politburo. Executive Decision 408 states that the party's role is not that of the state or government, and personnel decisions in government would prioritize merit over party affiliation. Lacking a substantial base, Asad pursued this in order to introduce more "reformers" into government-appointed positions.[28] Reformers in this sense were people willing to build the president's independent networks to offset the rival elites.[29] Yet, rather than Asad getting stronger, the opposite occurred.

When a new cabinet was announced in September 2003, the percentage of pro-president elements actually decreased. Key reformist Minister of Industry 'Issam Z'aim was falsely charged with corruption while other nonparty actors, such as economist Nabil Sukkar, were passed over for ministerial postings. Instead, the ruling party's representation in the new cabinet increased, indicating a setback for the president's agenda. Indeed, the 2003 cabinet reshuffle contained more members of the ruling party than the previous government.[30]

The cabinet reshuffle in October 2004 continued the trend of marginalizing Asad. Thus, while the president successfully lobbied the RC to agree to Executive Decision 408, the party weakened its practical application through cabinet appointments. Ignoring Asad's initiatives is not the exclusive purview of the party. The power centers influence extends into the day-to-day execution by the state's bureaucracy. For example, between 2000 and 2003 "some 1900 decrees, laws and administrative orders carrying Bashar's signature have been issued . . . very few have been implemented, a result of bureaucratic inertia or outright opposition by high-ranking officials."[31] Elites with extensive patronage networks within various politicized institutions rallying support throughout the system dilute the president's impact. The elites have not simply blocked the president by disregarding his pronouncements.

The president's attempts to nominate nonparty technocrats are another example of this dynamic.[32] The most prominent appointments have been 'Issam al-'Awwa's appointment as dean in Damascus University and 'Abdallah

Dirdari's appointment as head of the State Planning Commission.[33] As such, the president's chief strategy is to introduce changes in the education field so as to break the ruling party's control. Some, however, are not impressed by Asad's strategy of limiting the party's reasserted influence.[34] As one observer argued, "Bashar's presidency is similar to Sadat's. He is either going to carry out a coup against the elites or else he will be a toy in their hands."[35] Samir al-Taqi, former member of the Faysil wing of the Communist Party, made a similar point in a perhaps more nuanced manner. He argued, "Unless Bashar makes important leadership changes, the party will ably maintain its political hegemony within the system."[36] All unconsolidated presidents face obstacles and entrenched interests, which they must overcome if they are to effectively consolidate their presidency. In the case of Bashar al-Asad, Syria's ruling party's politicized character has proved to be more difficult than in other Arab states where the executive enjoys centralized authority.

This has also prevented Asad from building a counterelite base. The president has not been able to protect high-profile ministers or appointees to strengthen his position vis-à-vis the party's power centers. The patronage networks of some of the B'athist elites, such as 'Abd al-Halim Khadam and Mostapha Miro, proved far more extensive than Asad's.[37] Given the party's deep corporatist reach, it is unsurprising that elites housed there easily contain Asad. For every top-down appointment Asad makes, the party responds with years of experience, networks, and organizational attributes that offset these gains. While the president governs the most effective institution in the country, the party elites have been capable of blocking him, which effectively lessens his powers in a de facto sense. This has led some, such as Joshua Landis, to portray the struggle occurring in Syria as one between the old and new guard.[38]

Yet, understanding them as elites within politicized institutions is a better way to represent governance in Syria. As a former consultant argues, "Z'aim was removed, al-Rifa'i's ministry was stripped. There are no reformers left. The party hunts anyone near the president and he is incapable of protecting his people."[39] This competition is not about domination. The party elites seek to make the president dependent as he looks to incrementally advance his influence against the institutionally backed elites. This makes achieving a regime consensus difficult because of the inability to bring all the institutional interests together. Consequently, obstruction rather than cooperation has become a frequent hallmark of governance and this has hampered system adaptation.

The prevalence of multiple and overlapping politicized power centers increases the state's inability to respond with basic governing efficiency.

Syria's experience on the United National Security Council (UNSC) reveals examples of Asad's position among rival elites housed in competing politicized institutions. It also demonstrates the inefficiency that results in a government managed by power centers with poorly defined roles. Between 2002 and 2004, Syria was one of the rotating representatives on the fifteen-member UNSC. As a result, its role on the UNSC was spotlighted internationally. To vote against US-favorable resolutions, supported by the rest of the council, could be used as diplomatic fodder to isolate Damascus. However, approving measures that were seen as bolstering American interests invited domestic and regional criticism. Syria had voted favorably for UN Resolution 1441 in November 2002, which gave the final warning to Saddam to abandon Iraq's nonexistent weapons programs. When Bush launched the war the following March, Damascus rightly anticipated the war's fallout and pointed to the US's lack of strategic planning.

Syria became the region's most outspoken critic while the other Arab states tacitly supported the United States and tried to curtail domestic protests. Veteran ruling party elites, who experienced similar regional challenges under Hafiz's leadership, spearheaded the opposition to the war and decided to stand fast rather than capitulate to Western regional designs. In interviews with American embassy personnel, they conceded that Syrian predictions had been more accurate than those of the Bush administration.[40] Regardless, Syria increasingly became a focus of neoconservative attention with some, such as John Bolton, advocating regime change in Syria.[41]

Besides its stance regarding Iraq, the Syrian government was not unified. As the war unfolded, the struggle between power centers became publicly apparent. On May 22, 2003, the UNSC convened to vote on Resolution 1483, which legitimized the US occupation by creating the Coalition Provisional Authority (CPA). The resolution passed 14–0 during the meeting. Syria's UN representative, Faysil Makdad, did not attend the vote for the resolution. However, Makdad did show up in the afternoon to present Syria's affirmation. While Syria's vote on 1483 was noted into the UN minutes afterward, it was recorded officially as an abstention. According to a former Syrian political advisor present at the Regional Command's deliberation of 1483,[42] the confusion surrounding Syria's vote provides a unique insight into how its power centers interact when they disagree over an issue.

The party's RC met the evening before the vote. Asad was not present but indicated that he wished Syria to vote affirmatively. Two RC members, then vice president 'Abd al-Halim Khadam and then foreign minister Farok al-Shar'a, opposed the resolution. When a show of hands was given, all RC members supported the resolution while Khadam and al-Shar'a voted against it. Makdad was contacted and told the RC voted for the resolution. The following morning Makdad was contacted again by the Foreign Ministry, which claimed a mistake had been made. Perplexed by the contradictory signals from Damascus and unable to obtain confirmation of Syria's vote, Makdad did not attend the vote. When the president was told Syria abstained, he asked for clarification and was angered with the senior B'athists' interference. He ordered Makdad to the UN to record Syria's vote for the resolution. This anecdote was confirmed by Makdad who explained, "If we were given more time in the morning, we would have done this and raised our hands with the other people."[43] The confusion surrounding this UN resolution is rich with interpretative possibilities about Syria's political arrangements. Yet, it aptly demonstrates how the power centers interacted at that moment in time.

This example does not suggest that every decision is taken in such a conflicted manner, but it does show how Asad is contested. As 'Abd al-Hamid said, "Bashar is one of the equals while his father was first among them."[44] Entrenched elites, who are supported by politicized institutions, are capable of maintaining autonomy from the president. While Asad is not powerless, he does not command the position or ability to decisively exercise his constitutionally stipulated powers, which delineates formal hierarchies and duties between the presidency and the party. After all, the president can dismiss any appointed position in the bureaucracy and military according to Articles 95 and 109 of the Syrian constitution. However, the constitution does not confer any powers over elected positions such as RC members. It is worth pointing out, however, that the formal powers of the RC are not constitutionally enshrined. Rather, they are instead formalized within the party by-laws framework.[45] As such, this contrasts greatly with other regional presidential systems, such as Egypt. The RC can interfere blatantly against the president's stated will without constitutional authority and not face legal retribution. Hence, unlike in centralized political arenas, politicized institutions protect their leading elites.

Discussing power centers is potentially misleading. The key power center relative to the president is the party. Others that vie for influence are the bureaucracy, redundant security services, and competing military branches.

Nevertheless, the institutions are not monolithic blocs. The ruling party, for example, does not move against the president in unity. Also, reality indicates that "old guard–new guard" distinctions inaccurately depict the cleavage in Syria. Older elites have young clients, as patronage networks cut across generations. As every individual maintains separate and overlapping patronage networks, institutional power centers sometimes coalesce. Hence, one party member may be part of a reforming wing that supports the president's more liberal measures while another member may not view political change as advantageous to the system's evolution. Both belong to the B'ath but not to the same power centers within the politicized institution. Counting other institutions such as the military, the security services, bureaucracy, and regional elements throughout the country, hundreds of factions may exist. Hence, discussion of the ruling party as a power center identifies only the most salient and empirical cleavage. Power is undoubtedly more fragmented in Bashar al-Asad's Syria.

One could argue that the younger Asad has not yet consolidated his position and that power relationships will tilt favorably toward him in time. Yet, time alone will not accomplish this. The Syrian president will have to maneuver and restructure how he exercises authority over the state's governing organizations. As economist Nabil Sukkar argues, "There has not been much change in personalities within the party. When they disappear, will it change the dynamic? When an older member falls, he is not necessarily being replaced by a propresident figure. Most of the entrenched elites have powerful and influential crony capitalist links, which are not disappearing. In fact, it is more accurate to argue they are increasing."[46] As Sukkar's comments indicate, the president faces "entrenched elites" supported by politicized institutions that contain him. Because of their politicized character and the fact that executive authority is decentralized, the institutions can protect their elites. Asad has not been able to eliminate his opponents because an attempt to depoliticize the party is tantamount to attacking the political system. As Asad cannot remake the ruling party at this time, he will have to continue to compete with it.

Hafiz al-Asad politicized institutions to widen and strengthen the system's foundation during the 1970s. Institutional inactivity during the 1980s did not involve their enervation. Then as Hafiz al-Asad's death neared, the upper elites reasserted themselves and their institutions. Consequently, the Syrian political system has transformed to an informal oligarchy where the politicized institutions of the presidency, ruling party, and security services compete for influence and share power. While the presidency maintains wide constitutional powers, Asad seems incapable of asserting his control over the state's pillars. Hafiz al-Asad did not rule as an omnipotent puppet-master, but rather as the system's chief arbitrator among various institutional power centers. Bashar al-Asad, on balance, is not the system's arbitrator. He participates but not above the elites' politicized power centers. Being an arbitrator over politicized institutions contrasts greatly from being challenged by institutions that can accumulate power and actively participate in politics.

It is within these contexts that the central executives in Syria and Egypt pilot over different structural and governing dynamics. The degree to which the executive elites exercise authority over these organizations affects *how* co-optation occurs. This has important ramifications on the adaptability of each political system. The more decentralized executive authority, the more arduous a president must work to achieve the consensus required to adapt the system. This slows adaptation by making structural changes to the ruling coalition risky for the regime. Conversely, the more centralized authority that an executive has over the ruling coalition, the greater the ability the elites have in designing or obstructing a ruling consensus. To show the point further, executive centralized authority or the lack thereof also affects the character of elite co-optation. Specifically, in decentralized arenas, co-optation tends to be diffuse across the competing institutions while highly concentrated in centralized fields. Interelite politics and elite co-optation reveal these diverging institutional configurations.

ELITE CO-OPTATION AND COALITION CHANGE

Just as presidents constantly work on maintaining and increasing their influence—so, too, do other elites. Elites compete to be included or avoid exclusion from the political field. Thus, elites attempt to maintain and enhance their positions. Yet, in political arenas where the executive exercises centralized authority, elites can be included and excluded more arbitrarily within the ruling coalition. Because authority is structured in a centralized way, it reduces institutional protection and emphasizes personalities. Contrastingly, the multiplicity of power centers where the executive has decentralized authority implores a president to compete in the co-optation process more directly. This is because a president remains only one figure in the co-optation and shedding strategies that elites employ. Therefore, decentralized executive arenas increase elite resiliency because the structures, along with the personal patronage networks, must be weakened simultaneously in order to include or exclude elites from the ruling coalition. Older established elites are more difficult to remove because the institutions provide insulation, which favors their continued inclusion. This also makes introducing new elites to a repository's leadership difficult. In this regard, politicized institutions provide far more elite protection and allow for the proliferation of overlapping and competing power centers within such structures.[47] Consequently, since elite co-optation is occurring across many institutional locations in decentralized arenas, the process is more dispersed.

Elite co-optation and exclusion does reveal a distinct logic at work. Generally, the distance between an elite and a repository of power determines how high one climbs. The higher one is generally correlates with one's longevity within the system. Thus, the higher position an elite achieves, the greater the difficulty in being excluded. Yet, the degree of executive control over the state's organizations conditions how co-optation occurs. In Egypt, the prevalence of centralized executive authority made the dynamics of elite co-optation or exclusion a straightforward affair before the 2011 uprisings. It also concentrated the process in a single locale—the party of the government, the now-disbanded NDP. Egypt's elite arena was more changeable in terms of inclusion and exclusion because it was more centralized. This helped enable Mubarak to rule with limited challenges from within his political establishment for nearly thirty years. Centralized executive authority permitted a change in the ruling coalition as opposed to the collapse of the regime. In this way, it revealed Egyptian autocracy to be more adaptable than the Syrian variant. By contrast, elite co-optation occurs across Syria's decentralized executive arena and reveals another dynamic at play. State institutions such as the ruling party, multiple security agencies, the military, and the bureaucracy also are active areas where elites are co-opted and protected.

Elite coalition change is a strategy that reorganizes and redistributes power within the elite arena. Coalition change is a visible process because one actually observes new elites being introduced and older ones being removed. Therefore, concrete examples demonstrate this aspect of elite politics in Egypt and Syria. Bearing in mind the variations between the political arenas, it is easier to introduce and exclude elites in Egypt than Syria. Elite coalition change is elastic because personalities, rather than institutions, anchor the system. While the examples below are drawn from the cases prior to the 2011 uprisings, it helps explain why Egypt and Syria experienced such different outcomes during these uprisings. In Egypt, SCAF was able to use the system's centralized character to drop coalition members, such as the neoliberal economic team, as well as the president himself before they assumed the executive's central position during the transition. In only eighteen days, and without deploying massive violence against the protesters, SCAF changed the ruling coalition in order to preserve parts of the regime. Syria, however, experienced a protracted and violent uprising because executive authority over the state's institutions was decentralized. Asad's inability to change the ruling coalition and drop members, as well as the inability for a coalition member to replace Asad by sliding into the executive, did not give the Syrian state the option for a structural change. Rather, when confronted with regime survival or disintegration, the regime employed lethal force to remain in power.

EGYPT: THE CASE OF 'AMR MOSA

'Amr Mosa joined the Egyptian Foreign Ministry in 1958. He served as Egypt's ambassador to India and the United Nations before being appointed foreign minister in 1991. For nearly a decade, Mosa ably directed his ministry, and, indeed, exhibited charisma on both the regional and international levels.[48] Despite Mosa's prominence, he was not a direct client of the president. Instead, he was connected to one of the president's most trusted political advisor, Osama al-Baz. In this regard, Mosa was an elite but did not belong to the chief executive's elites.

Mosa's outspoken and frequent blunt depictions of the situation in the occupied Palestinian territories endeared him to many Egyptians precisely because they often clashed with Washington's unbalanced portrayal. He was also criticized frequently in the Israeli press, which increased his Egyptian (and Arab) popularity further. As this report demonstrates, Mosa's blend of charisma, opposition, and frankness is apparent. It summarizes:

> Queried whether Cairo would broker a meeting between Israeli Premier Ariel Sharon and Palestinian president Yasser Arafat, Moussa said the issue is not a photo opportunity for television cameras. So far, Moussa said, the attitude of the new Israeli government towards the peace process is not clear. On the fact that Israel and the new US administration have made it a condition that the Palestinian Intifada stop before resuming negotiations, the Foreign Minister said that it cannot be halted by pushing a button. Ending the Intifada depends on addressing the frustration felt by the people occupied due to the practices of their occupier.[49]

While Mubarak's statements often disagreed with Washington and Tel Aviv, he rarely or sharply distanced himself from Washington's influence in the view of Egyptians.[50] Additionally, Mubarak's statements rarely displayed emotional frustration toward the occupied territories' deteriorating situation. Thus, the population favorably perceived Mosa because he appeared frustrated while contemptuously addressing the Israeli government's actions. As a consequence, he was unpopular in Washington because he was "no ordinary Egyptian government official."[51] Mosa's popularity had Cairo's politically aware classes advocating his succession to Egyptian presidency before the 2011 uprising.[52] Petitions even circulated in Egypt demanding fair presidential elections with Mosa as a potential candidate.[53] Since the removal of Mubarak in February 2011, Mosa returned to the scene as a leading candidate for president. Yet, the arc of Mosa's career before the 2011 uprising becomes important in this instance.

In early 2001, with the second Palestinian Intifada escalating, populist Egyptian singer Sh'aban 'Abd al-Rahim's song, "I hate Israel and love 'Amr Mosa," dominated the airwaves and catapulted Mosa's status. Egypt's presidential elites appeared to interpret Mosa's increasing popularity as problematic. Mosa's popularity jeopardized his ministerial position. The appearance of autonomy from the presidency is credited with terminating his tenure as foreign minister. In May 2001, the much less charismatic, Ahmad Mahir replaced Mosa as minister. In fact, as Mahir was appointed, the Information Ministry broadcast that Mahir's brother, 'Ali, was appointed and doled out details of his brother's career before correcting the error.[54] As one Cairo journalist remarked with hindsight, "If you made a list of potential Foreign Ministers that could have followed 'Amr Mosa, Ahmad Mahir would not have been on it."[55] Mosa went from being a prominent elite to being shed from the political arena in a matter of days. However, at least his expulsion allowed for his continuation of politics outside of Egypt's domestic sphere.

Mosa became secretary-general of the Arab League in May 2001. He remained there until 2011. In many ways, he was the best possible candidate at that time. While his predecessor 'Asmat 'Abd al-Magid was capable, the Arab League needed to be rejuvenated, and Mosa's personality added considerable weight to the notoriously fragmented and popularly ridiculed organization. While Mosa's appointment as secretary-general appeared impressive, it effectively relegated him to a retirement track in Mubarak's Egypt. From an Egyptian elite perspective, his new position stripped him of his domestic power base and wreaked havoc on his patronage networks. Being secretary-general permitted Mosa to use his charisma and ability but in a way that could not directly challenge Mubarak domestically. It also maintained Egypt's prominent position within the league. Mosa's transfer, while paraded positively by the semi-official press, had profound overt and subliminal effects. However, it did not take long for his clients to react to the demotion.

Mosa lost his domestic elite status and ability to maintain a sizable patronage network when he was relieved as foreign minister. Upon assuming his post in the Arab League, he asked many of his most talented clients to move with him. A few of Mosa's clients went out of personal allegiance. Yet, if Foreign Ministry employees want to remain on ambassadorial career paths, they must be in the ministry. Hisham Badr, one of Mosa's ablest clients, exemplified the dilemma. Badr accepted Mosa's offer to manage his office at the Arab League temporarily. However, less than a year later, he returned to the ministry and accepted an ambassadorial posting to Japan. Badr confirmed that following Mosa to the Arab League was a "favor" because his networks depreciated after he was let go as foreign minister.[56] Mosa went from being surrounded by powerful clients to being discarded because he was no longer of any use to careers. Badr, at least, offered Mosa his services while others completely shunned the former foreign minister.[57]

Shortly after Mosa became the league's secretary-general, a publicly reported incident at Cairo airport exposed his ebbing domestic power.[58] Mosa and a prominent Libyan diplomat went to the Cairo airport to fly to Tripoli to dissuade Ghadafi from withdrawing from the Arab League in March 2002. However, the state-owned gas company grounded the Libyan jet by refusing to clear the plane's take-off until its $152 refueling account was paid. Mosa's entourage offered the equivalent in Egyptian pounds while the plane's captain offered Euros. The workers refused both currencies. The issue was resolved after Mosa promised to repay the company in dollars upon their return. Yet, for good measure, Mosa had to leave his personal ID as a guarantee before allowing the delegation to depart. While it is impossible to know the intentions of such a maneuver, it sent a public message that Mosa's authority was virtually nonexistent, since such a story would have been unimaginable just a year prior.

The case of Mosa offers an understanding to Egypt's elite coalition change. His distinguished career within the Foreign Ministry, links with the president's chief advisor, and considerable client base in the ten years as foreign minister should have protected him from easy exclusion. However, Mosa's charisma combined with increasing popularity led to his exclusion because the president and his chief advisors perceived his increasing autonomy as a threat. It is unclear who made the ultimate decision to exclude Mosa. That is also, ultimately, inconsequential. The point is that when Mosa was dropped as foreign minister, his removal was swift and unopposed in any institutional or ministerial corners. Indeed, it took less than forty-eight hours to dismiss Mosa and appoint Mahir. While introducing an elderly, ambivalent figure into a ministerial posting does not suggest elite arena dynamism, Mosa's straightforward exclusion does. Egypt's elite co-optation and removal is an easy task because of the executive's centralized authority over the system's elites. Executive centralization increases the flexibility for including and excluding elites—regardless of their formal positions of influence within the system.

In point of fact, there were no institutions capable of protecting Mosa from dismissal even if any incumbent elites had wished to do so. Executive elites, who are the main decision-making figures, excluded Mosa by offering him a transition into retirement as the Arab League's secretary-general in order to reconfigure the ruling coalition. By allowing him to continue in politics, while excluding him from Egypt's domestic elite arena, a gracious exit was Mosa's only choice. The unencumbered execution of the executive elites consensus as well as the effortless dismissal of Mosa demonstrates that co-opting and shedding upper elites did not tax the system's cohesion.

THE RISE OF GAMAL MUBARAK AND FALL OF THE EXECUTIVE ELITES

Even the president's closest executive elites are at risk of exclusion in a centralized ruling coalition. While they cannot be excluded as swiftly as Mosa was, the ultimate outcome remains the same. It also plainly reveals the ability to change the ruling coalition. In the case of three of Egypt's top ruling-party elites, the gradual process of elite shedding is reviewed, as is the incorporation of a new elite bloc. The process of including and excluding top elites occurs simultaneously in this example and demonstrates the adaptability of a ruling coalition when the executive exercises centralized authority.

For twenty years of Mubarak's rule, Safwat al-Sharif (information minister, 1983–2004, president of Shura Council, NDP secretary-general 2002–11), Yusif Wali (agriculture minister 1982–2004, NDP secretary-general 1984–2002), and Kamal al-Shazli (parliamentary affairs minister 1984–2005) were some of the longest-serving and most prominent party elites in Egypt. They were public figures as much for their resiliency as for their reputations as the notorious manipulators of the domestic political scene. Their tenures and proximity to Mubarak made them personalities with extensive patronage networks. The ranks of Egypt's executive elites were certainly more numerous than these three individuals. Yet, al-Sharif, Wali, and al-Shazli were arguably some of the system's most untouchable civilian political figures outside of the president's family prior to 2011.

These three senior elites' increasing marginalization coincided with the incorporation of the president's son.[59] Most elites enter on lower levels as a part of a patron-client relationship and incrementally develop themselves. Gamal Mubarak's entrance as an executive elite, at the expense of preexisting executive elites, is uncharacteristic but reveals the possibility. It is a prominent example that demonstrates the flexible quality of elite inclusion and exclusion in systems with centralized executive authority. Wali and al-Shazli[60] were excluded first while al-Sharif's duties were progressively split and reduced before the 2011 uprising.[61] While exclusion occurred rapidly in Mosa's case, the chief executive depended more heavily on al-Sharif, Wali, and al-Shazli's individual and overlapping patronage networks. Therefore, they could not apparently be excluded by decree. Their marginalization was more gradual. Yet, the declining trajectory is unmistakable. Without the institution of the ruling party protecting them, it was easier to exclude them than elites within decentralized political orders.

Before it was abolished in the wake of the 2011 uprising, the NDP was adjustable and malleable. This flexibility resulted because the party was depoliticized and incapable of asserting itself against the executive. As scholars demonstrate, politicians joined the NDP to gain access to state resources as opposed to being ideologically committed to the party's flimsy platform.[62] In other cases, big businessmen wanted to be leading NDP members and MPs to protect their business monopolies such as the case of steel magnate Ahmad 'Ezz.[63] Either way, the party was not a politicized entity that influenced or constrained the executive. It existed through the personalities that managed it. Rather than adhere to party protocol and guidelines, personalities dominated the party's processes while blocking the potential emergence of charismatic politicians. Hisham Kassem, who lost as an independent candidate in Cairo's Kasr al-'Aini District in the 2000 elections, described the NDP as a "no-man's wasteland devoid of a single mechanism capable of promoting internal democracy. It only consists of people with patronage systems protecting their fiefdoms."[64]

Years of tinkering with the electoral system by introducing legislation that transformed a party list to an individual candidacy system advantaged the NDP.[65] The party, because of its inability to distinguish itself from the state and its coercive instruments, had no incentive to develop. However, the ruling party received a message of rejection in the 2000 parliamentary elections, which suggested that it was out of touch with the people and in need of restructuring.

Three months before that election, the Supreme Constitutional Court (SCC) ruled that the existing election procedures were unconstitutional because of a lack of judicial supervision inside polling stations. Mubarak, unwilling and unable to legitimately contradict one of Egypt's highest courts, ensured that judges would be inside the polling stations in place of Interior Ministry personnel. Yet, this did not change the outcome in 2000. As judges manned sometimes near-empty polling stations, scores of hired thugs (*baltagaya*) and Interior Ministry figures repressively controlled the space outside polling stations as the party mobilized state employees and citizens with bribery and threats. In tandem with these tactics, the Interior Ministry transported the ballots to counting stations. Despite rampant interference, only 172 of 444 NDP nominated candidates prevailed (39 percent). The party's leadership (particularly Wali, al-Shazli, and al-Sharif), which prior to the elections emphasized its strict internal nominating process, allowed NDP "independents" back into the party's fold out of necessity.[66] The NDP independents boosted the party's nominated victors to a formidable 88 percent majority by securing 388 of 444 available slots. This revealed that personal resources and social standing—not party support—were rewarded in Egypt's parliamentary elections prior to 2011. Nevertheless, the 2000 parliamentary elections embarrassed the ruling party. They also provided a window of opportunity to justify changing the elites in the ruling coalition. The party's electoral failures introduce two coinciding alterations to the ruling coalition: the rise of Gamal Mubarak, and the decline of Wali, al-Sharif, and al-Shazli's political careers. While the elections exposed the party as a weak institution, the party was, in fact, used to change in the elite arena. Hence the ruling party could be hijacked and made into a vehicle for the ascent of new senior elites precisely because it was weak and incapable of defending itself.

Gamal Mubarak's political profile increased dramatically, but incrementally, after the party's parliamentary election failure in 2000. At that time, Mubarak was a newly appointed member of the party's twenty-five-member General Secretariat and focused on youth, technology, and development projects. He was also the chairman of the Future Generation Foundation—a project his mother, Suzanne, initiated in 1999. His investment firm, Medinvest Associates, facilitated his own independent political connections. In late 2000, the idea of an inherited succession scenario playing out in Cairo seemed unlikely. It remained a highly contested idea through the first part of the decade according to some government critics.[67] Nevertheless, Gamal Mubarak's accession (along with his group) into the top elite echelons while Wali, al-Sharif, and al-Shazli's careers eroded effectively demonstrates elite change in a centralized coalition. While the top elites appeared against Gamal Mubarak's rapid accession into their elite ranks, personalism rather than institutional considerations shaped the outcome.

Following the electoral debacle of 2000, the NDP needed restructured. The struggle to restructure the party shows the Gamal-led group's initial weakness compared with that of established NDP elites. The NDP began an internal reform process by revamping its platform and electoral protocols for nominations of local, district, and governorate positions. Interparty elections were held and called electoral primaries (*al-mugam'at al-intikhabaya*). With the president's son championing internal party reform, the younger NDP members' prominence increased as did that of the youth minister, 'Ali al-Din Hilal.[68] Despite the changes to internal party practices whereby open nominations were used to choose new members for local councils, other indicators showed that the president's senior elites—Wali, al-Sharif, and al-Shazli—still controlled how Gamal's reform agenda was implemented. For example, the president's elites interfered with the primaries' internal nominating criteria by personally selecting the candidates even though the party's by-laws stipulated that nominations were to be handled via elections by NDP members on the district and local council levels.

The electoral primaries before the Shura Council elections of July 2001 revealed how easily entrenched elites manipulated the younger Mubarak's initiatives at the outset. They also provided a snapshot of the power relationship at that time. As former NDP member turned dissident, 'Ali Shams al-Din, explains:

> The primaries did not help Gamal's faction other than in a public relations sense of advertising change. Actually, the protocol changes strengthened al-Sharif, al-Shazli, and Wali's positions against Gamal because it pitted selection of Gamal's faction against al-Sharif, al-Shazli, and Wali's nominations. Put simply, the entrenched elites won because the selection process ultimately came down to who had the most money to bribe figures such as al-Shazli or recommendations from State Security (al-Amn al-Dawla) where al-Sharif's networks originate. The fact that they could oppose Gamal demonstrates where elite power was concentrated at that time.[69]

Other research similarly shows that entrenched actors' manipulation easily thwarted the NDP's internal reform movement.[70] When the entrenched elites' manipulations failed, they resorted to overt interference during the primaries. In the case of Shams al-Din, a middle-ranking politician on good terms with the younger Mubarak's faction, the senior elites worked against him. Shams al-Din ran against the Wali-supported candidate, Nabil al-Qalmy, in the 2001 primaries. His opposition to the presidential elite was not tolerated. During the primary run-off, agents on behalf of Wali, al-Shazli, and al-Sharif contacted eligible party voters with instructions on how to vote, discouraged voters who were thought to be supporting alternative candidates from going to polling stations, changed the composition of the party electors committees, shut off electricity during voting, and employed thugs to intimidate people.[71] After losing the rigged primary, Shams al-Din paid for his insolence. As Shams al-Din explains, "You are expected to obey their orders. You cannot say no to Wali or al-Shazli. Immediately, they begin asking 'who is backing you?' or 'what are you seeking to gain?'"[72] He was dismissed from the party after opposing Wali's candidate in the primary. Shams al-Din's case is indicative of elite power configuration between Gamal Mubarak and the entrenched figures in mid-2001. This power dynamic changed drastically when the Gamal Mubarak ascendency project began in earnest.

The NDP held a party congress in September 2002. The party's weak structures were favorably altered for the rise of the younger Mubarak's group. The president's top elites witnessed attacks against their patronage networks, which determined the congress's outcome before the proceedings convened. Wali, al-Shazli, and al-Sharif each witnessed their leading clients being indicted on similar but unconnected corruption charges in August and September 2002. Agricultural Ministry official Yusif 'Abd al-Rahman (Wali's client), former chairman of TV news Mohamad al-Wakil (al-Sharif's client), and chairman of the Misr Exterior Bank 'Abdalah Tayal (al-Shazli's client) were arrested, effectively limiting their patron's bases to obstruct Gamal's inclusion. As Schemm reported in reference to 'Abd al-Rahman, "The arrest should be seen in the context of an attack on the minister himself."[73] What remains unclear is who authorized the seemingly coordinated campaign. The public prosecutor processed the indictments, but no paper trail exists that shows where the campaign originated. One, however, can assume the president tacitly granted his blessing, as some journalists insinuated. Khalil states, "All three have been affected in recent months by corruption charges against close associates—fueling speculation that the trio was being softened up to ease the ascension of new blood to the party's leadership."[74] If softening up three of the president's top elites was the objective, it succeeded because they proved unable to stop the encroachment into their portfolios. Al-Shazli's control of party membership was downgraded and split with Gamal-supporter Ahmad 'Ezz while his budgetary duties were split with Zakaraya 'Azmy (the president's chief of staff). Al-Sharif assumed the NDP's secretary-general position from Wali, who was demoted but kept his ministry. By arresting the senior elites' clients, positional changes of top elites occurred without producing any resistance from the party. As such, the isolation and dissection of individual networks and their inability to institutionally rally support weakened them to the degree that they could be demoted by the party congress with no response. As a consequence, Egypt's prominent elites accepted their demoted positions instead of risking dishonorable exclusion by trying to mobilize against it.

Gamal Mubarak, flanked by members of his network, took control of the newly established Policies Secretariat (al-Amanat al-Siyasiya) at the 2002 party congress. The body instantly became the most significant of the NDP's fourteen secretariats. Outside of the presidency, the Policies Secretariat became the most relevant body for policy creation in the country. As one NDP member argues, "The Policies Secretariat and its associated groups are the only place to be if you are interested in political change. It is the most single important policy organ in Egypt."[75] Combined with the senior elites' demotion, the structural insertion of the younger Mubarak's group expanded their power within the elite field. With the president's son heading the secretariat, close associates Hosam Badrawy (head of the education subcommittee), Mahmoud Mohy al-Din (head of the economic subcommittee), and Mohamad Kamal (head of the youth subcommittee) boosted the secretariat's networks. Ahmad 'Ezz became a steering committee head at the 2003 party conference, further strengthening its profile. Mubarak's group, each member with his own budding patronage networks, became the leading reformers and most enlightened politicians within the party ranks.[76]

While the younger Mubarak was certainly the chief patron, the group's continuing success derived from its penetration into the party. By being allowed to strengthen the secretariat, Mubarak's faction insulated itself from other top elites without necessarily politicizing the party. As such, while the Policies Secretariat became an influential actor after its establishment, the Gamal Mubarak-led group continued to easily counter attacks from declining senior elites.

Following the 2002 NDP congress, the weakened Wali, al-Sharif and al-Shazli continued to challenge Gamal's faction by choosing not to advise them when they made policy gaffes. For example, there were frequent occasions when senior elites were present when Mubarak's associate Hosam Badrawy advocated dismantling the national health care system and privatizing hospitals. While seemingly a plausible direction given the decrepit public health system, such notions are politically unpopular in a developing country with poor infrastructure and gross inequalities in the distribution of wealth. Yet, rather than advising Badrawy to present his suggestions in a more politically palatable fashion, they allowed him to publicly advocate his views and hence "hit the wall" with "the people."[77] As a result, this turned public opinion against the faction's neoliberal economic leanings. As Shams al-Din argues:

> The top elites [older presidential elites] portray themselves as coming from Egypt's clay. They understand what ordinary Egyptians want to hear. While they often employ a strategy of listening to the people and then implementing their own agenda, they do not advocate social cuts publicly. While these established elites cannot directly oppose Gamal or his comrades, they do small gestures that make it clear they do not want to help them politically.[78]

In a political setting where the ruling coalition is centralized, this is one of a few limited techniques for interelite opposition. Nevertheless, the executive's elites had few alternative options to respond to their depreciating positions. Because established elites were not engrained in the system structurally, they became easy to exclude from the ruling coalition.

The centralized character of the ruling coalition also made the appearance of overtly blocking the president's son potentially risky. Several NDP members, such as Yusif Wali's nephew Sharif, witnessed interactions between Gamal and the senior elites and detected an increasingly predictable pattern. As Sharif explains, "During meetings when Gamal suggests a measure such as repealing state-security courts, most of the top elites explained that his proposals were not practical during discussion but when Gamal persisted and the committee voted, everyone is in favor. Not a single Gamal-introduced initiative has been rejected by the higher party members."[79] This is certainly attributable to Gamal's being the president's son.[80] Yet, the former executive elites were marginalized at the expense of Gamal's inclusion and showed that they were ineffective at publicly challenging him.

In July 2004, the senior elites' exclusion deepened as Gamal Mubarak's faction consolidated their positions further. President Mubarak began having back problems in the summer of 2004. The then seventy-five-year-old president traveled to Germany for surgery and recuperation that lasted two weeks in late June—at the time his longest absence from Cairo since becoming leader. As the president received treatment and underwent surgery, the press detailed an imminent cabinet reshuffle. About halfway through his stay in Germany, Mubarak removed Safwat al-Sharif as information minister, a post he held for nearly twenty years. Al-Sharif maintained his position as NDP secretary-general but was demoted to the party's representative in the Shura Council. Given that al-Sharif's networks originated in the security services and his public service gave him control over the media, this may have been cause for concern. Instead, Mubarak effectively demonstrated that he was capable of removing one of the most powerful senior elites by a telephone call from Munich. After returning from Germany, the president finished reshuffling the cabinet. Yusif Wali was dismissed as agriculture minister.[81] He had been wholly excluded from the elite arena.[82] In 2006, al-Shazli was removed from all official duties and retired.

The 2004 cabinet contained a number of Gamal Mubarak's allies. The prime minister, Ahmad Nazif, a fifty-two-year-old Canadian-trained engineer, was the youngest person to fill the post since the Nasser era. Nazif had accompanied Gamal Mubarak on public relations' trips abroad to the United States in 2003. Policies Secretariat member Mahmoud Mohy al-Din was named investment minister. While he was the only high-profile Policies Secretariat member to be appointed minister, seven other lower secretariat members, such as Rashid Mohamad Rashid and Tariq Kamal, became ministers. With the previous executive elites marginalized, influence of Gamal Mubarak's Policies Secretariat was apparent in the new cabinet. The cabinet began executing its neoliberalizing agenda immediately.

By late August 2004, the cabinet announced the repeal of duties on approximately one hundred consumer goods. Most prominent in this field was the removal of 40-percent duty on cars between 1300 and 1600-liter fuel injection. According to *al-Ahram*, nearly 88 percent of vehicles in Egypt fall within this range.[83] Similarly, subsidies were halved on diesel fuel, which caused an increase in public transportation costs. In keeping with the Policies Secretariat's neoliberal economic discourse on modernizing Egypt, the reforms reflected willingness to rescind some lower-class populist privileges while expanding the secretariat's appeal with the critical middle classes. As one analyst suggested, the new economic reforms were "middle-class populism."[84] The secretariat and the government banked on economic reform as the tool to maintain and expand professional middle-class support even if this meant forfeiting the support of the working poor.[85] While it is impossible to know exactly what the role of the neoliberal economic policies was for igniting the 2011 uprising, there was an undeniable component to it because of the incredible inequalities they produced for the remainder of the Mubarak presidency.

Gamal Mubarak fully consolidated his positions as an executive elite by 2002. Subsequent annual NDP conferences left no room for doubt. In 2004, al-Shazli's usual prominence at the conference diminished. Party Secretary-General al-Sharif's most substantial contribution was to introduce Gamal Mubarak, who was frequently interpreted and praised throughout his speech by the party faithful.[86] Wali did not even attend the proceedings. While the conference emphasized economic reform, the Gamal Mubarak faction set the agenda and managed the press. Indeed, PM Nazif was the only non-Policies Secretariat member to brief the press most years. Political reforms were largely shelved. Thus, as Mohamad Kamal explained constitutional amendments to introduce presidential term limits or canceling emergency laws—key opposition demands—were "not on the agenda." Gamal Mubarak issued a statement in the party's paper that "political reform cannot be realized in unfavorable economic conditions."[87] The political and economic reforms the conference produced were limited. Yet, the Policies Secretariat's strength within the party appeared to be the 2004 conference's key outcome. The president's address stressed that the key objective was to introduce younger elements into the party with the aim of pushing them to take up positions of responsibility.

While the press and members of Gamal Mubarak's faction often reference this elite maneuvering as "old versus new guards,"[88] the process was far more complicated than the convention suggested. Given Gamal Mubarak's political advancement at the expense of established executive elites, rumors of hereditary succession became inevitable and routine.[89] The president's intentions remained unclear although he publicly denied accusations that a hereditary republic is possible.[90] While the party was weaker than the military (the usual channel of presidential recruitment), the depoliticized character of the military seemed to level the playing field for succession before the 2011 uprising.[91] However, the younger Mubarak's faction used the feckless party to create and extend their own power base.

Gamal Mubarak's Policies Secretariat and cabinet were the leading forces of change in the politics of Egypt between 2002–11. Although the party's structures went untouched, that faction officially conducted party business while the older personalities faded away.[92] It remained unclear if Gamal Mubarak would be elected as Egypt's president despite some party members' desires before 2011.[93] However, his faction's rise into the elite arena does reveal the dynamics behind elite coalition change in Egypt. Arenas where the executive exercises centralized authority over the ruling coalition made removing powerful elites and introducing new elites much easier than in systems that possess politicized institutions. This centralized system must, however, be compared with Syria's arena to understand the variance between the two systems' elite arena.

SUCCESSION AND THE CONTINUITY OF ELITES

Syria's political system is less pliable than Egypt's when it comes to moving elites onto or off the ruling coalition. While changes of personalities happen in Syria, institutions matter more because top elites can insulate themselves within their protective confines. This is primarily because the executive exercises decentralized authority in Syria. Hence, decentralization allows elites in the ruling party, security services, and military elites to enter an oligarchic power-sharing arrangement with the chief executive. This resulted because Hafiz al-Asad developed a decentralized ruling coalition to anchor political stability in the 1970s and 1980s. Although the Syrian arena experienced extensive political deliberalization in the 1980s, once those institutions acquired autonomy, the elites within them had an ability to reassert themselves in politically meaningful ways. When confronted with succession, the ruling coalition's senior elites united behind a cooperative strategy. All of the leading elites realized that none of them could easily slide into the position of the chief executive without upsetting the regime's balance. Thus, elites on the coalition accepted Bashar al-Asad because he bolstered their positions. The younger Asad was not a threat to their positions or institutional power bases. If anything, the weak president became indispensible for making the regime's ruling coalition function. Yet, this appears to go against conventional wisdom.

Hafiz al-Asad appears to have intended a hereditary republic since the early 1990s. His original heir apparent was his eldest son, Basil. While officially under command of Asad's cousin-in-law, 'Adnan Makhlof, in practice Basil al-Asad was in charge of the republican guards by the early 1990s.[94] Basil's succession, however, went unrealized after he died in a traffic accident in January 1994. Following his brother's passing, Bashar was recalled from London where he was pursuing ophthalmology training. As Perthes notes, "Following Basil's death, clear attempts were made by the regime's propaganda machine not only to transfigure and idealize Basil as the embodiment of all the good qualities of

Arab youth, but also to put the President's second son . . . in Basil's place."[95] Thus began Bashar al-Asad's gradual rise through the elite ranks.

Bashar al-Asad enrolled in Army Staff College at Homs where he graduated as a captain. He was promoted as a staff colonel in January 1999. He then became commander of Syria's republican guard. By 1999, he supervised military and air force intelligence. Yet, just because Asad formally commanded various units does not necessarily imply he actually controlled them. Although the younger Asad never held an official B'ath Party or government position before becoming president, he became responsible for a number of policy files between 1995–2000. One such file was Lebanon. He made his first official visit to Lebanon in 1995 and played a prominent role in Emile Lahod's victory in 1998's presidential election.[96] Additionally, Bashar al-Asad was marketed as wanting to modernize Syria. His chairmanship of the Syrian Computer Society, which emphasized Syria's need to introduce computers, Internet, and other IT services, reflected as much. Similarly, in his public comments, he lobbied frequently for state administrative reform while continuing to push for greater economic liberalization.

Many of the leading accounts suggest that Hafiz al-Asad's father wanted Bashar to succeed him and the political elites blindly implemented his dynastic ambition. Eyal Zisser, for example, argued that al-Asad's succession plans were an "open secret," credits the president with overseeing the ousting of the "old guard" in the army and intelligence services, attacking the remnants of his brother's loyalists, and transferring the important "Lebanon folder" to his heir's purview.[97] Others such as David Lesch and Flynt Leverett seem to have uncritically accepted this narrative of events.[98]

Despite Bashar's forays into the policy and military worlds, measures beyond Hafiz al-Asad's purview contributed to realizing hereditary succession.[99] This underscores a paradox in the leading accounts. The time period when al-Asad's health was at its worst coincides with when his most urgent presidential attention to senior elite maneuvers was required. On the one hand, the president was obsessed with his son's succession to the extent that he was ridding Syrian institutions of powerful elites and potential obstacles while carefully reshuffling the cabinet and promoting his heir through the system. On the other hand, he was so ill that he could not make basic public appearances or complete rudimentary tasks such as verbalize his thoughts intelligibly during a meeting.[100] A scenario in which a president's trusted elites are aware of his diminishing facilities and remain idle in the face of an uncertain or incomplete leadership succession is hard to imagine. Thus, to facilitate Bashar al-Asad's succession, elites forged an agreement that favored the hereditary transfer in 2000.

With the president's health in a steep and progressively incoherent decline from the mid-1990s, senior elites from across the institutional spectrum became the primary engineers of the younger Asad's ascendency. To ensure Bashar al-Asad succeeded his father required the disciplined implementation by the party, security services, military, and parliament. Elites from these organizations employed strategies that mixed coercion and co-optation to minimally shed older members perceived as obstacles to his impending presidency. The co-optation strategies consisted of a selective anticorruption campaign and a cabinet shuffle three months before the president died. The coercive element eliminated individuals as security raids helped condition the succession. Rather than invite a struggle for power that may threaten the regime's survival, senior elites compromised on their candidate to preserve the system.[101] Reconceptualizing Bashar al-Asad's succession as a process guided by senior elites activates their role in the collective consensus-making process.

The competing factions accepted the younger Asad because he ensured continuity and could not overtly threaten their interests. His semioutsider status must have appeared attractive. Indeed, becoming president did not award Asad an arbitrating role, and he did not gain autonomy from the ruling coalition. Rather, he was forced to interact with the top elites from politicized institutions as an equal. Had a more dominant figure within the system taken over, it could have disrupted elite cohesion and the influence that some elites had. Either way, near unanimity to remove dispensable personalities seemed apparent.[102] As such, Bashar al-Asad's elevation provides useful insights into elite coalition change in Syria.

The reason that the senior elites mattered is because Bashar's succession process was incomplete when his father died on June 10, 2000. He held neither an official government nor B'ath Party position. Speculation insinuated that the ninth B'ath Party congress would formally elect him to a high post. But his father died a week before the congress convened. While he had been promoted rapidly through the military's ranks, this did not afford him formal control of the elites within the institution. Hence, core coalition elites became the explanatory key for Bashar's succession.[103] The intelligence services and military were key centers that supported his candidacy. The succession was implemented easily. As Samir, an ordinary Damascene, commented on the lack of attention to the president's actual death, "This is not grief. It's politics."[104]

Elites from various institutions on the ruling coalition united in support of Bashar al-Asad's succession. After the president's death was announced officially, parliament convened within hours to glorify his reign. The body voted unanimously to amend constitutional Article 83 lowering the age of an eligible president from forty to thirty-four, which was Asad's age at the time.[105] In another example of regime caution, the security services went on high alert for the potential return of Rif'at al-Asad from exile in Spain. Airports and borders in Syria and Lebanon were secured.[106] Parliamentary speaker 'Abd al-Qadar Qadora stated that no individual would be permitted to "affect the security situation in the country" during the presidential transfer.[107] The ruling party's politburo also nominated Bashar al-Asad. The following day, Vice President Khadam promoted Asad from staff colonel to lieutenant general as well as the armed forces' commander-in-chief. Thus, succession was carried out by many different elites coordinating across the institutional arena to ensure security and cohesion. The speed of the transition also suggests the uniformity on the decentralized ruling coalition. As Quilty notes, "They began Bashar's succession ritual before Hafiz was even in the ground."[108]

The succession process continued formally at the ninth B'ath Party congress held on June 17–20. As a journalist covering the congress recalls, "The death of Hafiz al-Asad the previous week undermined the original agenda, and the congress was hurriedly transformed into a forum to legitimize the heir apparent."[109] Bashar was elected to the party's politburo and to his father's former post as party secretary-general. He also was given the title "leader of the party and people" by the congress. While the congress promised to be a platform for drastic change in the Regional Command (RC), only twelve new people were added. In addition to the four RC members who died or had gone into exile,[110] eight figures joined including Bashar, Miro, al-Shar'a, Naji Otri, Salim Yasin, then head of criminal intelligence Said Bkhitan, and Damascus party secretary Faruqabu Shammat. All except Bashar were insiders. Several entrenched figures remained in their posts including Tlas, Qadora, Khadam, 'Abdallah al-Ahmar, Soliman Kaddah, and Zahayr Masharqa. Hence, "the old guard was not overturned, but supplemented."[111] Despite advertising the first B'ath congress in fifteen years to be a forum for reform and change, continuity quickly became the hallmark.

The succession process also included Bashar's formal nomination from parliament, which occurred on June 26. A national plebiscite had to be held for the public to endorse or reject the parliament's nomination within ninety days. Rather than wait, then vice president Khadam scheduled the plebiscite on July 10. Bashar obtained 97.2 percent of the vote. Only .25 percent opposed his presidency.[112] Some observers noted that the high percentage did not reflect public support. Rather, it highlighted the support of the elites and their bases, which included the military, intelligence services, ruling party, and administration sectors.[113] On July 17, Bashar al-Asad officially became president. This established the first hereditary republic in contemporary Arab politics. Yet, the lead-up and unfolding of Syria's presidential succession reveal the workings of an oligarchic system rather than a centralized presidential selection.

Syria's succession in 2000 resulted from a clear consensus by the top elites from the military, intelligence services, and ruling party. There was tremendous continuity of the senior elite on the ruling coalition during the succession process. Indeed, no one challenged his succession.[114] Bashar al-Asad became president with the military and intelligence services supporting him as well as other core party figures. Yet, while resistance to Asad's succession was minimal, the established elites' opposition to his policies was frequent. Asad inherited his father's position, but found himself in the middle of a decentralized political arena in which he lacked the informal authority to initiate compromise on the ruling coalition.

The rivalry between existing senior elites and the emerging competition between institutions encouraged a compromise on a presidential candidate from "outside" the system. Asad may have had his father's name, but he was not seen as a "son of the system" in the way his brother Basil was.[115] Hence, the senior elites got a weaker president than if one of them would have assumed the presidency. While new presidents always must consolidate their power once in office, the situation was different for Bashar al-Asad. He was forced to compete with decentralized power networks strewn across institutions capable of empowering their senior elites. In this regard, Syria's senior elites encouraged a coalition amenable to entrenching and strengthening their positions and influence vis-à-vis the presidency. This decision to facilitate Bashar al-Asad's succession and his slow consolidation makes his presidency one of the competing politicized institutional power centers rather than the centralized arbitrator.

This leads to some tentative conclusions. Had a senior elite from the army or the ruling party taken over, it may have produced elite conflict. Rather than chance fragmentation or risk the system's survival, it is more likely that elites opt for a weaker president in order to help guarantee the ruling coalition's cohesion. When it comes to day-to-day political interactions, senior elites from institutions included on the ruling coalition will compete against one another for influence. Yet, if confronted with regime survival, they will band together in the collective interest of the ruling coalition's survival. In such systems, an executive that exercises decentralized authority makes autocratic adaptation a less feasible option. This is primarily because it is difficult to alter the ruling coalition. Because the Syrian system lacks the ability to change the coalition without inviting the collapse of the regime, the senior elites have to unify behind force to save the regime. Thus, as the 2011 uprising has shown, the coalition deployed force against the population because they tried to pressure the state to structurally change the ruling coalition.

MANAGING ELITES ON THE RULING COALITION

Coalition change is about circulating elites and redefining who is included and excluded. The management of the elite coalition is different. Coalition management aims to keep them dependent on the central patron. Thus, it is about keeping included elites loyal to the ruling coalition. This promotes interdependence and results in a cohesive elite center. Coalition management is difficult to empirically show because public examples rarely happen as with coalition change when actual inclusions and exclusions occur. But it is no less important. It regulates the uncontrolled assent of an elite and keeps potential dissenters loyal by threatening, obstructing, and blocking the emergence of alternative figures. Rather than circulate elites, it keeps them cohesive. The goal is to induce conformity toward the consensus of the ruling coalition's executive elites.

In Egypt, Mubarak's centralized position and the lack of politicized institutions with which to compete exempted him from participating in daily coalition management. With Mubarak's presidential office tailored to his specifications, the executive elites maintained control over lesser elites in Egypt's political field. Specifically, they directed and managed lower ones, who can include MPs, heads of party committees, or secretaries of governmental organizations. They and their client networks safeguarded the president's consensus while expelling those who might interfere with the status quo. Some of Mubarak's most trusted elites until the 2011 uprising were Zakaraya 'Azmy (head of the president's office), Safwat al-Sharif, Husayn Tantawi (defense minister), and 'Omar Suleiman (head of intelligence).[116] Each of the executive elites served different functions by overseeing ministries, government committees, parliament members, military links, or directing the security services. The commonality between the executive elites is that they are loyal to and nurtured by a centralized source of authority. Thus, they were never autonomous of the president.

The lack of autonomous elites protected by the politicized institutions ensured that the patronage networks of the lesser elites were easy to crush if required. Since there was no structural or institutional foundation on which to lean for protection or support, elites below the executive ring were at the mercy of a higher elite during the late Mubarak period.

Day-to-day maintenance is not public or reported in the news because of its subtlety, the lack of written evidence, and the porous character of human interactions. Nevertheless, insights from political participants into the dynamics of coalition management can be gleaned. For example, a middle elite in Egypt explained his experiences after nearly two decades in the arena. As a NDP member and prominent figure on several elected committees, Sharif Wali explained their relationships are rooted in informality and, at times, unpredictability. As he notes:

> Here you become trained in how to deal with one another. I know exactly where I am just by saying hello to my patron. If I meet him and am received coldly, I begin to ask if something is wrong. The idea is to close the opening between us as soon as possible. Then, I figure out who's created the problem. I never allow for a misunderstanding to widen. Others enjoy creating space between patrons and clients and then filling that space to separate you from power.[117]

The most common way to "create space" between upper, middle, and lower elites is through rumor spreading. For example, one elite spreads untruths to other elites about a client's intentions. If the matter is not addressed or rectified, the falsehoods take on their own life. They end up going beyond the control of one's patron.

One such example is the case of 'Ali al-Sawi, a political science professor from Cairo University. Sawi is an academic who writes critically about parliament. Because criticism rarely provides one a pass into the elite arena, Sawi used his connections with his mentor and former youth minister 'Ali al-Din Hilal to enter the elite ranks.[118] Hilal appointed Sawi as the NDP youth secretary for Cairo in 2000. After the appointment, Sawi indirectly confronted then minister of military production Mohamad al-Ghamrawi, who reacted by creating space between Sawi and Hilal.[119] The incident that apparently sparked the misunderstanding is linked to Sawi not accepting a phone call from Ghamrawi.[120] Offended that his call was rejected, he spread rumors that Sawi was too arrogant and thought himself entitled. Sawi understood that it was a pressure tactic on the part of Ghamrawi. He did not, however, contact Hilal to clear up such a trivial matter directly.[121] As time passed, the rumors intensified and were supplemented by bureaucratic obstructions to Sawi's initiatives. This, in turn, led Sawi to make a drastic decision. He wrote a letter of resignation, thinking that Hilal would protect him. To a degree, Hilal did. He called Sawi and told him that he could withdraw his letter and the matter would be dropped, to which Sawi temporary agreed. Then a day later, progovernment journalists came to Sawi and asked why he resigned and then withdrew his resignation, thus insinuating he was not good on his word. Angered at this point, Sawi told the journalists he resigned, which the Ghamrawi-allied journalists promptly printed on the edition's front page the following day. As a contemporary of Sawi in the Youth Secretariat points out, "Resignations are calculated risks. They indicate that you reject your fellow elites. If they backfire, then you are out."[122] Thus, after only three months as Cairo's youth secretary, Sawi left politics and returned exclusively to teaching and researching at the university.

This example points to the process of incremental elite coalition management in that it focuses on how a more powerful elite attacks a lesser elite. Ghamwari, either out of a lack of trust, spite, or pretension pressured Sawi into miscalculating by isolating him from his patron. Sawi misunderstood his patron's reach and did not understand his resignation would be a self-imposed exile from formal politics. This example of the unsavory side of elite coalition management, tactics of rumors spreading among the elite and using journalists as proxy were frequent practices in Mubarak's Egypt. Sawi miscalculated, but it was a powerful elite's ability to keep separation between him and his patron that contributed to the mistake. Sawi's formal political experience lasted three months and his return to ordinary life has been uninhibited.

Coalition management is also present in Syria. Yet, elite management tends to be contained within an institution's patronage network rather than on a nationally public stage. For example, B'ath elites handle patronage networks within the party while security services and the military oversee their members. Given that several networks compete within any institution, committees and meetings provide a formal area for elite management while other informal means likely exist. For example, Hafiz al-Asad "ruled by telephone" to keep apparatchiks personally accountable.[123] While my Syrian field research did not uncover any Egypt-like examples, there are examples of elites attempting to keep other elites dependent within existing institutions.

While Bashar al-Asad is constitutionally entitled to dismiss any elite appointed to government office, actors use their politicized institutions to reduce the president's ability to use such measures. In this way, the president's continued inability to assert full control over the political arena has reinforced decentralized character of the system. As one former consultant explains, "Senior party leaders believe in the independence of the B'ath. They need Bashar but they need his position constantly weakened to keep the party independent from his control."[124]

In Syria, managing elites on the ruling coalition differs greatly from Egypt. The president is involved in elite coalition management as he is forced to personally protect the nominees that he chooses for governmental positions.[125] Asad's appointments tend neither to be B'athists nor have traditional bases in the system. Rather, they are unaffiliated individuals with professional experience outside of Syria. Their lack of an internal political base makes them susceptible to being undermined by the well-positioned and institutionally supported elites. Senior elites supporting politicized institutions attempt to make the president's appointees dependent on them, not him. If they cannot, they attempt to marginalize the president's appointees. Therefore, coalition management becomes a control mechanism for competing power centers. This is what causes friction between elites from different institutions but cohesion within the politicized bodies. Thus, coalition management differs depending on whether the executive commands centralized and decentralized authority over the top elites.

When the risk of an elite potentially defecting from the consensus increases, overt management tactics by the institution's elite attempt to prevent it. During one of the summer's twice-weekly RC meetings in 2003, the command's deputy president Suleiman Qaddah used such tactics against another RC member to prevent defection. A discussion turned into an argument as then prime minister Mostapha Miro opposed Qaddah openly regarding the party's internal policy. The root of the argument related to an underlying tension connected to Miro's pending demotion as PM.[126] Qaddah interpreted Miro's opposition as potentially threatening as the PM insinuated that he was tempted to align with the president against the party. Qaddah responded to Miro by reportedly saying, "If you pursue such action, your career is over. You are either with us or you are gone." Miro chose the party. Two months later, Miro was demoted but assumed the position of heading the party's labor organizations. This placed him in care of nearly one million B'ath members.[127] Whether Qaddah could exclude Miro is inconsequential. Miro chose to remain within the party's fold rather than avoid expanding the rift with his party colleagues and risk life outside the B'ath. While Miro was likely to lose his office, elite coalition management within the party ensured his continued loyalty to it. Qaddah's ultimatum led to Miro's continued co-optation to the party. The process described above depicts management within one institution rather than at a system-wide level. Rather than contribute to overall system adaptation, this management process is directed at keeping the B'ath cohesive and prepared to compete with other politicized institutions in Syria.

Within decentralized ruling coalitions, elite coalition management produces cleavages at the system level that make the process diffuse and obstruct adaptation on day-to-day policy matters. Rather than work together, elites on the ruling coalitions tend to their power bases—be they the office of the president, the ruling party, or the security services. Because elite coalition management is such an atomized process, it permits co-optation to occur across the spectrum of competing institutions. There is no specific location or institution for those looking to be included into politics to find a home. Those looking to be included have options and various networks from which to choose.

An opposing trend appears when the ruling coalition is centralized under executive authority. There, management is geared toward preserving executive power. In such a case, it makes management a wider but concentrated systemic process. The executive's elites do not represent or tend to their institution constituencies as much as they do to the affairs of the executive. While infighting does occur, it is more likely to happen at the highest levels of the ruling coalition rather than at the institutional level. As a result, elite co-optation and inclusion tend to fall within the ranks of the single-party vehicle. Hence, the more centralized executive hierarchy and a ruling coalition, the more adaptive the political system. This underscores an integral difference between authoritarian systems with centralized and decentralized executive authority.

Elite management of the coalition is a much less visible process than coalition change. Yet, when seen, it does help explain autocratic adaptation. Frequently keeping elites affirmed to the political center—whether institutionally or personally—increases the likelihood of cohesive elites developing a stake in a system's continuation. Coalition management ensures that elite politicking is a structured process of affirmation and loyalty to a system or an institution. Hence, the efforts and energies of elites are put into the service of continuity. Yet, this process produces the perpetuation of the type of executive authority rather than contributing to advancing political development. While some theories assume that authoritarian structures inevitability lead to an all-powerful leader, the cases of Egypt and Syria demonstrate a more structured process reinforces different types of executive authority, which, in turn, conditions the character of elite co-optation.

CONCLUSION

Analyzing elite co-optation and political arenas is an imprecise endeavor. While coercive force shows how a system's elites wish to focus power, changing and managing the ruling coalitions reveals how they expand and adapt their authority. Given the different types of executive authority in each case, it is unsurprising that co-optation occurs differently in the ruling coalitions. The key variation for how authoritarian systems co-opt and shed elites is the degree in which the executive exercises centralized authority.

In centralized ruling coalitions, the executive elites have more control. Irrespective of the home institutions to which the executive elites belong, their loyalty overlaps and connects to the centralized executive. Without institutions that can protect their personnel, a ruling coalition becomes easier to alter and transform. Thus, the lack of autonomous structures facilitates the autocratic adaptation. Rather than take on a state organization, only a person's individual patronage networks and linkages require their attention to exclude someone. This is because patronage networks become transferable as elites can more easily move from one network to another. The lack of institutional anchors allows for the rapid alteration of the ruling coalition, which is essential to autocratic adaptation. But, more importantly, centralized authority also leads to the resolution of political crises without state violence against society becoming a strategy to regain political control. As the 2011 uprising revealed, Egypt's military was capable of altering the ruling coalition and then assuming the centralized executive position at the political hierarchy's apex. They accomplished this by forcing the former chief executive to resign. Thus, regime change was avoided in favor of a structural change to the ruling coalition.

Decentralized coalitions give elites from the different state institutions greater autonomy from the executive's control. Because the executive does not possess centralized authority over elites from the state's leading institutions, competing power centers offer elites from these structures the option of protecting their positions and their patronage networks from executive encroachment. Among the elites, loyalty becomes to their home institution rather than the wider coalition. Hence, the president seeks to domesticate the ruling coalition's elites. He may be forced to not only attack the patronage networks that exist within institutions but also the institutions themselves. Such a move can be tantamount to attacking the regime itself in a decentralized political context. Since this perpetuates the decentralized character of the party, the security services and the military are left to include new recruits and remove their own. Co-optation, therefore, is a diffuse process. Furthermore, top elites can oppose the president and one another without suffering exclusion or repercussions. This is not to argue that senior elites are so insulated that they can never be dismissed. However, it would take a drastic shift of existing power relations to enable the president to depoliticize the current arrangements. In turn, this seems to bolster elite resiliency because each power center is capable of resistance against other centers.

This type of system comes with consequences. A decentralized ruling coalition hinders the elites' abilities to develop and execute a system's consensus. This slows the adaptation process because decentralized authority makes policy debates difficult to coordinate because of the varying interests at play. While this obstructs autocratic adaptation on a day-to-day basis, it can lead to elite unity if the regime is threatened. As the case of Bashar al-Asad's succession revealed, elites from across the ruling coalition rallied together to ensure a predictable transfer of power. Similarly, because potentially changing the ruling coalition could lead to regime collapse, the regime unified in deploying lethal force against protesters during the 2011 uprising. Without an option to change the ruling coalition in a time of crisis, the ruling coalition chose force as it messily tried to see its way out of the crisis. Not only does this reveal the state's weakness, but it also emphasizes the ruling coalition's lack of flexibility to adapt.

Thus, the prevalence of a decentralized ruling coalition, as in the case of Bashar al-Asad's Syria, produces a more diffuse and less amenable environment with regard to the inclusion and removal of elites. The presence of multiple power centers provides some form of insulation for the senior elites who compete over regime consensus. There is, however, an irony to these dynamics. When the ruling coalition is decentralized, all of its constituent institutions—including a relatively weak president—are necessary and indispensible for maintaining the regime. Alternatively, the case of Egypt shows that executive elites are advantageously positioned to reorganize the political field because of a centralized ruling coalition. The system relies on looser and more flexible personalized attributes that make alterations to a ruling coalition more tenable. The irony, in this case, is that such coalitions can be so centralized that it can result in the rapid removal of the president and the insertion of a new executive body, such as SCAF, without leading to the regime's collapse. In regard to changing and maintaining elites, centralized and decentralized executive authority matters greatly for co-opting and shedding elites from the ruling coalition. The following chapter addresses the topic of nonelite individual inclusion and co-optation to further illustrate the differences.

4 ADAPTATION AND NONELITE CO-OPTATION

BY MOBILIZING AND INCLUDING NONELITE GROUPS, ruling elites extend state power into society. Until 2011, Syria and Egypt's political systems were both postpopulist authoritarian systems that diverged because of the degree of executive centralization over state organizations. It remains unclear what will become of these political systems in the aftermath of the Arab uprisings. However, because of these structural differences, nonelite co-optation in both systems has differed in the past. Specifically, how does the degree of centralized executive authority affect nonelite co-optation? When elites in state institutions are under centralized control, the executive's elites can more easily co-opt groups because there are no institutional obstacles when new blocs are incorporated. This leaves nonelite co-optation to occur in one location—usually the ruling party. Elites in other state institutions, such as the military or security services, do not compete to include social groups. Such arenas make changing the ruling coalition an efficient process. As a consequence, this increases the ability of ruling elites to adapt the political system.

Conversely, in political arenas where decentralized executive authority over elites prevails, it leads to competition between elites backed by power centers. As a result, co-optation is less concentrated because elites in politicized institutions all try to bring outside nonelites into their organizations. Because power is shared between competing institutions, it is harder for elites to alter the ruling coalition without the assent of its disparate members. This slows an autocratic regime's ability to adapt to challenges or to initiate change. While nonelites in Egypt tend to be channeled largely through the regime's single party, nonelites in Syria are dispersed throughout the system's pillars—party, presidency, parliament, and security services. As such, nonelite co-optation in Syria is more diffuse compared to Egypt.

PARTY CO-OPTATION IN EGYPT

Egypt and Syria are noticeably different despite being grouped similarly in the literature on the politics of Middle East. And, yet, the variance between them prior to 2011 has not been explored sufficiently. Before its uprising, Egypt's ruling party was better at co-opting activists and the middle class. Conversely, the party in Syria proved better at incorporating the rural masses. At the very least, the strengths and weaknesses of the two systems differed before 2011. It is clear, though, that the executive body's centralized authority advantaged Egypt's ruling elites to change the ruling coalition when confronted with a political challenge. This was particularly evident through the protests that forced the removal of the president before the military's Supreme Council assumed day-to-day rule during the transition. A major factor that enabled the executive elites to change the coalition with such ease stems from the weakness of the ruling party.

The National Democratic Party (NDP) in Egypt was never an institutional anchor capable of resisting centralized executive authority. When Sadat engineered the NDP, he specifically designed it not to be a counterweight to the presidency. The country's last president, Hosni Mubarak, continued the trend of increasing the presidency's autonomy and informal powers at the expense of other depoliticized institutions and portfolios. The ease with which the ruling party incorporated the president's son and his associates revealed the inability of the party's established elites to defend their space. Despite this, the party did have a functional use. Rather than serving a decorative purpose, the NDP was where co-opting outside groups into the political system occurred.[1]

In the last decade of Mubarak's rule, there was no location as active in non-elite co-optation than the party's Policies Secretariat (PS). This increase in power within the party could be credited to the personality of Gamal Mubarak.[2] The NDP created the PS at its Party Congress in September 2002. When Gamal Mubarak and his group of technocrats such as Mahmoud Mohy al-Din (Economic Subcommittee head), Mohamad Kamal (Youth Subcommittee head), and Hosam Badrawy (Education Subcommittee head) began advocating reforms, they broke with the party's traditional policies of free education and health care as well as protectionist economic policy. For example, Mohy al-Din lobbied for floating the Egyptian currency in January 2003.[3] Badrawy argued that the national education system needed to be dismantled before it could be reformed.[4] Irrespective of the members' clout, the proposals the secretariat sent to parliament revealed continuity with the authoritarian status quo rather than change.[5]

Occasionally, the PS's ideas were not even their own. One example is the legislation that established the National Council for Human Rights (NCHR). The NDP secretary-general, Safwat al-Sharif recognized the council as the secretariat's "brain-child" in April 2003 even though it was not.[6] Regardless, there was little doubt of who ran the NDP in Hosni Mubarak's final years. The PS stage-managed most of the party's conferences as well as planned its electoral strategy from 2004 until the 2010 parliamentary elections. As I wrote at the time of the 2004 NDP annual conference, "From those briefing the press, to the applause Gamal received after his opening speech, it was evident that the group consolidated NDP leadership."[7]

During its period of influence, the secretariat's emphasis remained on economic reform. Gamal Mubarak lamely justified this by arguing, "Political reform cannot be realized in unfavorable economic conditions."[8] While the younger Mubarak insisted on adhering to the mantra of economic reform first, other PS members offered ambiguous statements of political liberalization. As PS member Mohamad Kamal argued, "There are no red lines, no taboos whatsoever covering any issue related to political reform."[9] Despite the seeming openness to political reform, few liberalizing measures were ever proposed. This led most experts to argue that the secretariat was redesigning itself as Egypt's latest authoritarian incarnation. As El-Ghobashy argues:

> Lectured for decades on the imperatives of delaying democracy, Egyptians today are being sent an updated version of the same message. Instead of young modernizing officers in khakis bent on reforming the rottenness of palace politics in 1952, today it is "young" modernizing technophiles in trim suits telling Egyptians to wait until the economy is liberalized and the population is safely democratic before embarking on any political experiments.[10]

While the secretariat's approach was not innovative, the PS's did contribute to the politics of nonelite co-optation through its Higher Policies Council (HPC).

Gamal Mubarak oversaw the secretariat's seven subcommittees.[11] The subcommittees, in turn, consulted with the 123-person Higher Policies Council (HPC).[12] The council's mandate was to assist in debating potential policies and suggesting possible reforms. It was to serve as the secretariat's brain trust. While the PS rapidly established itself as the country's preeminent political force outside of the presidency, the HPC got to view the process from up close.

The HPC was the party's latest body designed to co-opt nonelites. In doing so, the HPC took unaffiliated but publicly visible and respected groups and transformed them into agents of authoritarian continuity. Many academics, economists, and former diplomats served on the HPC. They performed a legitimizing role as well as helped to link the secretariat to society. Members portrayed debate within the HPC as open; all ideas were entertained, regardless of their applicability. One member, economics professor 'Adil Bishay, described the HPC as "the country's greatest think-tank." As he noted, "Heated debates break out. Members occasionally disagree before a subcommittee head reports the findings of the discussion to the PS's steering committee."[13] Conceptually, the HPC encouraged innovative thinking by including outside, unaffiliated nonelites with a range of expertise to help prioritize the PS's reforming options. As Bishay concludes, "The HPC brings people from outside the government to work for the country. Nothing like these forum discussions existed before so this is a healthy development. Any situation where ideas are exchanged in an unrestricted environment is positive. Nothing pleases me more than to see initiatives discussed by my subcommittee debated in the Shura Council and passed into law."[14] Indeed, the HPC's strengths were that it did include socially respectable figures freely debating the PS's direction. Several HPC initiatives, such as calling for the cancellation of military decrees and abolishing hard labor, were all hailed in the national press.

However, other HPC members complained that the council complemented and reinforced the existing authoritarian structures. Hala Mostapha, who is the editor of a prominent journal published by Egypt's leading think tank, felt the HPC was a step in the right direction and admitted that free debate was encouraged in its sessions. But she remained skeptical throughout her time on the HPC:

> The steering committee promised us a liberal body but now the secretariat has adopted an authoritarian style. They are becoming what they told us they were against. In the beginning Gamal Mubarak was accessible to all HPC members. He attended the subcommittees' plenary sessions, listened, and debated with us individually. Now he only shows up to the public sessions. He enters and exits surrounded by guards who do not let you talk to him. After the public sessions, we report to our individual subcommittees where his appointed heads run the meetings. They write the reports for the PS steering committee. They intentionally omit information to suit their personal interests, even inserting things that never happened. These subcommittee heads [Ahmad 'Ezz, Badrawy, Mohy al-Din, Kamal] filter what information gets to Gamal. They make sure there are walls between Gamal and us.[15]

Mostapha stopped going to subcommittee meetings, denouncing them as cosmetic.

But the HPC's subcommittee meetings were not a waste of time. The secretariat was a mechanism for bringing public intellectuals into service of the Gamal Mubarak succession project. While the council allowed open debate, the elites around Gamal ensured that the debate remained irrelevant. "It took about six months before I realized the HPC was a tool for co-optation," recalls Mostapha before saying, "Its intention was to select liberal-minded intellectuals not formally in the party and bring them in [so] to control them. When you place individuals in such a structure, they disappear."[16]

Senior NDP members, however, were surprised by but ultimately unconcerned with such an interpretation. Former Youth Minister 'Ali al-Din Hilal focused on the allegations of co-optation. As he argued, "No one on the council is paid. The establishment of the HPC was an opportunity to bring apolitical people into the dialogue. Co-optation is about obedience but everyone in the secretariat has total freedom to speak and engage with the reforms."[17] Hilal also noted that some individual members' frustration stemmed from an inaccurate perception of politics in Egypt. As he explains, "Most of the people that meet Gamal Mubarak think they are going to be a minister two months later. When that does not happen, they are dissatisfied. I think we need to ask why do they want to interact with him? I do not feel sympathy for these people. You interact with someone when you need to. It is work, not a social gathering."[18]

When one joined the HPC, he or she automatically became card-carrying members of the NDP. Hence, many university professors, academics, businessmen, lawyers, journalists, and economists went from being unaffiliated members of the educated middle and upper classes to party members. In the process, they transferred from being apolitical nonelites to members of the political establishment. For many, this was an unimportant factor when given the opportunity to serve their country. Given that many of their colleagues were also signing on, some may have even felt pressure to join. Yet, many previously unattached individuals also saw the HPC as a doorway into politics.

The illusion of power, self-absorbed ideas of personal importance, a stagnant career, and greed likely factored into the decision to participate as well. In any political system, acquiring higher public office and gaining proximity to power also provides added security for one's livelihood and the security of one's family. When asked why she remained on the council if it was so flawed, Mostapha confessed, "There are social rules and norms. Once someone is asked to serve, the commitment must be honored." After further probing, she conceded, "If I resign from the HPC and the NDP, my political career is over. Finished. I am not ready to completely leave the system for good. The situation could change and if I am outside, it is not easy to rejoin because I chose to disassociate myself."[19]

Unaffiliated nonelites, who build reputations and maintain their independence over the years, may not necessarily have a choice in the first place. When the government approaches them and asks if they wish to join, they risk future exclusion if they decline the offer. If they join and then defect, they ensure permanent exclusion. By joining the ruling party's touted reforming wing, one's status alters. Viewed from this angle, if one harbors political ambitions, then the decision is never left to the free will of the individual. It is unrealistic that the HPC was designed exclusively to be a tool of co-optation. Yet, some HPC members' fear of resigning showed the extent to which considerations of co-optation were present or perceived. Through the PS and its affiliates, the NDP expanded its power throughout the professional and urban nonelite layers of society during its first years in existence. As the secretariat jockeyed for power, its reformist edge dulled. Regardless, the body's effects were apparent.

The NDP was never a political party in a classic sense. The party's structure was loose. It maintained wildly ambiguous objectives, arbitrarily enforced its command structure, and had little discipline in its membership ranks. There was never a decisive committee that sifted through party applications, set established membership procedures, or determined worthiness. Rather, the party recruited and excluded to meet the demands of a given moment or objective. Since its creation, the NDP was depoliticized and existed as the venue for distributing patronage as well as co-opting the politically ambitious. However, it was precisely the weakness of the party's structures that allowed it to co-opt upwardly mobile, urban, middle-class nonelites without threatening the cohesion of the executive elites on the ruling coalition.

Co-optation can breathe vitality into a centralized ruling coalition. As was seen, the process of recruitment and inclusion had less to do with the NDP's legitimacy and more to do with people wishing to connect to the state. Outsider nonelites were not attracted on the basis of strengthening the party, but rather to favorably structure future changes such as attempting to resolve succession. Outside of the NDP or the executive's office, attracting and integrating unaffiliated groups of individuals into the ruling coalition rarely happened in Egypt before 2011. However, because executive authority was centralized in Egypt before 2011, the ruling party was one of the few places that one could be co-opted. The flexible inclusion of nonelites into the party reflected the ruling coalition's high disposition to autocratically adapt. Perhaps nowhere more than the HPC is this flexibility on display. This, by contrast, does not apply in the case for Syria's ruling party.

PARTY CO-OPTATION IN SYRIA

The mechanism for nonelite group co-optation differs in Syria. Besides the ruling B'ath Party's 1.8 million members, seven other parties comprise the Progressive National Front (PNF). Hafiz al-Asad initiated the PNF in 1972 to bring disparate political groupings under B'athist control. This made the opposition parties subservient to the ruling party in exchange for parliamentary and ministerial representation. The continuing effect of the PNF is that it fragments the opposition parties. Additionally, Syria maintains an agricultural union that allows the ruling party to penetrate villages in rural areas.[20] Corporatist entities, such as the agriculture union, do not to have the autonomy or lobbying influence of the B'ath, the security services, or the presidency. They, and more than one million members, do, however, exist to support the party. In doing so, they reinforce the ruling party's autonomy. In this respect, the B'ath Party was and remains more of a genuine social organizing experiment than any corporatist attempts in Egypt's political field. The party can maintain both its cohesion and prominence among the various power centers. This strength makes it difficult for the presidency to depoliticize the party apparatus. Furthermore, any indication that the president intends to restructure the party, and try to exercise centralized control over it, is met with resistance and opposition. Because of the decentralized ruling coalition, institutional gridlock between various competing organizations frequently occurs on day-to-day policy matters. Yet, it makes altering the coalition difficult to do because all of its constituent parts become indispensable.

Co-optation of nonelites into the ruling party, which is the key strategy of Egypt's elites, plays out in a different way in Syria. Given the bureaucratic requirements for full B'ath membership and the party's internal elite configurations, it is difficult for the party's leadership to parachute in a block of unaffiliated cadre. Similarly, the president cannot will into existence B'athist-sponsored councils as is routinely done in Egypt. B'athists join at a young age and are socialized. As such, established individuals outside the system do not often join government-sponsored councils and think tanks, much less become members of the ruling party. Yet, there are exceptions to the rule that illuminate Syria's ruling party differences from Egypt.

An example of nonelite co-optation was the Committee for Reforming the B'ath. In January 2004, the party commissioned the body and charged it with preparing a list of priorities for the June 2005 party congress. This was to be the first congress held under Bashar al-Asad's presidency. Many analysts felt it would be an important measurement of the president's position vis-à-vis the other institutional power centers.[21] 'Abdallah Ahmar, who served as the party's National Command Head until June 2005, chaired the body's four subcommittees. The subcommittees included two ideological groups for pan-Arab unity and Regional/Local leadership. The remaining subcommittees evaluated the party's content. They included a Socialism Subcommittee and a Democracy or "Freedom" Subcommittee. The Regional Command (RC) reviewed all of the subcommittees' reports and incorporated changes when preparing the congress's agenda.

The subcommittees had a year to complete their tasks. Of the four subcommittees, three had influence in that their recommendations would guide change for the congress. The fourth organ, the Freedom Subcommittee, was consultative. Its recommendations could be adopted or dismissed at the RC's discretion. The reason for its consultative status is that it was the only one that included opposition and independent figures. The remaining subcommittees were comprised entirely of party members. As an independent member of the Freedom Subcommittee explains, "We were told to say what we wanted but that it was not our job to reform the party."[22] The Freedom Subcommittee included a mixture of B'ath Party members, military officers, and independent figures. It also was a cross-sectarian mix that included Sunnis, Shi'as, Christians, and 'Alawis. Its members were Ahmad Barqawi (ex-B'athist, philosophy professor at Damascus University), Samir al-Taqi (surgeon, former member of the Faysil wing of the Communist Party), Michel Kilo (civil society activist), Husayn al-Owdat (ex-B'athist, opposition figure), Samir Hassan (B'athist, dean of literature in Damascus University), Marwan Sabah (B'athist, consultant for the Information Ministry), Hamid Mar'ai (opposition, member of Committee for Friends of Civil Society), Major-Gen. 'Ezz al-Din Idris (a figure in the B'athist ideology branch), and Gen. Mohamad Yehia Sulayman (faculty director of the National Defense School).

The Freedom Subcommittee met almost weekly throughout 2004. The non-B'athist figures participating on the Freedom organ reached an agreement whereby they could leave without retribution if they were unsatisfied with the subcommittee's direction or progress.[23] Members such as Kilo successfully lobbied for their reports to be published and publicly circulated. Samir al-Taqi and Ahmad Barqawi published their contributions on the *All 4 Syria* electronic newsletter.[24] Al-Taqi argued, "We made it clear from the beginning that we were here to save the country, not the B'ath Party. Our reports were not managed. We discussed everything. We spoke about the military and its structures, the role of the shadow economy, potential social tension, and the ethnic and confessional impact on our history and future development."[25] Individual members' papers addressed topics such as conceptual approaches to democracy and explored the effects of popular democracy on the economy, civil society, and state structures. At the conclusion of a year's work, the subcommittee submitted a final report to the party.

Samir Hassan was placed in charge of amalgamating the numerous discussions and papers into a working paper that the RC could use to determine an agenda of priorities. The final report generated controversy in Damascus. This revolved around the fact that the final report was not made public, and there were rumors that the party would not convene its congress. One Western diplomat suggested that "the Freedom Subcommittee had lots of bluster in the beginning but as time wore on, people started shutting up. As for the report, it is known that it was written from above, and that the party discarded the opposition figures' individual papers."[26]

Al-Taqi disagreed. He felt that the final paper was a fitting summary of the subcommittees' efforts. Even if the report did not live up to expectations, the original papers are still consulted and ready for use in the event of any party restructuring. In his view, just because some of the more liberal ideas were not in the final report does not mean they are unusable in the future. While the committee's members produced useful ideas, the impact of their efforts depends on the outcome of the political struggle. Depending on which institution (presidency, party, or military-security complex) accumulated the most influence on this issue of party reform determined how the final report was implemented. Given the lack of progress since the 2005 congress as well as the 2011 uprising, progressive ideas were dropped from policy discussions.

The limited co-optative capacity of the subcommittee in comparison to Egypt's HPC is evident. The Freedom Subcommittee consisted of a cross-section of society. While a few of the subcommittee members were B'athist, some of its members were not. They belonged to a part of the civil society movement that survived the Damascus Spring in 2001. People such as Kilo or Mar'ei were primarily concerned with cultural developments.[27] Kilo frequently comments on Syrian politics in the media while writing weekly for Beirut-based newspapers and journals. Samir al-Taqi is a surgeon. Once a member of the politburo of the Faysil branch of the Communist Party, al-Taqi is now loosely affiliated with Walid al-Mo'alim, then deputy minister of foreign affairs.[28] Yet individuals such as al-Taqi or Kilo cannot fairly be considered co-opted by the party because of their participation in this subcommittee.

If Syria's political field mirrored Egypt's, individuals that were approached would have become members of the ruling party de facto. The incorporation of independent members would have neutralized them, as their efforts became absorbed into the system's service. Yet, in Syria, nonelite individuals were offered an opportunity to join a party committee without conditions. No one was forced to accept formal institutional affiliation. In fact, it is unlikely that the party, with its rules for degrees of membership, could have easily accepted outside figures becoming instant members. The party's members are arranged in extensive, overlapping, and, at times, conflicting patronage networks. Indeed, injecting fresh or charismatic members in higher positions could disrupt these networks.

Simultaneously, many of these unaffiliated, nonelite figures did not see joining the party as the best way to improve Syria. As al-Taqi argues, "We would not join the party, our role is to criticize the party. By participating on the Freedom Subcommittee, we reinforce our independence and maintain open dialogue. If I were a member of the party, they would not need me."[29] One might reasonably deduce that al-Taqi or Kilo might not have been appointed to the subcommittee if they were party members. They and the other subcommittee members are useful for developing ideas to reform the system in contemporary Syria. But, as a politicized institution, the party serves a different function. This allows the governing party to reach out and interact with these figures without formally including them. Hence, the inclusion of nonaffiliated nonelite figures is not as prominent or concentrated as in Egypt.

Rather, the trend in Syria focuses on nonelite figures being consulted and used but not incorporated formally into the system's structures. This indicates that in authoritarian systems where authority is decentralized among the members of the ruling coalition, interactions between the state's institutions and independent nonelite personalities does not result in formally incorporating the latter. The consequence of such a measure is that nonelite individuals are diffusely spread across the system between the politicized institutions such as the party, military, intelligence services, bureaucracy, PNF, and parliament. In this vein, the institutions become more important rather than personalities that make them up.

EGYPT'S COUNCILIZATION

One way that elites in Egypt's system won over a wider segment of society in pre-2011 Egypt was by establishing national councils. These councils dealt with issues such as women's rights, human rights, and other concerns often viewed as foreign priorities. Steven Heydemann sees these initiatives as particularly illuminating as authoritarianism in the Arab world continues to update.[30] Andre Bank developed the notion of councilization in relation to the Arab world's two constitutional monarchies, Morocco and Jordan. In the case of Morocco, Bank argues:

> These unelected bodies existed or still exist in different areas. . . . It is an attempt by the king to institutionalize his rather informal powers and to create something of a parallel government structure. Thereby, a hybrid system develops in which the exact spheres of responsibilities are not clear and in which Muhammad can bypass the formal procedures that have developed in Moroccan politics over the last decade. Overall, this constellation allows for various ways of penetration and intervention by the king.[31]

Councilization is not just a monarchical option. It is also visible in Egypt, where it fortified the autonomy of the centralized chief executive and helped usher in Gamal Mubarak's participation. While the Mubaraks' executive elites were not a royal court, the government did display an ability to harness national councils as a means of expanding state power into society. The strategy sought to invite divisions among groups working in such fields as human rights while fragmenting and nationalizing oppositional discourses of discontent. Its purposes were to reach out to a key regime constituency—urban middle-class professionals—and reduce the activism of civil society. Egypt's two most prominent national councils are the National Women's Council (NWC) and the National Council for Human Rights (NCHR). By examining the NCHR,[32] I illustrate how the use of councils facilitated nonelite group co-optation by penetrating a targeted segment of society.

The establishment of the NCHR in 2003 represents an example of the state attempting to assuage domestic concerns without changing its existing practices. It also attempted to market Gamal Mubarak's secretariat as the reformist future to a social support base. This perceived key constituency was the educated but politically inactive urban professional class. Lastly, and a peripheral reason, the council was established to appeal to foreign calls for reform.

After the cabinet approved the creation of the NCHR in May 2003, the justice minister laid out the council's composition and mission. It was to have twenty members, to be affiliated with and appointed by the president, and to foster a culture of human rights. It would also examine pertinent legislation and ensure Egypt's compliance with international human rights agreements. The president, subsequently, attached the NCHR to the upper house of parliament (Shura Council).[33] Nevertheless, the council's affiliation to the ruling party blurred the mission and sapped its potential autonomy.[34] Parliamentarians created the council on June 16, 2003. Law 93/2003 stipulated that the NCHR would be state funded, possess no legislative powers, and consist of a chairman, a deputy, and twenty-five members.[35]

The NCHR was purposefully designed to serve as an advisory body. Former NDP parliamentary whip Kamal al-Shazli described the limits of the council's authority by saying, "It [NCHR] is merely a consultative council with no power to draw up any plans."[36] While NDP MPs "heaped praise on Gamal Mubarak's policy secretariat, and encouraged the NCHR to stand up to NGOs that exploit the human rights issue to tarnish Egypt's image," analysts noted that its powers did not extend beyond "requesting cooperation" from governmental agencies and "recommending" cases for prosecution.[37] As such, inconvenient or inexpedient council advice could be legally ignored or shelved by the prosecutor general's investigative services. Indeed, even requesting cooperation seemed unlikely to be beneficial because the NCHR was not endowed with any legal redress. Hence, the agencies asked to cooperate with the NCHR could not be held accountable if they declined.

Rather than hinge the NCHR's domestic and international legitimacy on lesser-known personalities, the Shura's appointees represented a "who's who" of Egyptian politics. Former UN secretary-general Boutros Boutros-Ghali became the council's chairman while respected international lawyer Ahmad Kamal Abul-Magd was nominated as its deputy. The additional twenty-five council members could have been generally described as socially active and respectable figures.

The appointment of independent human rights activists also added some degree of credibility to the NCHR. Bahey al-Din Hassan, the director of the Cairo Institute for Human Rights Studies (CIHRS), and Hafiz Abu Sa'ada, the director of the Egyptian Organization for Human Rights (EOHR), were considered the NCHR's opposition members. Abu Sa'ada is a deeply symbolic appointment. He runs the best-known domestic human rights NGO in Cairo. He was also arrested and held for six days in December 1998 because he authored a report about the al-Kosh incident of August 1998.[38] Although these appointments failed to impress civil society activists, their presence intended to appeal to inactive professionals who viewed them as outside of the government's control. On closer inspection, however, the council revealed a different story.

The appointment of Hassan and Abu Sa'ada was not wholly unexpected. In May 2000, when the Justice Ministry was initially preparing to launch the NCHR, an article traced the council's development to Paris in March 2000 where Abu Sa'ada pitched the idea to Mubarak's chief of staff, Zakaraya 'Azmy.[39] In the same article, activists denounced the potential ramifications for Egypt's human rights NGOs, but Hassan indicated that such a council would be a positive step. The Shura Council apparently approached other activists to find out if they would be willing to serve. Others approached, but not appointed, included Nagad al-Bora'i,[40] and Hisham Kassem, then manager of the independent daily *al-Masri al-Youm*.[41] While the appointees were prominent, they were hampered by institutional constraints rather than abilities to research, assess, and call for action.

Some of Abu Sa'ada's colleagues from other organizations branded him as an "opportunist."[42] Others argued that Hassan and Abu Sa'ada "lost their independence" when they joined the NCHR.[43] For their part, Abu Sa'ada and Hassan defended their membership. As Abu Sa'ada stated, "If you do not join, you can have no impact at all. I could not say no until we examine how the Council operates. If it is inactive, I can resign."[44] Hassan made similar arguments.[45] The argument over co-optation and members' reputations even reached the NCHR's chairman, Boutros-Ghali, who brushed off the criticism by saying, "There is not a single representative of the government on the council. My personality alone is an obstacle to the government's pressure. I said 'no' to the US government [when UN secretary-general] so I can say 'no' to the Egyptian government."[46] While this debate raged, it neglected to spotlight the various constituencies that the NCHR reassured. The value of the NCHR lies in its middle membership, which was an attempt to achieve two interconnected aims.

First, the NCHR middle members included leading and well-known lawyers, journalists, bureaucrats, doctors, and intellectuals. Each of these professionals had his or her own social network. The government sought to woo the professional class by bringing prominent professional figures to reach out to these social segments. For example, Osama al-Ghazali Harb,[47] editor of al-Ahram's *al-Siyasa al-Dawliya*, and NDP MP Mostafa al-Fiqi were appointees. As government-inclined yet moderate pundits, both enjoy positive social reputations domestically. Hosam Badrawy, a NDP MP and Gamal Mubarak associate, was also on the council.[48] Popular Wafdist MP Monir Fakhry 'Abd al-Nor represented opposition parties.[49] Lawyer and women's rights activist Mona Zolfiqar also served as an active voice.[50] Likewise, then press syndicate head Galal 'Arif ensured that journalists had representation.

Secondly, the council neutralized the human rights debate by diluting civil society's monopoly over exposing abuses. The NCHR provided a semiofficial platform from which its socially respectable members transmitted an incrementally liberalizing argument to various constituencies. In this vein, the target audience was not the upper-class businessmen or the countries' numerous urban and rural poor. Rather, the NCHR spoke to urban professionals who, while perhaps concerned with human rights issues, are not consumed by the debate's contours. By adding its voice to the human rights debate, the government nationalized and partially co-opted the debate—thereby winning the support of this nonelite group of the population.

The NHRC had seven working subcommittees. They represented political, social, economic, civil, and cultural rights as well as legislative matters. The remaining subcommittee verified citizen and institutional complaints. An eighth subcommittee was slated to deal with international regulations, but it remained unclear if it ever was constituted. Hence, seven of the eight subcommittees maintained the tasks of human rights education and dissemination. Only the Complaints Subcommittee handled violations. In light of the NCHR's lack of legal powers, little of substance transpired.

The NCHR published its first annual report on Egypt in April 2005. The report's release was handled in a questionable manner. A meeting scheduled for mid-April for the NCHR to circulate and discuss the 358-page report was never held. Instead, Abul-Magd called an ad hoc meeting. Bahay Hassan, who was traveling at the time, characterized the move as consistent with how the body operates. He stated, "The report was adopted at a meeting called on short notice and sent to the president without making it available for its members to read. The report was completed to tell the people it has been done."[51] When asked if the report dealt with the al-'Arish detentions,[52] Hassan said, "I have neither read nor know what is in the report. Only those around Abul-Magd know its contents."[53] Hafiz Abu Sa'ada claimed that the report did address the al-'Arish arrests and that the NCHR was publicly releasing the report in Arabic, English, and French "in a few months after the president and parliament have the opportunity to review our recommendations."[54] While the NCHR looked frail intellectually, its operation appears to confirm the state was presenting an illusion of reform rather than actual reform.

The NCHR was not designed to be, and did not become, the regime's tool for including opposition. It did not have enough seats to co-opt very many people. Yet, the NCHR served an important political purpose. While the council did not pretend to possess power, its creation was largely about that. The primary purpose of establishing the NCHR was to expand and redistribute regime power. While it is debatable that it ever achieved such aims, it did muddle the discourse over human rights.

The Policies Secretariat and the NCHR advertised that the government was moving in a liberalizing direction. By wrongly attributing the NCHR's genesis to Gamal Mubarak's secretariat, the ruling party marketed that group as its enlightened wing. By reaching out to professionals, the council's establishment tempered discontent while expanding professional class support for the younger Mubarak. In reaffirming existing supporters as well as adding new ones among this potentially wavering social base, power seemed to increase during that time. Similarly, in adding an official voice, the NCHR redistributed power because the human rights field was redefined into "moderates" and "rejectionist" camps. Cultivating such a distinction, the human rights debate became nationalized because the NCHR weakened the criticism by independent human rights groups. Even if a few or even most human rights NGOs disregarded the council, it failed to invalidate the NCHR as an incremental development for the politically inactive middle class.

Human rights violations such as in the northern Sinai towns during the fall of 2004 remained routine. One could argue that human rights abuses increased in Egypt until the 2011 uprising. Yet, handling domestic violations was not the NCHR's mission. The NCHR was rhetorically active in areas that concerned Egypt's urban middle-class professionals. In this vein, directing attention to international violations in Palestine and Iraq, which complemented media coverage, also helped the council satisfy its intended domestic audience. Failure to resolve the Arab-Israeli conflict helped keep the NCHR's focus abroad rather than at home. Whether the NCHR was capable of assuring long-term support was not an important question. For the many urban middle-class professionals who did not harbor political ambitions, the establishment was a form of nonelite co-optation in that it was seen as working on the issue. Rather than being an exemplary expression of co-optative politics, it was preemptive inclusion by nationalizing the discourse.

While in the previous examples there is a focus on forcing a formal institutional affiliation, the strategies of councilization in Egypt demonstrated an increasing sophistication of autocratic adaptation. In this example, the government did not employ the older strategies of bringing independent people and forcing party membership on them. Yet, the council still wedded prominent figures to the system's structures. One could also say the NCHR's closest affiliation was with the ruling party although it did not require its members join the party. In a sense, this newer strategy attracted a base through acquiescence rather than formalized membership to a structure. Apart from the traditional co-optation tactics of dominating formally "independent" entities such as trade unions, NGOs, and professional syndicates, executive elites in Egypt attempted to create parallel entities within the system with national councils. In the cases of the opposition or independent figures that joined the NCHR, the government proved capable of recruiting individuals from prickly NGOs into a state-affiliated entity. They, in turn, helped expand the regime's social power among a key constituent. In hindsight of the 2011 uprising, such strategies now seem like useless exercises. Yet, the inevitability of popular protest grabbing the initiative and forcing state elites to alter the ruling coalition is rare. It is entirely possible that such strategies do work until unpredictable and outside forces change the structural playing field of politics. Syrian elites, by contrast, use a different strategy for empowering associations in hopes of expanding their power.

CONTROLLED ASSOCIATION EXPANSION IN SYRIA

The adaptation strategy of councilization, as seen in the previous example, is not employed by Syria. Bashar al-Asad tried to introduce people connected to him from the Syrian Computer Society (SCS) into the governing structures after assuming power, but the efforts produced mixed results.[55] While the people brought in through the SCS have become part of the elite, it has been a failure in its intended scope. In Bank's words, the "attempts to bolster his power base have not been successful in the sense of creating a constellation in which he would acquire hegemonic powers over all other members of the core elite."[56] Asad is getting more powerful, but he does not possess an ability to restructure the coalition's political arrangements. The extension of Lebanese president Emile Lahoud's term, which required a Lebanese constitutional amendment, strengthened the president's position domestically vis-à-vis the key elites within Syria's politicized institutions.[57] However, the system has maintained its decentralized character where elites from all the ruling coalition's institutions are necessary for the state to remain viable. The 2011 uprising showed this more than ever. Perhaps because of the executive's decentralized authority, the strategy of councilization has not been adopted. Instead of using councils, however, there has been a controlled expansion of charitable associations.

To frame associational life in Syria is difficult because NGOs are not legally recognized. There are two reasons for this. NGOs, by Syrian political definitions, are seen as open to foreign funding and involvement in domestic political activities. Hence, associations—and not NGOs—operate in Syria. Perhaps this is a matter of semantics, but this is how associations characterize themselves in Syria. Since the United Arab Republic (UAR) with Egypt (1958–61), Laws 93/1958 and 1330/1958 have governed associations and charities. These laws define what associations are and restrict their activities by criminalizing political activism. Yet there has been some expansion within the association field in contemporary Syria.

The establishment of associations is one noticeable trend under Bashar al-Asad's leadership. According to the Ministry of Social Affairs, Syria maintains 586 associations. Fifty of them were created between 2002 and 2004.[58] As a founder of the Syrian Young Entrepreneurs Association (SYEA) explains, despite the increase in associations, "there are only about five that matter."[59]

The new associations focus on channeling younger people into the public sphere to tackle issues such as rural poverty, women's development, entrepreneurship, and environmental preservation. In a country defined by state-led development, state elites have proven not to have the requisite specialized training to engage with the issues that some of the new associations address. Despite a flourish of newly registered associations, the quickest and easiest way to be granted a license remains an association's connections to upper elite figures. For example, the most important associations developed under Bashar al-Asad all operate under the patronage of his wife, Asma.

FIRDOS (Fund for Integrated Rural Development of Syria) was founded in July 2001. It is regarded as the "pioneer" in the revitalizing association field. The purpose of FIRDOS is to reduce and eliminate rural poverty through projects that target financial, educational, and basic infrastructural needs overlooked or neglected by the state. One of FIRDOS's key contributions is its willingness to offer microfinance loans to undercapitalized rural businesses. Modernizing and Activating Women's Role in Economic Development (MAWRED) was founded in April 2003. It aspires to train, employ, and develop women's professional and entrepreneurial skills so they can be better incorporated in the economy. MAWRED initiated a project to consult and support struggling businesses in the hope of spurring creativity that translated into profits.[60] The aim of the project was to increase independence in business among the lower members of Syria's social strata.

SYEA was established in January 2004. Sami Moubayed, a Damascene businessman and university professor, was a leading member among the group's twelve founders. Moubayed explained that Syria has an environment conducive for unbridled entrepreneurial growth. SEYA facilitates an organizational outlet for younger businesspeople to meet and network.[61] As he argues, "We are similar to FIRDOS and MAWRED. We are independent and sort of a junior Chamber of Commerce."[62] In many ways, the strategy of expanding Syrian associations is a means of expanding the power of the president's office because the focus is on neglected areas of state development. Hence, it is an attempt to link development to the presidency as opposed to the state's elites from the traditional institutions.

On closer inspection, these new associations are neither all that free, nor do they maintain staff with the required technical expertise in their specific fields. Although access to state money and the ability to push paperwork through rigid government bureaucracy is a benefit, associations connected to the president's wife forfeit independence. Moreover, those in charge of the day-to-day operations of each prominent association maintain other connections with the senior elites from other state institutions. For example, daughters of prominent figures participate and contribute to FIRDOS and MAWRED's development. For example, Dima Turkmani, the daughter of former minister of defense, Nora al-Shar'a, daughter of former foreign minister, and Reem Khaddam, daughter of former vice president, are all members of FIRDOS or MAWRED. People affiliated with these associations feel that focusing on their family connections misrepresents the good work being done. As one FIRDOS member states, "It is incredible how smart and energetic these women are. Who cares who their fathers are. They care about Syria and its future dearly. They are not out for personal gain or wealth."[63] There is no reason not to believe this statement. These individuals are concerned with Syrian development and graciously donate their efforts.

Yet, the striking feature is that the likelihood of these associations carving out an autonomous space is small. Being daughters of the senior elites is a double-edged sword. While it allows them the leeway to establish associations and to pursue such activities, it also makes the organization susceptible to control. If one of these organizations interferes or proves detrimental to the Syrian political establishment, their efforts are easily curtailed. As one analyst remarks,

"The associations here do good work. Unfortunately, the president's wife has pulled back so they are suffering at the moment. But, it is not like these groups were ever in anything but safe hands."[64]

A second consideration is that while those with personal connections to senior elites can more easily circumscribe bureaucracy, they may not always be experts in their chosen field. Some Syrians living abroad have returned to work in these associations. Attracting these expatriates was a key element of the president's early agenda. Yet, despite these western-trained Syrian expatriates returning to work on development, some do not possess the required field credentials. As a former consultant connected to the projects argues, "I read some proposals and in many cases they did not have the expertise to reduce rural poverty. Sure, they were optimistic and hard working, but FIRDOS and MAWRED operate without a compass. It is not rule of experts, but instead a lack of experts."[65] Because of the direct and indirect control exercised over the expanding associational arena, it seems unlikely that the problems these groups hope to combat will be effectively overcome. Additionally, no definitive measurements credibly indicate how these associations affect social co-optation other than involving new people. The expansion of the sector, then, suggests that the presidency has been unsuccessful in building linkages around the ruling party and security services.

The associations are not as visible as they were a few years ago. The legislation proposed to alter the association law to officially permit NGOs has been stalled. This keeps these groups hampered from receiving external development aid. Keeping these new associations closely controlled through people connected to the senior political elites in an ambiguous legal arena produces several different strategies for the associations. The formal and informal controls senior elites maintain over associations make the probability of their becoming a new space for independent activity unlikely. For example, the associations receive state funding. Yet the introduction of quasi-official associations sponsored and operated by relatives of regime members does not have the social co-optation reach of the councilization strategy in Egypt. While the new associations indicate that the government is reaching out to include new figures, it does so slowly and in a manner that it controls completely. Accordingly, reaching out to new people is done in the hopes of developing individual networks rather than attempting to win over an apolitical economic class.

One conclusion is that Syria's existing institutional field is resistant to the addition of other potentially politicized entities that could also vie for influence. In Egypt's centralized arena, the addition of numerous NGOs, councils, and committees is frequently used as an adaptation strategy. Yet, in Syria, a complementary trend is absent because of competing power centers within and among the decentralized ruling coalition. Such entities block the emergence of energized associations or councils. Hence, only controlled entities that cannot threaten the political equilibrium between upper elites from the different institutions on the ruling coalition are permitted to operate. Hence, Asma al-Asad's associations would be blocked if they upset the political balance in the president's favor. In Syria, neither political nor apolitical associations are welcome regardless of their sponsor. In Egypt, the system can flexibly incorporate new entities precisely because they can be included as easily as they are excluded. The big difference between associational life in Egypt and Syria is that in the former there is more room for NGOs so long as they are not political. In the latter, there is simply not enough room given all the existing competition for policy influence among the repositories of power on the ruling coalition.

ELECTED NONELITES: PARLIAMENTARY DIFFERENCES

While Egypt and Syria's parliaments lack autonomy, both assemblies distribute patronage and absorb figures into the system. The processes whereby this happens, however, differ significantly. In Egypt, many independent parliamentary candidates join the ruling party and officially designate themselves as NDP members after they win their election. In Syria, by contrast, party membership is not a prerequisite. In fact, the law cordons off one-third of its seats to independents. This section highlights these differences of nonelite co-optation by focusing on the dynamics of how agents are brought into parliament.

Until the 2010 election, Egypt's lower house of parliament (Maglis al-Sh'ab) comprised 444 elected and 10 presidentially appointed members. Parliamentary elections were vigorously contested under Mubarak's rule, despite the opposition's inability to compete with the ruling NDP.[66] The reduction in opposition representation in parliament following the 1987 election can partially be explained by a change in the electoral law away from a proportional representation list system in 1990. The 2000 election stood out as a fairly typical election under Mubarak. The legal opposition parties obtained seventeen seats, or 4 percent of the total. The Wafd won seven seats, the Tagam'u six, Nasserists three, and the Liberals one.[67] True independent candidates won twenty-one seats with the Muslim Brothers winning seventeen of those.[68] At that point, it was the group's largest total since 1987. This left the NDP to accumulate 388 seats, establishing a dominating 88 percent majority.

The low opposition figures can also be explained by the NDP independent phenomenon. Newly elected MPs, who were not the party's official candidates, would join the NDP after their election. In the 2000 parliamentary elections, official NDP candidates won 172 (38 percent) out of 444 contested seats. Another 216 independent candidates joined the party following the election, giving it an 88 percent majority in parliament. Of the 216 independents that joined the party, 181 were originally members who did not receive the party's official nomination and contested elections anyway.[69] A large number of independents also joined after the 2005 parliamentary elections. According to published totals, the NDP official candidates only won 145 (32 percent) of the 444 races they entered.[70] The injection of 166 NDP independents increased the NDP's parliamentary bloc to 311 seats total (71.4 percent). The NDP's 2005 electoral performance indicated a further decline in the party's ability to officially nominate candidates that win outright. It hardly was a surprise that independents who win parliament elections join or rejoin the party in Egypt. The independents joined in order to have access to the government's resources or gain proximity to the president's centralized reach for guiding policy. Independents would have been marginalized from the patronage networks without formal NDP affiliation. In this manner, joining the NDP became the most logical choice. Yet, it also imparts a key element of control.

Before the 2011 uprising, Egypt's parliament was not an active legislative body like those found in competitive democracies. Rather, parliament was expected to pass legislation that the executive elites forwarded to the chamber. 'Amr Hashem Rabi'a, a parliamentary analyst at the al-Ahram Center for Political and Strategic Studies, notes, "Nearly 95 percent of the legislation passed in parliament comes from the government. The other 5 percent is derived from the parliamentary members themselves."[71] NDP MPs were expected to vote for legislation even when it went against their interests. An example of this was seen when the parliament voted on the second phase of a Value Added Tax (VAT) in 2002. As independent MP and leader of the Karama movement, Hamdin Sabahy, recalls:

> When the legislation was put to a vote, all the opposition and independents were against it. Also, a majority of the NDP MPs were initially against it. Many of them are businessmen and an increase in a VAT would result negatively as their products would be more expensive. They were arguing that it was not fair

and against the people but then the parliamentary speaker intervened and said this initiative came from the president's office. When it was put to a vote, all the NDP MPs raised their hands to allow the bill to pass.[72]

In this example, the NDP's parliamentary leadership proved capable of enforcing conformity, even when its members opposed a bill they perceived as contrary to their financial interests.

Official affiliation with the ruling party facilitated a parliamentarian career during the era of the NDP. This is because ruling-party affiliation secured the benefits of patronage and allowed parliamentarians to pass along these benefits to their clients. In the process, executive elites asserted control over individuals. The incentive of co-optation also encouraged candidates who did not get the party's official nomination to rejoin it after winning as independents. The Syrian parliament is also an arena for co-optation. The process of co-optation is as vital in Damascus as in Cairo. Yet, the key difference relates to a MP's institutional affiliation.

The Syrian parliament is similar to Egypt's in that it is not an independent or active body. As with the Egyptian parliament, the Syrian legislature has, in the words of Perthes, "remained at the margins of political life. From the mid-1970s to date, all laws that were passed by parliament have been introduced by the government, and never have government bills been defeated."[73] While the incentive of access to state funds encouraged Egyptian independents to join the ruling party, a different trend is at work in Syria. Rather than hold elections where independents and legal opposition parties compete for the available 250 seats, the seats are allocated prior to the election. Nonelite individuals are co-opted into the political system through the mechanism of predetermined independent slots.

Syrian parliamentary elections have been held approximately every four years since 1973. In 1990, electoral legislation widening parliament's "representation of interests" as it introduced "a new element of political participation by forces outside the regime elite."[74] In the 1990 parliamentary elections, the parliament was expanded from 195 members to 250 seats with 83 seats reserved for independents outside of the Progressive National Front's lists.[75] As Perthes notes:

> The regime expended considerable effort in encouraging independent candidatures. There was no competition between independents and front-party candidates, and voters still had no choice as far as the PNF list was concerned.

It was clear in advance that the PNF would secure seats for all its candidates and maintain about the same number of deputies as it presented on the outgoing council. But there was considerable competition among non-PNF candidates. . . . Many candidates had marked views and independent opinions, but none of them represented anti-regime opposition. Most candidates actually confirmed their allegiance to the President, crediting him as the leader who had put Syria on the path to democracy.[76]

In both cases, election to parliament likely meant co-optation. In Egypt, however, membership in the ruling party became vital only if one wished to have access to state resources and proximity to the chief executive. In Syria, independents are expected to be loyal but are not expected to apply for party membership. A closer examination of recent parliamentary elections in Syria further reinforces this point.

The 2003 parliamentary elections proved little different from any of the previous or subsequent elections conducted since 1990. They were, however, the first conducted under Bashar al-Asad's presidency. The ruling party was allocated 135 seats while the remaining PNF parties were guaranteed 32 seats. The independent candidates were allotted their predetermined 83 seats. By one account, the 2003 elections witnessed the fiercest electoral competition in terms of money spent on campaigns among independent candidates in the post-1970 era. One estimate put the money spent by potential candidates at more than one million dollars ("a huge amount by Syrian standards").[77] Despite low voter turnout and the public's preoccupation with the imminent American-led war on Iraq, the independents that won were largely businessmen. Many figures with connections to the ruling elites were among them. *Middle East International* described the parliament following the election as "a parliament without opposition."[78] One key development was noticeable, however. In response to calls by the political establishment for businessmen to be more involved in the reform process, parliament witnessed increased representation by businessmen, including the fabulously wealthy Salih al-Malih (Aleppo), Khalid al-Ulabi (Aleppo), Zuhayr Dab'ul (Damascus), Mohamad Hamsu (Damascus), and Hashim Akkad (Damascus).

Regardless of the money these independent candidates spent to get into parliament, they became parliamentarians without becoming members of the ruling party. One businessmen MP clearly indicated in an interview that joining the party was an undesirable move. Hashim Akkad is an independent MP from Damascus. He has served in parliament since 1994. Akkad's understanding of contemporary Syrian politics and Bashar al-Asad's presidency reveals how independent MPs represent one of the system's co-opted wings. Akkad's empire is expansive. He claimed to have business interests in textiles, soft drinks, pasta, advertisement, information technology, telephone exchanges, trucking, car rentals, conference organization, restaurant services, trade houses, construction materials, and an oil company that specializes in drilling and field services (his company owns "several" oil rigs).[79] Akkad, whose office was festooned with framed pictures and sayings of Hafiz and Bashar al-Asad, notes that when the younger Asad came to power, there was a distinct change in style to a "more open-minded approach." While he conceded that the older politicians have some wisdom to bestow, he feels no one was indispensable. Someone like then vice president 'Abd al-Halim Khaddam is "capable at his job. But if he is no longer any good, he will be removed."

While Akkad spoke mainly in generalities, he was transparent in his feelings about the president. As Akkad argues, "The president does not want any obstacles on the way to reform. If some are hurting the country, he will remove them constitutionally. But, it must be stated, people are happy with his progress. The president has made no mistakes—in foreign or internal matters—since coming to power."[80] Akkad feels that the economic-reform process is accelerating at a "very fair" pace. He argues that he had not heard any complaints from the business community and emphasizes that the Syrian parliament "makes the country better because we force people to account."[81] Perhaps, Akkad's independent status drives a desire to remain included. Yet, being an independent in his case clearly indicates aligning with the president against elites from the ruling party.

The Syrian and Egyptian parliaments were both arenas of nonelite co-optation prior to the 2011 uprisings. They provided the executive elites in these systems with an opportunity to invite competition between prospective nonelites. Once elected, they and their interests were insulated so long as they publicly expressed their loyalty and availed their social capital to the system. However, an important difference between Syria and Egypt emerges in methods of bringing nonelites into parliament. In Egypt, nonelite co-optation into parliament was achieved through joining the ruling party. The main avenue was the actual act of affiliating with the ruling party. The few true independents that entered parliament could act as opposition members, but if they attempted to attack the political status quo, their prospects of maintaining a career in politics declined quickly.[82] In Syria, parliamentary inclusion is more straightforward and overt. The B'ath and the other emasculated PNF parties maintain their positions virtually unchallenged through predetermined seat allocation. The system invites competition between independents to become elected without having to join the party.

This difference seems to stem from the NDP not ever truly being an ideological party with internal institutional mechanisms to enforce internal discipline or grant it autonomy from the presidency's reach. By encouraging "independent" candidates who prevail in parliamentary elections to join the ruling party, the party maintained its dominance and refreshed its membership by including new figures and reaffirming the loyalty of existing ones. Also, by encouraging independents to officially join the ruling party, it prevented MPs from joining another party or affiliating themselves with a political trend that opposed the establishment.

Conversely, the Syrian parliament operates within an arena in which the ruling party is more institutionally entrenched. The B'ath Party maintains strict rules and timetables for full membership. Thus, the inclusion of new powerful nonelites could disrupt the balance of the ruling coalition's decentralized networks. To circumnavigate this predicament, Hafiz al-Asad included independent nonelites and elites by designating a space for them as independent MPs. His son continues to build on this political arrangement. As shown through the Akkad example, this has not led to opposition blocs but rather to newer avenues for economic elites to be co-opted—without formal party affiliation—into the political system.

NONELITE CO-OPTATION AND THE SECURITY SERVICES

The security services can also co-opt nonelites in some instances. Yet, the security establishments operate differently and according to the degree to which executive authority is centralized in Egypt and Syria. In Syria, while the security services monitor individuals and opposition movements, they are politicized blocs that compete in co-opting outsiders. The services co-opt people in order to safeguard their autonomy so they can contribute to or obstruct other elite initiatives on the ruling coalition. To do this, individual branches target and groom activists as sources of information.[83] Comparatively, the professionalized but depoliticized security services in Egypt is used to reinforce their apolitical roles in that centralized system. It remains unclear what role the newly reconstituted security services (al-Amn al-Qawmi) will have in post-Mubarak Egypt.

Until the 2011 uprising, the head of Egyptian intelligence, 'Omar Suleiman, had a public profile because of his handling of the Israeli-Palestinian portfolio. There were even, on occasion, campaigns calling for him to run for president before the uprising. This was primarily an attempt by the opposition to force the regime to pull away from the Gamal Mubarak option, which it failed to do until the protests in 2011. President Mubarak attempted to placate the demonstrations by appointing Suleiman vice president during the initial days of the protests. That ultimately proved unsuccessful at disarming the popular mobilization. Suleiman retired from public life when the military forced Mubarak's departure on February 11, 2011. Irrespective of his fate, Suleiman had been a key player in Egyptian foreign relations. While Suleiman was a strong political force, his ability to impact policy was directly linked to his relationship to Mubarak.[84] Even members of the NDP's Policies Secretariat indicated that Suleiman's political role was not institutionally based. In the words of Mohamad Kamal, "Is Omar Suleiman powerful? Yes, he is. Does he have a strong say in politics? Yes, but any talk about Omar Suleiman drafting domestic policy or competing for power is pure exaggeration and fiction."[85] Besides this intelligence head's active role, the other services showed a different modus operandi in Egyptian society before January 2011.

State Security (Amn al-Dawla), which was affiliated to the Ministry of the Interior, played a less participatory role than Suleiman in developing the ruling coalition's policies. For example, the services did not have a popular presence in society. In fact, they were nearly universally despised. Also, the services were not capable of co-opting outsiders that could help them institutionally rally resistance against presidential initiatives. Rather, State Security played a more traditional and predictable role in Mubarak's Egypt. While State Security was informed of on-the-ground opposition figures and groups, such as the Egyptian Movement for Change (Kifaya),[86] dissidents were not called in to discuss their movements unless they triggered instability.

State Security gathered information through informers and interagency research rather than through developing relationships with activists to provide information. As activist 'Aida Saif al-Dawla explains, "State Security know us by face. During demonstrations they address us by our names and say things like 'you should be careful, your health is not strong enough to cope with this excitement' but they do not approach us unless they want to arrest us."[87] Rather, Egypt's security services relied on disruptive organizational tactics as well as intimidation as opposed to reaching out to activists. For example, between November 2004 and February 2005, human rights activist Ahmad Saif al-Islam had two laptop computers stolen from his home in separate break-ins in Cairo's Bolaq al-Dakhror neighborhood. Saif al-Islam blamed the security services and filed charges with his local police station, but it failed to produce an investigative response into the matter. Instead, the police argued that local thieves were responsible. Without leads, they did not attempt to apprehend the culprits.[88] Saif al-Islam's work with the Hisham Mubarak Legal Center as well as his decades-long activism always keeps him on State Security's radar. Yet, rather than detain Saif al-Islam, the security services allowed him to operate before disrupting his efforts. In many ways, this tactic was less provocative legally than it would have been if the security services arrested activists. Instead, disrupting activists' work helped sever their linkages to the wider society. Keeping small groups of activists isolated by not allowing their groups to connect in a horizontal way achieved this desired aim without resorting to overt force or involving the state's legal arm.

The Egyptian security services rarely "invited" activists to extract information from them. Instead, when one was called in for an interview with the services, the approach was to intimidate and to draw a hierarchical distinction between the summoned citizen and those who govern. Indeed, those individuals that State Security did question were treated like subjects, rather than citizens. One published encounter told of a researcher who was approached by State Security after examining electoral violence in the Delta region and was told patronizingly that security services were well prepared for social discontent. As the officer said, "This is not Algeria or Iran you know. Everything is under control. . . . We will never make the same mistakes as them."[89] While this is only one case, Egypt's security services did not seem to rely on invited outside help or on independent outsiders for the analysis of social phenomena.[90] While torture remained the key tool to extract bogus confessions, instilling fear as a deterrent was State Security's purview. It was not trying to co-opt unaffiliated nonelites.

In Egypt, elite and nonelite co-optation was overwhelmingly practiced and located in the ruling party. State Security did not participate in recruiting outsiders as their entryway into politics, nor did they reach outside to co-opt nonelites. They certainly used street informers, who are not officially employed by the services, but that is distinct from adding someone onto a patronage network from which an institution actively participates in forming policy. In Syria, however, different trends are apparent.

The security services in Syria are politically active and do attempt to participate--even if by obstructing the governing process. Being politicized, they are autonomous from the ruling party and the presidency. The services do not seem to strive for dominant control of the ruling coalition, but do constitute an institution capable of influencing or blocking initiatives from other elites.[91] Hence, the security services engage in competitive co-optation in which they try to groom opposition figures as sources of information and clients.

Security agencies in Syria develop dissident and opposition contacts to provide information and assistance. The purpose seems to be to effectively claim someone so that other elites and institutions cannot. This affords the services direct access to a particular dissident while providing access to information on a movement or community. Yet, such information and assistance are not strictly limited to questions about an individual's activities or group. Pro-democracy activist 'Ammar 'Abd al-Hamid agreed that the services develop clients from among the opposition. After a six-month fellowship at Brookings Institute in 2003–4 where he met with the then US vice president and assistant national security advisor, political security asked 'Abd al-Hamid to pay it a visit upon his return to Damascus. 'Abd al-Hamid claims he met with the agency's second-in-command. Initially, he was confused about his meeting with security. In his words, "I thought they were bringing me in to question me or threaten me, but instead they tried to use me as a consultant. They knew I met a Turkish academic at a conference, and they kept asking why all these Turkish delegations were coming to Syria, what they wanted, and why there were increasing ties between Syria and Turkey. I had no idea because I only met the person once."[92] 'Abd al-Hamid said that his dealings with security had been amicable until that point despite the fact that they had taken place against his will. He said that the agency "tried to establish a friendly rapport with me. They [security] invited me to their headquarters and then tell me 'you should come around to the house for tea and meet the family rather than come to the office.' The moment you strike up a friendship with these people, you become part of their network."[93]

'Abd al-Hamid's comments suggest that the agencies try to participate in politics. As they have relatively little control over the party or president's maneuvers with other governments, they seem at a loss for information and analysis. They develop contacts with unaffiliated opposition figures not only to watch them but also to secure information from them. With regard to politics, the services also appear to co-opt outsiders to stay abreast of developments.

Another example of opposition-security services cooperation is similarly revealing. Shortly after the Damascus Spring ended with the arrests of activists such a Riyad Saif and Ma'mon Homsi in June 2002, American political pressure increased on Syria. The most frequent criticisms were Syria's relationships with violent Palestinian groups, its presence in Lebanon, and its chemical-weapons programs. Demands for the US Congress to apply sanctions on Syria grew by the day. With Bashar al-Asad battling elites in the ruling party and security services for policy influence as the looming threat of a war in Iraq increased, the American pressure coalesced to a crisis point. The security services began to reach out to its unaffiliated intellectuals.

The interactions between Sadaq al-'Azm and Bahjat Sulayman expose the politicized role of the Syrian security services.[94] Sadaq al-'Azm is Syria's most prominent and respected intellectual. Educated at Yale and a frequent visiting professor at American and European universities, al-'Azm hails from one of Damascus' most historic families. Al-'Azm teaches political philosophy at the University of Damascus and the American University in Beirut. In the winter of 2002, an employee of then foreign intelligence chief Bahjat Suleiman approached al-'Azm to arrange a meeting. Suleiman's conduit was a former student of Al-'Azm. The professor agreed to meet the intelligence chief more out of curiosity than fear. Al-'Azm continued to meet and discuss politics with Suleiman frequently until the latter retired in spring of 2006. Al-'Azm saw the security director's interest in such issues as "going beyond the theoretical stereotype."[95] According to al-'Azm, Suleiman was eager to learn about the potential fallout from the US's war on Iraq as well as the potential ramifications of sanctions. He felt that Suleiman expressed genuine concern over the American sanctions as he worked to develop ways to communicate with the United States.

Suleiman published an article in the pro-Syrian *al-Safir* newspaper in Lebanon, which represented a culmination of his meetings with al-'Azm. In the article, the first time a Syrian security figure penned an article under his own name, Suleiman devised a strategy to change Syrian-US relations as he detailed the Syrians' understanding of American pressure.[96] While Suleiman's opinions in the article did not wholly reflect al-'Azm's thinking, it is a unique case of a security director publishing an article after consulting an unaffiliated client.

Suleiman's article prompted much debate in Damascus, and several responses were published in Lebanon's *An-Nahar* paper in the form of a debate.[97] Although impressed at Suleiman's unconventional approach, Al-'Azm noted the surreal character of the meetings. As al-'Azm describes, "At no time was there a whiff of 'we [Syrians] all need to cooperate to get out of this mess.' It is always about them [the ruling elites/regime]. You feel like a spectator."[98] The relationship between al-'Azm and Suleiman is one variation of opposition–security service cooperation, which is ongoing in Damascus as the services expand and develop contacts for information. It is within this context that their activist contacts also occasionally assist with problems. This demonstrates another variation of this co-optative relationship. Occasionally, it seems that relations with the security services can be mutually beneficial.

Activist Haytham al-Malih was once called in by political security to intercede and prevent social unrest. Al-Malih is the eighty-year-old head of the Human Rights Association in Syria (HRAS) and a longtime opponent of Syria's B'athist rule.[99] Because of his Islamist sympathies, President Hafiz al-Asad ordered his imprisonment from 1980 to 1987. Al-Malih's human rights organization remains illegal, and he is routinely under a travel ban. His relationship with the security services is well known and his insolence toward the former political security director, Ghazi Kan'an, is well known in Damascus.[100]

After the European Union protested the travel ban against Al-Malih because of Damascus's refusal to allow him to address the German parliament in December 2003, Kan'an called al-Malih in for an "interview." Kan'an informed al-Malih that he was "a good man" and gave him his passport back. Kan'an asked if he would pay him a visit before he left to "chat" about his lectures. Al-Malih declined the offer. Three days later, Kan'an called him. He asked for a meeting again. Al-Malih, now perturbed, said, "I told you I am preparing to travel. I simply don't have the time." Sensing al-Malih's abrupt tone, Kan'an replied, "Well, have a nice trip. I will see you when you get back," and he hung up the phone. Kan'an did see al-Malih when he returned and reinstated his travel ban.[101] Despite these seemingly tense interactions between the activist and the security director, al-Malih tries to use the services as much as they use him for information about his social activism.

In March 2004, violence erupted at a football match between Kurdish and Arab fans in northeastern Syria when the Arab contingent allegedly taunted the Kurds with posters of Saddam Husayn. The riots continued for four days, spreading throughout the northeastern provinces of al-Qamishli and al-Hasakah before heading south to the western Damascene suburb of Dummar. By the time the violence died down, twenty-two Kurds were dead and more than one thousand were detained. Schools were closed, and the security services enforced a curfew. During this unrest, al-Malih visited al-Qamishli and al-Hasakah and met with various directors of different security agencies, governors, and Kurdish tribal leaders. By the time the riots were poised to spread to Damascus, al-Malih was brought in by the security agents to stop the violence. All traffic to Dummar was blocked, so he got out of his car and walked the remaining three kilometers and brokered an agreement to get the rock-throwing to cease before the riot police deployed. Al-Malih met with security and Kurdish leaders and got both sides to withdraw. Al-Malih's involvement was clearly instrumental in preventing "things from getting bloody," as he put it.[102] Do people such as al-Malih, who maintain connections with security directors, realize that they are nominally co-opted when they resolve political stalemates?

Al-Malih did not seem to think in these terms. Activists have agendas, and if cooperating with the security services to achieve their agendas is necessary, it is an arrangement some are willing to accept. Others, such as women's rights' activist M'an 'Abd al-Salam, argue that depicting activists or opposition figures' dealings with the security services as positive is an injustice. 'Abd al-Salam maintains that cooperation is less of a choice because activists are constantly under an indirect repressive threat. 'Abd al-Salam agrees that there is competition between the services to cultivate activist links. He describes it as a competition for influence to see which agency is capable of developing or including various opposition figures. But while some activists cooperate because they see it as an exchange to achieve their aims, the security's relations with activists are the services' way of policing behavior without resorting to violence. As he argued:

> They have no problem keeping friendly lines of communication open or contacting someone when they need to use him for a problem. But this is a one-sided relationship—when a dissident does his job, then it is finished. It is forced co-optation. Activists deal with the security services because they see it benefiting Syria. But once they bring you in, you are marginalized. It does not turn into a dialogue between equals. The services use people and turn it into good propaganda for the regime.[103]

This reading of activists' cooperation with the security services offers a different perspective. It reveals that the security services are proactively involved in establishing links with activists to understand political domestic and foreign developments, monitor behavior, and use activists' grassroots efforts to diffuse social tensions. The security services remain politicized and, therefore, co-opt various activists and opposition figures operating in Syria in order to protect their autonomy. Cooperation between activists and security services takes many forms.

In some cases it is the need for information. Other instances show that activists actually participate with the services to resolve domestic unrest.

The main objective for any security service in an autocratic setting is to ensure that the population is policed, disciplined, controlled, and prevented from igniting instability.[104] Yet, in Syria, the security services go beyond this role by actively gathering information from co-opted activists that they use to ensure their influence is not curtailed in relation to the other institutions such as the presidency or ruling party. While it is difficult to single out a popular domestic case of the security services overtly blocking the state's other institutional actors (as was shown with the B'ath Party), many Syrian analysts claim that it is happening. One case, if ever proven, that undisputedly demonstrates the Syrian security services' politicized role is its possible unilateral decision to assassinate former Lebanese prime minister Rafiq al-Hariri on February 14, 2005.[105]

Syria's security services differ from their Egyptian counterparts because of the politicized role that they play. Without a single arbitrator to balance the ruling coalition, elites in the coalition's institutions have proven capable of asserting themselves against one another as they compete for influence. In this context, the political field gravitated to an oligarchy. Hence, the best representation of the current political system in Syria is a system of rule in which institutional centers of power on the ruling coalition compete.[106]

Egypt's security services, by contrast, are depoliticized because of centralized executive authority. The services' role falls outside the boundaries of where politics is practiced. Instead, they play the more routinized role of keeping opposition activists contained. Before 2011, security services in Egypt did not seek out activists for their opinions about governance, bilateral relations, or trends within groups. Similarly, the security services did not enlist the help of a known opponent to preemptively solve a situation of social unrest. Information was gathered internally and operations were conducted cohesively. So far as friendly relations between activists and security officers, this trend was utterly absent in Egypt. The lines between security services and activists were more transparent and delineated in Egypt.

Conversely, security services are politically active and autonomous agents in Syria's arena. Their politicized institutional base affords them the ability to protect their influence as they compete with one another for activist contacts. As blocs on the decentralized ruling coalition, the security services demonstrate an ability to assert themselves vis-à-vis the other institutions, such as the ruling party and the presidency. This dilutes the chance for a concentrated location for nonelite co-optation. As executive power is decentralized among multiple institutions, nonelite co-optation becomes amorphous and spreads the competition for clients across many state institutions.

Before concluding the section on the security forces' abilities to co-opt opposition in Egypt and Syria, it must be noted that these states are thoroughly repressive. One only needs to recall the case of Khalid Sa'id or Hamza al-Khatib to glimpse the inhumanity of the hammering fists of these apparatuses.[107] Although one can present the Egyptian and Syrian security services' choice of options as becoming increasingly sophisticated as they use coercion in more selective and targeted fashions, repression remains a viable and all-too-frequent fallback strategy for containing and encouraging fragmentation in opposition groups.

The Egyptian state's repression of the Muslim Brothers following the group's 2005 legislative electoral gains exposed the depths and range ruling elites went to halt opposition it could not defeat politically before the 2011 uprising.[108] The type of coercion used against the Muslim Brothers also starkly contrasted that which was employed against the extraparliamentary movement Kifaya. For example, usually the security forces surrounded a demonstration but did not repress it. When the security services did repress protesters, the result—more often than not—was the fragmentation of Kifaya. In this sense, the security services' targeted and selective use of repression served as a disruptive tool to induce fragmentation among a group's ranks. It was a strategy that worked all too well for the likes of promoters of democracy and social justice until the security services were physically beaten by popular protesters during the eighteen-day battle for Egypt. As El Ghobashy showed regarding the Egyptian uprising, "Al-'Adli's police force did not melt away in the face of a popular onslaught. It fought for four straight days on nearly every street corner in every major city, before finally being rendered inefficient by the dynamism and stamina of exceptionally diverse crowds."[109] The point of this discussion is that the role of state repression against opposition was increasingly being used if the manipulation of the legal framework failed to sufficiently contain and control opposition. Hence, while choosing to emphasize the character of nonelite co-optation by the security services, one must not forget that the job description of security services in autocratic settings is always to coercively contain or fragment opposition groups.

CONCLUSION

We learn much by examining the relationship between the degree of the executive's centralized authority and the ability of elites on the ruling coalition to co-opt, mobilize, and neutralize nonelite individuals in Egypt and Syria. Co-optation of nonelite individuals was occurring in Egypt and Syria before the 2011 uprisings, but it transpired differently. The key difference between the two systems was the presence of centralized and decentralized ruling coalitions. Specifically, it displays the variance of how elites on the varying coalitions participated and organized politics. In Egypt's centralized arena, official affiliation was important while in Syria's it was not. This concentrated co-optation primarily in Egypt's now-defunct ruling party while spreading it across the spectrum of politicized institutions in Syria. The political system that has a higher capacity to adapt maintains a centralized arena where executive elites can include new nonelites and exclude older ones easily. Such governments also can adapt to crises more efficiently by creating structures to incorporate groups. The ability to change the ruling coalitions is the key for autocratic adaption. However, it is in highly centralized arenas that formal institutional affiliation seems necessary.

Maintaining a weak ruling party and a professionalized security-military complex reinforces the centralized character of the chief executive's power. It nurtures the inability for elites in these institutions to counter the influence from that office. The president's centralized power bolsters the executive elites' flexibility to constitute or reconstitute the ruling coalition so that no agent supported by a structure can readily challenge its rule without ramifications. The individuals that choose to participate in politics do so without the support of viable institutional support. Thus, a system with one centralized repository of power simplifies the interconnected processes of coalition changes, co-optation, and adaptation.

Similarly, centralized arenas encourage the employment of new strategies such as national councils. These councils provide the executive elites with a means to participate in and muddy the problematic debates. The process of councilization helps increase informality in a way that elites connected to the president can bypass and ignore existing state institutions. It also expands the executive elites' power by marketing the advancement of incremental political reform and change. Rather than produce reform, however, it masks a process whereby it attracts undecided, apolitical, urban professionals into a role of political acquiescence.

Executive-centralized political orders also help to confine politics to a particular locale into which only the ruling party can recruit new nonelites. This facilitates the executive's ability to keep the security apparatus from connecting to social actors or from getting involved in politics. Keeping the security services depoliticized and separate from the political field keeps them loyal to the executive and emphasizes their role as defenders against nascent opposition figures and movements.

Without elites in politicized institutions, the ability to channel, neutralize, and exclude political participants makes adapting the ruling coalition easier. While this can be viewed as a lack of political development, the opposite is also true. Centralized rule and the absence of countervailing repositories of power aid and abet autocracy. While theories deride personalized political orders as traditional, centralization provides a tremendous aptitude for adjusting to changing circumstances. Particularly, when adapting under a guise of a reform project or a popular uprising, a political arena based on centralized executive authority actually facilitates the elites' abilities to manage and control change. This is because it allows executive elites to remake the ruling coalition and change its composition without disrupting the centralized character of politics. One only needs to look at SCAF's ability to insert itself into the centralized position of Hosni Mubarak as well as its ability to remove other coalition members as evidence of the adaptive qualities of centralized authority. This was achieved without the military firing a shot on the population, as it emerged from the crisis with its honorable reputation intact.

Conversely, a political field where an executive exercises decentralized authority produces different outcomes for co-optation and changing the ruling coalition. Under the leadership of a president confronting many challenges while building a state, Hafiz al-Asad nurtured a political order built on active and politicized pillars. Asad deliberalized politics but did not depoliticize the repositories of power. His son and successor now confronts these repositories, which compete against him over the direction of future policy—even if that means confronting obstructionism. While this interaction does not lead to a competition for absolute dominance, it produces institutional gridlock between the presidency, the ruling party, and the security services. The competition between the ruling party, multiple security services, and the presidency actually hinders the ruling elites' ability to include nonelites in an even or concentrated process. Hence, remaking the ruling coalition is made extremely difficult to do.

Competing politicized institutions also make striking a governing consensus difficult. While the situation remains fluid, unless one institution establishes an arbitrating role, it seems unlikely that the Syrian system will be able to adapt to emerging problems or govern in an efficient manner. Because politicized institutions seek to safeguard their influence and interests at the expense of other politicized institutions, governing is more challenging. The effects of decentralized power produce slow and inefficient adaptation. This does not imply that a politicized institutional system is in danger of collapse or failure. Syria's uprising in 2011 seems to bare this out.

When confronted with a disparate and diffuse popular movement for change, Syria's decentralized executive order was not able to alter the ruling coalition in order to placate the crowds. Rather, a decentralized coalition facing the prospect of regime change encouraged its members to band together. This led to the grave mistake of only being able to deploy force to stop the uprising. Whether such a strategy will be successful in the long-term looks uncertain at the moment. However, the lesson is clear. Decentralized ruling coalitions are not easy to change when confronted with an existential challenge because change to the coalition is tantamount to the deconstruction of the regime. Without an option to structurally change the ruling coalition, regime elites can only resort to violence against their own people. This just shows that adaptation is made more difficult because nonelites are not brought in or excluded in a systematically hierarchical fashion.

5 THE 2011 UPRISINGS AND THE FUTURE OF AUTOCRATIC ADAPTATION

AFTER ACHIEVING INDEPENDENCE, both Egypt and Syria experienced military coups where the new elites attacked the economic foundations of the ancien regime. After displacing the traditional landed and commercial upper classes, the new rulers rallied support through populist economic policies that appealed to broad swaths of the public. Specifically, the new ruling class expanded the rights and privileges of rural farmers and urban workers. Initially, infrastructural improvements, industrialization, and redistribution of wealth produced sizable economic growth. During this period, state elites negotiated an agreement with society that purchased political acquiescence in exchange for delivering economic benefits to the population. Yet, state-led growth eventually proved unsustainable. Capital accumulation faltered because of planning flaws, inefficiency from an overcentralization of the economy, and use of the public sector industry for populist payouts. Economic liberalization (*Infitah*) projects reorganized the political and economic spheres during the 1970s, which meant the agreement between the state and society had to be renegotiated.

The shift to economic neoliberalism ushered in an era where the existing authoritarian structures remained, but the ruling elites served different, even contradictory, interests from the populist era. This produced greater economic inequalities and the exclusion of previous members of the ruling coalition. Farmers and laborers were usually the first members excluded as the ruling elites began to more frequently represent the interests of the business class. In fact, the business class became the major base of support for the political system. If populism can be described as authoritarianism of the left, the neoliberal projects redirected the regime's orientation to the right and were conservative. Altering the ruling coalition without extending political rights was a delicate balancing act because it encouraged social instability. Neoliberal authoritarianism also included international alliance shifts and managed political openings. All of these new policies provided occasions for disruptions to the existing economic, social, and political order. Executive elites with more centralized authority over their ruling coalitions were able to more extensively pursue neoliberal economic policies. The chief task for executive elites was to manage the ruling coalitions with minimal repression and to remain in control.

As the leaders jettisoned popular sectors from the ruling coalitions, they used authoritarian controls and structures to fortify the systems. Autocrats in both systems contained opposition, sought to control the implementers of regime policy, and propagated "catch-all" nationalist ideologies to anchor their projects. More important than these policies, the leaders developed and designed institutions that structured the amount of authority the executive could exercise. Egypt and Syria were on similar trajectories in that they were populist before they began experimenting with varying degrees of neoliberal authoritarianism. However, this similarity masked the key difference in the degrees of executive centralization and decentralization.

Do autocratic neoliberal systems eventually evolve into bureaucratic authoritarianism,[1] make the leap to democratization, return to populism, or can they remain suspended in the postpopulist phase? The answer remains unclear. The popular mobilizations and uprisings in the Arab states appear only to further complicate the clarity of the situation. While some of the uprisings may be considered revolutions because they successfully removed longtime rulers, has the social class hierarchy or the way in which executive authority works been altered? Only time will provide the details that enable a fuller explanation. Neoliberal authoritarianism may not indicate where such states are heading, but the model has given rise to inaccurate assumptions that become accepted only because they are repeated.

One convention holds that Syria is essentially Egypt, just not as advanced. The reasoning suggests that it is only a matter of time before Syria adopts neoliberal economic policies similar to Egypt. Yet, reality has not conformed to the assumption. This book's research drew out this notion further by demonstrating that autocratic neoliberal regimes can be utterly different. After all, Egypt and Syria do not resemble one another in degrees of executive centralization, co-optation styles, or adaptive qualities. This is because whether the executive's authority is centralized or decentralized affects the co-optation of elites and nonelites into the ruling coalition. This determines whether a ruling coalition is easy or difficult to alter, informs how many people participate in the political process, and whether co-optation is concentrated or diffuse across the state's organizations. The ability of executive elites to introduce changes to the ruling coalition, and thereby to carry out adaptation, is thus a consequence of whether rulers were able to structure centralized executive authority. Only focusing on the neoliberal authoritarian trajectory as an explanation other than for a general development pattern is misleading because of the variance these systems can have.

The 2011 Arab uprisings reveal the differences in the ability of autocratic regimes to adapt. The list of outcomes is proving unique in all the countries that experienced sustained protests in 2011. From Tunisia to Egypt to Bahrain to Yemen to Libya and Syria, the uprisings are leaving an indelible mark on these systems as they press into the future. Social scientists do not need to predict the exact details of these uncertain futures. But, we do need to provide an explanation for why the outcomes vary in the ways they do.

In the case of Egypt's centralized executive arena, unanticipated but relentless popular protests in Cairo's Tahrir Square as well as other major squares across every major city overwhelmed the Interior Ministry's security apparatus. By physically defeating the security forces in pitched street battles over four days, protesters effectively shut down the country. This caused the military to intervene and deploy personnel and armored vehicles into the streets on January 28. During the tense days after the military deployed and before Mubarak stepped down on February 11, the NDP faded from existence.[2] The party's paralyzed state was complemented by the disappearance of the police and security forces. As the standoff continued, Egyptians and the world watched anxiously whether the military would open fire on the protesters. The military, which has extensive economic interests and has served as a regime's core since 1952, reiterated the promise that it would not. Time eventually ran out for Mubarak and his executive elites as the Supreme Council of the Armed Forces (SCAF) nudged them out the door. Many assumed that with Mubarak exiting, the regime would go with him. However, the military salvaged the regime. It could do this because the executive's centralized lines of authority allowed for the ruling coalition to be altered in the face of a crisis.

SCAF slid into the position of the chief executive and drastically altered the ruling coalition. First, the despised neoliberal economic team that surrounded Gamal Mubarak was dumped. This officially lay to rest the notion that Egypt would experience a hereditary transfer of power from Hosni to Gamal Mubarak. It also sought to sacrifice those that introduced such gross inequalities into the system. Many ministers that represented the neoliberal team fled to places such as Dubai while others, such a Yousif Botros-Ghali, have just disappeared. Those

that stayed in Egypt, such as Ahmad 'Ezz, are currently imprisoned and await-
ing trial. Then, SCAF targeted the equally hated Interior Ministry. Its minister, Habib al-'Adli, was arrested and charged with fraud, money laundering,
and ordering security to fire on protesters. He was convicted on the former
charges and sentenced to twelve years in prison. If he is found guilty on the latter charge, he could face the death penalty. After Mubarak's forced departure,
the dreaded State Security were renamed National Security, but the extent that
the body has been reformed seems superficial to date. In addition to dropping
these constituents from the ruling coalition, even President Mubarak became
a casualty. After Mubarak's faux-resignation speech on February 10, then vice
president Omar Suleiman appeared and read a brief statement saying Mubarak
had stepped down the following day.

In a mere eighteen days, Egypt went from a model of authoritarian durability under Mubarak to experiencing an historic political revolution. Yet, the
revolution remains unfinished as the rigid class structure that underpins Egypt
remains intact.[3] In some cases many of the revolutionaries themselves have un-
consciously participated in the replication of the class hierarchies.[4] The larger political transition has been fraught with complications. It remains unclear where
Egypt will end up. SCAF's lack of transparency, the uneven ability of the political
forces to compete, and the many procedurals debates about a new constitution
and elections are but some of the outstanding issues. None of this bodes well for
the emergence of democracy. Furthermore, given the role of the United States
and the world community in conditioning economic aid to the advancement of
neoliberal economic policies, Egypt's transition may end up producing continued autocracy.[5] Thus, the transition will prove to be a missed opportunity for
Egyptians to realize greater democracy.

While many are relieved to see Mubarak and his cronies gone, the revolutionaries did not aspire to change one autocracy for another. However, centralized executive authority helped structure the initial outcome. Confronted
with various options, SCAF could replace leading executive elites—including
the president—in order to preserve the regime. In fact, the protests provided
SCAF an opportunity to eliminate its coalitional rivals before resituating the
military at the center of the executive during the transition. One can anticipate
the military's influence in Egypt's posttransition period will be considerable—
if not formalized into the political arena.[6] Yet, irrespective of its future, we can
explain why Egypt experienced the type of rapid and swift outcome to its 2011
uprising. SCAF's ability to insert itself and alter the ruling coalition produced

a structural change to the regime rather than regime change. The distinction is important. The centralized authority of the executive structurally favored this outcome and allowed SCAF to opt against using force to maintain the regime. Such an outcome reveals that centralized executive authority lends itself to a high capacity for autocratic adaptation. Contrasted with Syria, the variance between the two cases could not be plainer.

If Egypt stands as an exemplar for highly centralized executive authority facilitating adaptable autocracy, Syria exists at the other end of the spectrum. After initially claiming that the Arab uprisings' diffusive effects would not penetrate his country, Bashar al-Asad watched as the southern part of the country rebelled against forty-eight years of B'athist rule. While Dera'a was the most restive in the beginning, protests also emerged in Latakiya, Homs, and on the outskirts of Damascus in Domma. After initially attempting to placate the protesters with new reforms, including repealing martial law, Syria's decentralized ruling coalition had quickly reached an impasse. Unfortunately, it carried limited options. Unable to resolve the dispute with their society peacefully or politically, the elites on the ruling coalition opted to use violence to quell the protests. The fact that no executive arbitrator has the authority or capital to alter the ruling coalition's membership to deflate the protesters' frustration forced the elites to band together in a disciplined and unified way. The members of the decentralized ruling coalition perceived the challenge from society as existential. Either the coalition remained intact or the regime would collapse. There was no soft out as in the case of Egypt. Unwilling and unable to change the ruling coalition, state-society relations were reduced to a zero-sum game as the state tried to stop the protests.

Initially, the sights of tanks advancing on the towns as snipers shot from rooftops suggested that the state would be able to dictate an end to the standoff. The regime also propagated fears of sectarianism to keep its urban bases in Damascus and Aleppo loyal. For the most part, they did. Damascus and Aleppo have not yet joined the revolt in a large or sustained way. Similarly, despite some defections in the military, the ruling coalition held together in a disciplined way. The ruling coalition, however, was standing with the executive rather than behind it. If there was evidence to suggest that oligarchic rule prevails in Syria, the way in which the ruling coalition unified during the 2011 uprising seems to confirm it.

Employing state violence is a risky strategy and not a preferable or first recourse. Yet, the ruling coalition's only real options were piecemeal gestures for reform or violence in the absence of being able to alter the ruling coalition. Because the executive participates in a decentralized manner on the coalition, there was no option to change it without inviting the deconstruction of the state. The use of violence has not produced the anticipated ends of the elites. Rather, it has led to a stalemate, as the state obviously does not have the repressive capacity to pacify the entire country at once. The military and security services seem to rush around the country trying to put out the most urgent threats. Secondly, the state's use of force is providing protesters with a way to see past the very scare tactics of sectarianism that the regime is spreading. This ongoing uprising is producing the emergence of two Syrias. In the docile Syria, people pine for the quietness and worry about the outbreak of an Iraq-style sectarian civil war while in restive Syria the protesters become more resolute and capable of overcoming obstacles for collective action, which includes the sectarian dimension. While the elites on the ruling coalition use of sectarianism to induce obedience has worked in some respects, their use of violence redraws the line that distinguishes the state from society and renders sectarianism a secondary concern.

It is hard to picture a scenario where this works out well for the Asad family, the wider ruling coalition, or the Syrian state. While the regime does not maintain the repressive capacity to overwhelm the protest movement, the state does not appear on the brink of collapse. Additionally, given the dynamics of decentralized executive authority, it appears unlikely that the ruling coalition can be mended during this crisis. It does, however, remain to be seen that the coalition can survive if normalcy returns to Syria. Hence, while the principal members of the ruling coalition may survive the uprising, it is less clear if they will be able to remain in power over the longer-term. The country is in for more trying times in the face of diplomatic isolation, condemnation by allies of the state's use of violence, and the flow of refugees into Turkey. Yet, the major point of this discussion is that the reason Syria took this turn as opposed to an Egyptian or Tunisian-like path has to do with the character of executive authority. Because the executive exercises decentralized authority, and therefore shares power with the elites from key institutions on the ruling coalition, it left the Syrian elites in a place with no real good options. Unable to restructure the coalition for fear of deconstructing the state, violence and further fragmentation will likely define Syria's future. The lack of ability to adapt to political crises is thus directly conditioned by the decentralized character of executive authority.

This book began by discussing the periodic and public confrontations between the United States and Arab governments over reform and democratization. The conclusion shows that US-Arab reform debate is as misguided as the

"Syria is Egypt" convention. This is because the American discourse wrongly frames regional governance patterns by equating most Arab systems as similarly authoritarian. While the "Syria is Egypt" convention proves erroneous, American calls for general "reform" have been badly conceived. The use of democratization as an all-purpose solution has appeared in various guises such as projects to aid civil society and USAID missions for the past four decades.[7] George W. Bush's administration (r. 2001–9) simply amplified the volume on the refrain of an already broken record. The distance between US rhetoric and on-the-ground Arab governmental action has rarely been further apart. To draw less attention to this discrepancy, the current US administration appears to want to walk back from such an adversarial approach.[8] Barack Obama went so far as to imply that he does not view Arab leaders through the democratization lens. When asked if he thought whether Mubarak was an authoritarian leader in 2009, he stated, "No, I tend not to use labels for folks."[9] Yet, even a cursory examination of the documents exposed by WikiLeaks shows the extent that democratization dominates the analysis at the State Department.[10] While the Arab uprisings provided the United States an opportunity to scrap sixty years of the failed policy of supporting regional autocracy, the case-by-case approach will eventually show that this policy survived the uprisings. Despite its shifting rhetoric, the US administration is pathologically against the empowerment of Arab populations given its actions thus far.[11]

The American government's fundamental understanding of Arab states is that current actions or faulty elections are what is blocking some inevitable transition to democracy. Rather, it is the structure of these political systems, which conditions their ability to change. Without crediting how much authority the executive commands over the ruling coalition, it is unlikely productive policy prescriptions will result. By highlighting the differences between these political systems, this comparison sheds light on the limitations of previous academic and policy research. It also invites people to reconsider their analytic frames. Egypt and Syria are in the same region and share a political history and experiences, but none of these factors suggest that one state reflects the other—time lag or not.

EGYPT AND SYRIA: JUST DIFFERENT

Neither Egypt nor Syria is democratizing, and neither is likely do so in the wake of the 2011 Arab uprisings. It is not impossible, but it is unlikely. This book's findings are not the first to advance the claim that democracy in the Arab world is not likely to emerge in the near term. For example, Kienle showed how economic liberalization usually accompanies a contracting political sphere.[12] Ehteshami and Murphy documented the reversals experienced by Arab populations in relation to democratization paradigms.[13] Others such as Heydemann[14] and Bank[15] have elucidated the various strategies and tactics that maintain authoritarian rule.

When discussing authoritarian durability, the debate takes place against a backdrop of reform. I would argue that this "reform" process is better understood in terms of thinking about autocratic adaptation. Daniel Brumberg noted long ago that leaders never willingly undertake policies that could eventually lead to their losing power.[16] Unlike he suggests though, this has less to do with free will and more to do with the constraints imposed by whether ruling coalitions are centralized or decentralized. All political elites have an interest in adapting political systems, but structures and histories, rather than unencumbered rational actors, condition what is possible. In this vein, the vast differences between Egypt and Syria are in how the executive exercises authority, how this affects co-optation, and whether this enhances or hinders the ability of executive elites to alter the ruling coalition. This explains which autocratic regimes can change to overcome political challenges and which ones cannot.

In this respect, the ruling coalitions of the two states were never similar in terms of introducing changes or adaptation. Varying degrees of social homogeneity and heterogeneity, struggles over national and regional identity, and differing levels of industrialization are only some of the historical legacies that Egyptian and Syrian leaders faced after emerging from colonization. Despite these differences, social scientists have largely compared Egypt and Syria with an eye toward the similar. There is some basis for this given the temporary convergences between the two postcolonial states. For example, the states unified and seemingly disregarded these differences in 1958. But the union quickly failed. Emerging from the UAR in 1961, both states advanced populist regimes and rhetorically championed Arab nationalism in their foreign policies. After the B'ath Party came to power in 1963, Syria's leaders pursued a populist regime, as Nasser intensified populism by increasing the state's command of the economy in Egypt. Between 1963–70, both states also exposed Arab nationalism, had military officers in leadership positions, and were subjected to a major military defeat in 1967. Egypt and Syria's paths seemingly continued to resemble one another by 1970. Six weeks before Hafiz al-Asad came to power in Syria, Anwar Sadat took over the presidential reins in Egypt.

Initially, Sadat and Asad were weak presidents but for different reasons. Sadat struggled vis-à-vis the entrenched Nasserist elites, who were housed in politicized institutions. His lack of executive authority, in turn, constrained his ability to alter the ruling coalition. Asad, for his part, had the military's support, but he lacked political pillars for which the state could ward off another coup. Both presidents also wanted to lead their countries away from state-led development. Another commonality is that Israel occupied land belonging to both countries, which led Sadat and Asad to launch a joint war to reclaim their territory in October 1973. The similarities did not stop there. Sadat inherited a massive single party that was organized, politicized, and autonomous of the new president while Asad took over an ideological, but smaller, ruling party in an unconsolidated state. This left both leaders to inherit regimes in which neither president had full control. Sadat and Asad embarked on limited economic liberalization programs, purged political opponents, and created new institutions and constitutions to consolidate their rule. Despite the difference in party size, both systems appeared to be similarly oriented in terms of governance styles and objectives. And yet, after the 1973 October War, the countries appear to drastically split off into different directions.

Sadat's deception toward Syria during the 1973 War revealed the first foreign policy signs that Egypt was abandoning Arab nationalism in favor of an "Egypt First" approach. Following the hostilities, Sadat used his newly acquired legitimacy windfall to negotiate with the Israelis and realign as a US client state. This decision unleashed an economic liberalizing project, which radically reordered the Egyptian economy. Private investment and loans approved by its superpower patron further encouraged Egypt's redirection. Economic changes produced significant changes in Egypt's institutions as the composition of the ASU changed toward a more business-friendly class while the military became more dependent on the executive through various subsidies and economic opportunities for military officers. It was not, however, solely a product of the economy.

Sadat also began a highly political process that sought to accumulate as much authority for the executive as possible. He decapitated the ASU. Arrests as well as the frequent ministerial and party appointments produced personally loyal public servants as he dismembered the single party in favor of a managed multiparty area in 1976. The NDP, which eventually replaced the ASU, never functionally developed into a politicized structure. Hence, Sadat destroyed the system's old power relationships in favor of a centralized executive arena that deemphasized the ruling party's role to potentially contribute. Similarly, Sadat depoliticized the security services and military by hollowing them out. He reconfigured the chain of command to lead to and from his office. While this professionalized the armed services, it also contributed to the rise of an arena where the executive exercised centralized authority over the ruling coalition. It was this arena that Hosni Mubarak inherited in 1981 and maintained until popular forces overwhelmed the coercive apparatus in 2011.

In Syria, the aftermath of the 1973 October War proved less amenable to accelerating the postpopulist experiment. Not only could Asad not choose to align with the United States, but he also could not sell the idea of peace with Israel to the elites running and defending Syria's underdeveloped state because of the B'athist pan-Arab ideology. Because the ruling coalition was decentralized, he could not betray it without threatening the state's collapse. Exasperating these constraints, Syria became embroiled in the Lebanese civil war where it was forced to defend itself from Israeli military threats, a near-civil war against the Muslim Brothers, and internal splits within the Asad family as a "brother-against-brother" competition for the presidency surfaced. Given the differences with Egypt's context, Asad had different options at his disposal. Without an ability to centralize executive authority over the ruling coalition, he chose an option that favored the state's survival. Consequently, he strengthened the presidency, the B'ath Party, military, and security services to anchor the Syrian political system and protect the state. In doing so, Asad created a decentralized ruling coalition where elites from these institutions maintained some autonomy. This made the chief executive participate and compete with other power centers on the ruling coalition. Besides not easily allowing the executive to alter the ruling coalition, it also made autocratic adaptation more difficult.

Although they were inactive in the 1980s and early 1990s, elites in the ruling coalition's institutional power centers reasserted themselves as Asad's death neared in June 2000. This left executive authority in Egypt and Syria to look utterly different in the lead up to the 2011 Arab uprising. Namely, the presidency, the ruling party, and the military/security services compete for influence on Syria's ruling coalition while the elites that comprise the executive in Egypt have a greater ability to dominate the state's ruling coalition. Syria was more oligarchic while Egypt was more of a hierarchically autocratic system. Yet, the divergence in Egypt and Syria's political establishments can be traced to the 1970s. How Sadat and Asad built their political arenas at that time, as well as the domestic and international constraints that cemented these constructions, produced centralized executive authority over the ruling coalition in one case but not in the other.

EXECUTIVE AUTHORITY AND ELITE CO-OPTATION

After establishing varying degrees of executive authority in Egypt and Syria, it is possible to examine its effects on the ability to co-opt new members. The ability to co-opt elites and nonelites conditions whether autocratic adaptation is an efficient or arduous process. Given that Egypt and Syria maintain diverging dynamics for how executive authority structures each state's ruling coalition, it is not surprising that their adaptive qualities also differ. Elite co-optation puts this differing capacity for autocratic adaptation on display.

Egypt's ruling coalition is easier to adapt than Syria's because the executive exercises centralized authority. This means that new elites can be introduced and excluded more rapidly than in Syria. Because Egypt's executive controls the state's organizations, it leaves individuals brandishing extensive patronage networks to continuously compete with other elites to maintain their positions. Rather than a person's official positions in a structure such as a party or the security services, connections to the chief executive determine an elite's status. This leaves the system personalized. As a consequence, a long tenure in the ruling elite is by no means sufficient insulation against exclusion. This was evident in the case of 'Amr Mosa, whose ten years as foreign minister was abruptly terminated. In this situation, when he was relieved of his duties, he could not draw on institutional support and his patronage networks all but disappeared overnight.

In other instances, Yusif Wali, Safwat al-Sharif, and Kamal al-Shazli were all members of the highest echelons of Egyptian elite politics for more than twenty years. Yet, in the decade leading up to the 2011 popular uprising, attacks on their patronage networks considerably weakened them. Just as these executive elites could quickly be excluded from a ruling coalition, they could also be rapidly elevated into the ruling coalition. Gamal Mubarak and NDP's Policies Secretariat served as an example of this—the rise of the former president's son and his group of technocrats showed how easily individuals could parachute into the top elite strata. High levels of depoliticized institutions, which could not counterbalance the president's centralized control over the ruling coalition, made the Egyptian elite arena easy to change before the uprising. Centralized executive authority also helps explain why SCAF could change Egypt's ruling coalition during the uprising in order to preserve the regime without resorting to state violence against society.

An analysis of Syria's elite arena produces different findings. While Bashar al-Asad maintains the constitution's most powerful office in the country, institutions on the decentralized ruling coalition such as the ruling party and the security services are capable of obstructing his objectives. These bodies are active in the process of co-opting elites and nonelites (unlike Egypt). This also makes it difficult for Bashar al-Asad to exclude elites that oppose him. Syria's UN vote on Resolution 1483 was a manifestation of this—Asad ordered that Syria accept the resolution, and his party's Regional Command respected his wishes by voting overwhelmingly to do so. Yet, high-ranking party members such as Farok al-Shara' and 'Abd al-Halim Khaddam intervened against the president. The Foreign Ministry, where al-Shara' was based at the time, even ordered Syria's UN representative to vote no. After some confusion and embarrassment for Syria in the UN, Faysil Makdad registered a noticeably late "Yes" vote on the resolution. The aftermath produced no retribution against Khaddam or al-Shara' even though they disobeyed a direct presidential order. In this example, top elites opposed the president but were not removed as a consequence. This is because elites in state institutions are protected structurally rather than operating as individuals in politics.

The decentralized character of the executive authority and the multiplicity of organizational stakeholders discourage the executive's tampering with the ruling coalition. Hence, it is difficult to bring a group of new elites into the party or to alter its composition because this would threaten the party's role in the oligarchy. For the same reason, it is difficult to achieve agreement between elites from these politicized institutions on day-to-day policies. This factor slows the regime's ability to adapt. In fact, it makes non-regime-threatening decisions extremely difficult to resolve because of the number of participants protecting their turf. This demonstrates that Syria's ruling coalition is more based in organizational considerations and more oligarchic in character. It also makes co-optation a diffuse process as the elites in politicized institutions compete for new members and clients.

Yet, there is a flipside to the inefficiency of Syria's day-to-day autocratic adaptation. When confronted with a regime-threatening crisis, such as a leadership succession or a popular uprising, the inability of the elites to be able to alter the ruling coalition tends to produce uniformity. While in the case of Bashar al-Asad's succession, the decentralized ruling coalition seamlessly implemented the regime consensus, the coalition coalesced around the decision to use gratuitous state violence against Syrians citizens in another instance, as seen during the 2011 uprising. Because the chief executive exercises decentralized authority within the political arena, the elites in Syria's ruling coalition cannot alter its composition without threatening the collapse of the state. Without options to

structurally change the ruling coalition, they forestall regime change with violence. It is a proposition that reveals the state's weakness and also invites the
end of the regime. Yet, it seems to remain a more preferable option for Syrian
elites than altering the ruling coalition. It remains to be seen if such a strategy
will work and if Bashar al-Asad can remain in power after the rebellion ends.

EXECUTIVE AUTHORITY AND NONELITE CO-OPTATION

As elite co-optation varies between Egypt and Syria, so does the inclusion of
nonelites. Nonelite co-optation occurs in both Egypt and Syria, but differently.
The key distinguishing factor between the two systems is the executive's centralized or decentralized authority, which contributes to how politics is organized. Official affiliation—as seen in the example of the NDP's Higher Policies
Council—was important in Egypt before the uprising but not present in Syria.
Centralized authority granted executive elites the ability to easily create new
structures to incorporate groups by affiliating newly co-opted individuals to
the ruling party, which was the preferred location for inclusion before the 2011
uprising. Formal affiliation also determined who was and was not included
and could participate within the system. A party, such as the NDP, which was
loosely organized around individuals with patronage networks proved unable
to resist the executive's authority. Those who chose to participate in politics
prior to the uprising did so without institutional support or protection. That
could only emanate from President Mubarak or the executive elites. The party's
flexible character helped maintain the dominance of the executive's centralized
authority in such a way that no state organization could readily challenge the
office in any sustained way. In the end, it took popular mobilization to overrun
the political apparatus.

Similarly, before the uprising, Egypt's area encouraged the development of
new bodies to formalize the informality such as national councils. These councils provided such regimes with additional tools to engage in problematic issues.
In doing so, it permitted the state to quasi-nationalize debates that civil society
groups may have previously monopolized. This process of councilization—as
seen in the National Council for Human Rights—helped expand regime power
by marketing the advance of incremental political reform and change. Rather
than existing as true reform, however, it masked a mechanism of attracting the
participation and acquiescence of undecided, apolitical, urban professionals.

Executive elites that exercise centralized authority also concentrate co-
optation in that only the ruling party can recruit new nonelites. This excludes

the security services, the military, or civil society from developing a politicized character that allows opposition to the executive to develop. It reinforces and contributes to the continuation of centralized authority. It also allows the executive to prevent the security apparatus from connecting to social actors or getting involved in politics. Keeping the security services depoliticized and separate from the political field keeps them loyal to an executive as well as maintains them as the defenders of the regime against emerging opposition figures and movements outside the system.

The absence of politicized institutions contributes to autocratic adaptation by helping to channel and exclude participants. While this indicates a lack of political development, it also enhances a system's ability to adapt to challenges and crises. While some deride personalized political orders as traditional, centralized executive orders display tremendous resilience and efficiency at adapting to changing circumstances. Though such regimes adapt under the guise of a reform project, a ruling coalition in which politics remains based on individual patronage networks actually facilitates the ability to manage and control change. These characteristics also allow an authoritarian system to remake itself and change its composition without altering the underlying characteristics of authority. While it remains to be seen what Egypt's transition will produce, SCAF has undeniably inserted itself into the centralized position as the executive. After it did this, SCAF was able to drop key constituents from the ruling coalition as well as a president that has served longer than any Egyptian leader since the reign of Mohamad 'Ali (1805–48). By changing the ruling coalition, SCAF preserved the regime and, perhaps, increased its role in the system. Irrespective of the outcomes of Egypt's half-revolution, half-military intervention, the military is poised to influence politics for many years to come. It remains to be seen if the transfer the centralized authority to the next ruling executive and his elites is an enduring characteristic of the Egyptian system.

Conversely, decentralized executive authority produces a different outcome. Syria's decentralized ruling coalition encourages competition between elites from the state's rivaling pillars. Since Bashar al-Asad came to power, he has competed with other elites from state organizations. While failing to become the arbitrator over the ruling coalition, his struggles have produced governing gridlock among the presidency, the ruling party, and the security services. Because of the competition among Syria's institutions, autocratic adaptation has become an inefficient process. In Syria, competition among the ruling B'ath Party, redundant security services, and the presidency actually hinders the system's ability to evenly include nonelites in the concentrated process. In this system, nonelite and group co-optation occurs across the organizational field. Competing politicized institutions also make consensus politics problematic while increasing the likelihood of obstructionism.

While the situation remained fluid before the uprising began in March 2011, the Syrian system has proven it lacks the ability to adapt to existential problems in an efficient manner. Given that no single player on the ruling coalition possesses the authority to remake and alter it, the regime chose to collectively band together against society. Because there was not a strong executive to alter the coalition, the ruling coalition was reduced to deploying violence to hold the regime in place. It remains unclear what the long-term future for the Syrian state is in its current form. This does not imply that the system is in danger of collapse or failure, but it is hard to see how Bashar al-Asad and leading elites can remain in place long after the violence ends. While the future is unclear, the ongoing uprising plainly reveals the Syrian state's inability to remake the ruling coalition. Arenas where the executive exercises decentralized authority face more difficulties when adapting because of the unregulated way that participants contribute to politics.

A CHANGEABLE DESTINY

Since the 1970s, centralized executive authority has shaped Egypt's political arena while a decentralized ruling coalition characterized Syrian politics. Nevertheless, it would be wrong to assume that Egypt and Syria are forever locked in their current trajectories. There is, of course, the potential for the levels of executive authority to change. This would likely depend on one group of elites being able to impose their will over other elites to reconfigure the political order. Given how much change has been unleashed because of the Arab uprisings, politics seems to have a new lease on life in some Arab states. Hope and frustration now permeate the air and the mobilization is producing uncontrollable outcomes for the incumbent regimes. Indeed, popular protests forced SCAF to remove Mubarak and restructure Egypt's ruling coalition. To those who study or who have ever lived in Egypt, this was unimaginable given the thoroughly repressive impulse of the security services until early January 2011.

However, the most striking feature of the post-Mubarak landscape is the ability of SCAF to govern without many direct challenges to its authority. Many people object to SCAF's handling of the transition. They criticize the ongoing military trials, allegations of torture, the incitement of sectarian strife, and the general lack of transparency. But still, most opinion polls continue to show SCAF generals favorable among the population. Indeed, some even seem to think a general as president may be an acceptable outcome. Despite the democratic exuberance of the media's coverage, the days of centralized executive authority appear alive in Cairo. That being said, the protest movement has done an admirable job at maintaining the initiative and forcing concessions from SCAF. While it remains to be seen if SCAF will follow through on their promises, it suggests that popular mobilization will continue to be a force in the future. What, then, does the future hold for centralized executive authority? After parliamentary and presidential elections are held and the military steps back behind the curtain of power, will we see a more decentralized ruling coalition emerge? Or can we anticipate that Egypt's next president will have Mubarak-like authority at his disposal? One suspects that the former is more likely, but a lot will depend on the protesters' resilience and ability to continue to extract concessions and empower the economically impoverished classes, who also raged against Mubarak in late January 2011.

If Egypt is to experience a true revolution, institutions need to be built, power and wealth redistributed, and the rigid social hierarchy needs to be dismantled. If these prerequisites are not fulfilled, destiny will continue to favor some type of centralized or decentralized elite coalition. This would not be democracy. Rather, politics would continue to be an elite-only occupation where the sharp divide between those who govern and those who are governed continue to be apparent. Thus, it will likely produce more continuity than change. While the situation would unlikely resemble Mubarak's Egypt, it would remain fundamentally autocratic. Only time, agency, and the unpredictable interactions of humans with their structural legacies will reveal the dynamic.

Syria's ruling coalition appears likely to remain decentralized in the near-term. But, a decentralized ruling coalition is not destiny. Indeed, just as Sadat used shrewd political timing and opportunities to implement changes to the system he inherited, Bashar al-Asad could pursue a similar path by eliminating elites entrenched in state institutions before gutting the organizations into depoliticized bodies. In fact, before the March 2011 uprising began, developments indicated that this strategy was underway. Given the maneuvers at and after the tenth B'ath Party congress in June 2005, it was arguable that Asad consolidated his presidency at the expense of the oligarchic elites that obstructed his leadership during his first five years.[17] Despite this, Asad never depoliticized the state's pillars. If he ever does depoliticize the coalition's organizations, he may choose to destroy existing pillars and replace them with ones subservient to the executive. Yet, even if Asad engineers such a change, he will still need some type of institutions on which to extend and channel the executive's authority.

This may be all for not because of the 2011 uprising. While Bashar al-Asad seemed to recently be enjoying more authority compared to his earlier years as president, the uprising has swung the pendulum back in favor of decentralization. As the crisis deepened over the months that the Syrian regime was at war against demonstrators in a number of restive areas around the country, the Syrian executive seemed to blend with the party, security services, and the military rather than stand out above them. At times, Bashar al-Asad did not even appear to be in control of the state.[18] Seeing that Bashar al-Asad obviously could not change the ruling coalition, the regime appears to have decided to collectively fight its way out.[19] This does not indicate Bashar al-Asad's authority has increased vis-à-vis the other elites in the decentralized ruling coalition. Rather, it underscores how much he continues to need the coalition for the state to function. Thus, while Asad may have accumulated some political capital to eventually depoliticize the ruling coalition over the past few years, the protracted character of Syria's uprising has reversed that progress.

The point of this discussion is not to predict the outcome of power struggles in Syria. Rather it is to emphasize that Syria's decentralized executive authority, which was established and constructed during the 1970s and 1980s, is not a structural trap. The Syrian state is not condemned to one path. Human agency, international and regional events, and the ability to alter and redesign power relationships in the future will determine the types of changes Syria witnesses. Yet, alterations to the political system will, undoubtedly, produce changes in the state's ability to co-opt and shed coalition members, which will affect autocratic adaptation. With that being said, executive elites are more efficient when they possess centralized authority over the ruling coalition. In addition to providing clear lines of who can and cannot participate, it facilitates adapting the system to challenges and crises that arise during the course of governing. As is apparent in contemporary Syria, the state still does not maintain an ability to adapt to an existential threat without resorting to violence.

THEORETICAL LESSONS

According to democratization theory, disciplined and routinized institutions that follow impersonal lines of authority depersonalize politics. Authority begins to flow to and from an office rather than a person. As a society becomes more complex in its composition and interests, institutions channel and organize politics and help the system respond to crises. Democracies, therefore, are models for adaptation. Democracies, however, do not hold the monopoly on adaptation. In authoritarian political systems, whether the executive exercises centralized control over the organizations and the elites is crucial for adaptation. As decentralized executive authority in Syria shows, politicized institutions force their elites to engage one another, which often produces governing gridlock and obstructionism. This makes co-opting elites and nonelites a diffuse process as the organizations' elites compete for clients. It also complicates autocratic adaptation. Executives with decentralized authority lead political orders that inhibit, rather than facilitate, adaptation.

Decentralized executive elites co-opt elites and nonelites, but differently than systems with centralized executive elites. In the case of Mubarak's Egypt, the state did not lack institutions. Egypt had every conceivable governing platform, but those organizations lacked autonomy and the ability to resist executive authority. In the absence of having institutions that can protect their elites, the political system was made up of a multiparty system dominated by the executive's office. With the security services also out of politics, executive elites were in a position to freely manipulate, shuffle, and rotate elites and nonelites. Politics consisted of individuals whose institutions are unable to rally on their behalf in the face of executive appointments, demotions, or policy changes. Because politics remained rooted in personalities, the ruling coalition was more easily adaptable. It gave executive elites centralized authority and provided them the ability to confront and overcome challenges by adapting without forcing the regime to collapse. In this respect, Egypt's political system was more adaptable than Syria's. If one compares the outcome of the 2011 uprisings in Egypt and Syria, this becomes blatantly true. While in the short-term neither system is on a path toward democratic reform, how much authority the executive can exercise will continue to influence the efficiency of an autocratic state.

Neo-patrimonial autocracy is categorized as a development of personalized or traditional politics. In the literature (particularly on the Arab world), the theory is primarily viewed as a social phenomenon that is inherited from the colonial period, which, in turn, affects contemporary economics and politics. Yet, the existing literature does not substantially account for how differences in neo-patrimonial regimes manifest themselves in political institutions. The institutions and the elites they house are assumed to be weak. Such theories fail to point to the amount of variance in regimes that are blending concepts of traditional and legal-rational types of governance. Some autocratic regimes possess more traditional than legal-rational characters while others maintain qualities that are more legal-rational than traditional. Yet, the central fact is that both types are currently classified as neo-patrimonial regimes. In this book, I have examined how neo-patrimonialism affects institutions depending on the degree of centralized executive authority. This is not an attempt to discredit the existing literature but rather to build on it by using it differently than currently exists.

The work of many scholars, who cogently argue that political science should study authoritarianism rather than transitology, remains relevant. As Thomas Carothers argued a decade ago, the transition and democratization literature was important for understanding the initial upheavals in the political and economic areas of the post-Cold War period, but "it is increasingly clear that reality is no longer conforming to the model."[20] Those theories have exhausted their course for understanding politics in the age of American empire. Indeed, rushing to refocus on democratization will likely cloud, rather than illuminate, our understanding of the changing character of authoritarianism in the Middle East. Instead of rushing behind the excitement of a potential revolution, our efforts will likely be better spent examining how the authoritarians reconstitute themselves.[21]

Syria and Egypt are both states with a history of autocratic rule despite being at different stages along the postpopulist trajectory. Even though the similarities dominate as a focal point of inquiry, too many differences persist in terms of how these systems adapt and remain viable. Indeed, substantial differences characterize each state's arrangements of authority, style of co-opting elites and nonelites, and adaptive qualities. These differences should be emphasized when comparing Arab political systems. The field should do away with general democratization and modernization theoretical frameworks once and for all and begin to creatively explore the theoretical differences between these systems. By describing these systems as possessing centralized and decentralized executive authority, I highlighted differences in Egypt and Syria's institutional types, abilities to co-opt, and capacity for system adaptation. The fact that one seems more efficient than the other is a valuable contribution.

As noted in the book's opening pages, there is a quiet but continuing struggle between Western and Arab governments. Both sides argue that democracy will result. Nevertheless, this is unlikely. The question of how to interpret such a struggle and its potential outcomes was this inquiry's inspiration. The essential problem that became apparent was that seemingly similar authoritarian

regimes have different adaptive qualities. This variance in adaptation is attributable to the differences of centralized and decentralized executive authority.
Hence, it is erroneous to view autocratic rule in the Arab world as monolithic
or overly similar. Instead of relying on coercion as the central means to maintain order, the constant management and change in the ruling coalition tells us
more about how autocrats adapt.

It is within this context that an autocratic system adapts and overcomes
challenges that could threaten its durability. Any political system with established patterns of behavior is more likely to adjust and adapt its arena rather
than drastically alter the foundations of governance. Some elites in Arab states
are structurally advantaged to do it better than others, hence, the difference between Egypt's SCAF altering the ruling coalition and shunning violence while
Syria's ruling coalition hung together and deployed violence to preserve the regime. Without a doubt, political systems that fail to adapt court instability, but
changing the fundamental structures of power is not always an option. For the
time being, executive elites and ruling coalitions in Arab states have chosen to
attempt to autocratically adapt rather than reform their relationships with their
polities. Rather than understanding Arab political systems on the verge of collapse or being weak, we should recognize that the different regimes can sustain
themselves by making adjustments to the regime's ruling coalition. It is within
this framework that I have attempted to show that autocratic adaptation is inextricably linked to the centralized authority that an executive exercises over
elites housed in state organizations.

Authoritarianism, and all its individual variations, remains a central topic
to study. Through examining the process of renewal, inclusion, and maintenance of elites and nonelites vis-à-vis institutional considerations and executive authority, co-optation explains why such systems can adapt. It also explains
why this form of governance continues to be relevant even in the age of popular
mobilizations, uprisings, and potential revolutions. Rather than viewing such
a process as reform, autocratic adaptation will remain a better framework for
studying governance in the Arab world during the twenty-first century.

REFERENCE MATTER

NOTES

Introduction

1. Di Lampedusa, 21.
2. Heydemann, "Tunisia."
3. Heydemann, "Upgrading."
4. Brinks and Coppedge, 463–89.
5. El-Ghobashy, "Praxis."
6. The term "revolution" has become highly contentious. This is, perhaps, a function of the abuse of the term "thawra" in the Arab experience as well as by academics and the media to describe any and all movements that dislodge an incumbent leader as "revolutions." The various "colored revolutions" in the post-Soviet states between 2000–2005 are cases in point. On the one hand, bestowing the term "revolution" on these events grants the utmost amount of credit and legitimacy to the courageous populations that challenged and overwhelmed long-serving autocrats, who are often backed by the world's lone superpower. This is no small feat and recognizes their agency. Yet, it is worth noting that elites positioned in state institutions pushed out the dictators, when they realized their options were deteriorating. In the cases of Tunisia and Egypt, this led to military interventions. Yet, calling these interventions "coup d'etats" is equally misleading. Until more extensive social changes occur, it seems safe to refer to the protests as "uprisings."
7. Gause, "Middle East Academic Community."
8. Cooley and Nexon.
9. Ambrust.
10. Obaid.
11. Al-Qassemi.
12. Khalidi.
13. Stacher, "Egypt Without Mubarak."
14. Activists reference this as the advance of the "counterrevolution."
15. To be fully accurate, the peacefulness of these transitions is debatable. The UN claimed 219 people died during Tunisia's uprising. The numbers are higher in Egypt. Immediately after Mubarak resigned the government claimed 365 had died. By April

2011, the Egyptian government said increased the number to 846 with more than 5,000 injured. While the demonstrators were largely peaceful, state agents did attempt to forcibly remove the protesters, who defended their space. When confronted with clashes, the internal security services did not just melt away. They were physically defeated.

16. L. Anderson, 2–3.

17. Haddad.

18. Springborg, *Mubarak's Egypt*; Cook, *Ruling But not Governing*.

19. "Popular Protest in North Africa," 16.

20. Baker, 55–56.

21. Ouda, al-Borai, and Abu Saada, 24.

22. Kienle, "More Than a Response."

23. Goldberg.

24. Brownlee, "Heir Apparency."

25. Ricciardone.

26. IMF Country Report No. 10/94.

27. Scobey, "Scenesetter."

28. El-Ghobashy, "Egypt Looks Ahead."

29. Beinin and El-Hamalawy.

30. Beinin, 14.

31. D. Shehata, "Fall of the Pharaoh," 28.

32. Henry and Springborg, "Tunisian Solution."

33. al-Hamalawy, "General's Budget."

34. "Egypt's Interior Minister Seeks Riot-Control Budget."

35. "Mubarak Mocks Opposition."

36. El-Ghobashy, "Praxis."

37. Ibid., 3.

38. Levinson and Coker.

39. Interview, Kamal, March 21, 2011.

40. Interview, Hilal, March 20, 2011.

41. "Secretary Clinton Calls Egyptian Vice President Omar Soliman."

42. "Egypt's Military Plays Neutral Role."

43. Carapico, "No Exit."

44. Quinlivin, 134.

45. Kerr.

46. Hinnebusch, *Authoritarian Power and State Formation*, 281–86, 291–99.

47. Leverett, 28.

48. Zisser, *Commanding Syria*.

49. Stacher, "Reinterpreting Authoritarian Power," 198–212.

50. Sachs.

51. George.

52. Interview, Kilo, September 30, 2003.

53. Those thought to be close to the president are his brother, Maher (head of Republican Guard), brother-in-law, Asif Shawkat (former head of Military Intelligence and deputy-chief of staff of the Syrian Army), and cousin, Rami Makhlouf (Syria's richest businessman). See Shadid, "Syrian Businessman."

54. "'Day of Rage' for Syrians."

55. "Interview with Syrian President."

56. Yacoubian.

57. Rosen.

58. Habib.

59. Ibid.

60. "What Happens if Assad Goes?"

61. O'Donnell and Schmitter, 41.

62. McFaul, 213–14.

63. Bunce, 190.

64. Habib.

65. Tilly, 443–44.

66. See Lucas; Richards and Waterbury, 275–308.

67. Comparing monarchies in the Middle East has a literature. See Herb. If a comparative trend is evident, scholars comparing republics has tended to stress similarities such as "socialist republics," or "populist authoritarian regimes" rather than explore differences among them.

68. Ayubi, *Overstating the Arab State*, 196–223; Richards and Waterbury; Henry and Springborg, *Globalization*; Bill and Springborg, *Politics of the Middle East*.

69. Interview, Salah, February 9, 2004.

70. Adaptation is a system's ability to absorb political change. As a consequence, adaptation is distinct from reform. Developments that may cause a regime to adapt include but are not limited to technical developments, economic liberalization, the multiple transnational facets of globalization, and an external patron demanding democracy. With particular reference to regime adaptation to economic liberalization and the rise of technocratic governments, please see Fleron, 43–85.

71. By institutions, I mean the organizations of state. Namely, this includes the office of the presidency, the ruling party, the security services, the military, and parliament as well as state-affiliated councils and government sponsored NGOs.

72. Interview, Hilal, March 2, 2004.

73. Interview, Shab'an, March 24, 2004.

74. D. Shehata, "Fall of the Pharaoh," 31–32.

75. Jackson and Rosberg, 17–22, 270–71; Bill and Springborg, 71–73, 118–20; Brooker, 36–37.

76. The literature makes another observation: in lesser-developed countries that

have colonial legacies, bureaucratic institutions (executive, bureaucracy, military, police) tend to be stronger than political ones (parties, parliaments). This is one explanation for the predominance of authoritarian rule.

77. Wedeen, *Ambiguities of Domination.*

78. Wedeen, *Peripheral Visions.*

79. Posusney and Angrist.

80. Schlumberger.

81. Pratt.

82. Brownlee, *Authoritarianism in the Age of Democratization.*

83. Heydemann, "Upgrading Authoritarianism."

84. Soliman; D. Shehata, *'Auda al-Siyasiysa.*

85. Ouda.

86. Qandil.

87. Chehabi and Linz, 37–40.

88. Sharabi.

89. Lichbach and Zuckerman, 4.

90. Chilcote, 15.

91. For example, notable single-country works on Egypt include: Springborg, *Family, Power, and Politics in Egypt* and *Mubarak's Egypt*; Waterbury, *Egypt of Nasser*; Bianchi, *Unruly Corporatism*; Vitalis, *When Capitalist Collide*; S. Shehata, *Shop Floor Culture and Politics in Egypt.*

Concerning Syria: Wedeen, *Ambiguities of Domination*; Heydemann, *Authoritarianism in Syria*; and Hinnebusch, *Syria: Revolution from Above.*

More recent selections include Rutherford, *Egypt After Mubarak.*

92. Numerous examples exist, such as Richards and Waterbury's *Political Economy of the Middle East*; Ayubi's *Overstating the Arab State*; Korany, Brynen, and Noble's *Political Liberalization and Democratization in the Arab World*, vol. 2; Norton's *Civil Society in the Middle East*, vols. 1 and 2; Henry and Springborg's *Globalization and the Politics Development in the Middle East*; and Hinnebusch and Ehteshami's *Foreign Policies of Middle East States.* A recent addition is Michele Penner Angrist, ed., *Politics and Society in the Contemporary Middle East.* While all these works make necessary and useful observations on Egypt and Syria, among others, they are presented in a manner that makes any comparisons implicit, rather than overt.

93. There are a number of historical studies such as by Poliak. Also, old travel books are prevalent such as by Irby.

94. For example, Kerr; Gerges; Seale, *Struggle for Syria.*

95. Hinnebusch, "Liberalization in Syria"; and Kienle, "Return of Politics?" 97–131. Both scholars have written separate books on Egypt and on Syria.

96. Lenczowski, 29–56.

97. Issawi, "Social Structure"; Hinnebusch, "Politics of Economic Liberalization," 111–34.

98. Heydemann, *Authoritarianism in Syria*, 18–23.

99. A complete list of the people that I interviewed is in the References section.

Chapter 1

1. Brownlee, "Authoritarianism," 45.

2. "Freedom in the World 2011."

3. "Map of Freedom 2011."

4. Huntington, *Third Wave.*

5. Vitalis, "Democratization Industry," 46–50.

6. Harik.

7. See Fish; Stepan and Robertson.

8. Some prominent examples include Salame; Norton; Brynen, Korany, and Noble. None of these authors claim that civil society or transitions produce a democracy. But these works, like many of the democratization studies, apply to a linear, spatial, and temporal process that can only eventually lead to democracy.

9. Wedeen, *Ambiguities of Domination*, 26.

10. Heydemann, "Defending the Discipline," 103.

11. Lindsey.

12. Carapico, "Foreign Aid," 379–95.

13. Gause, "Can Democracy Stop Terrorism?" 62–76.

14. "Remarks by President George W. Bush."

15. "Arab Human Development" Reports.

16. Stacher, "Egypt: Anatomy of Succession."

17. Kienle, *Grand Delusion.*

18. Pool, 53.

19. International Crisis Group, "Reforming Egypt," i.

20. Dunne, 132–34.

21. Cook, 91–102.

22. Wittes.

23. Dunne.

24. Brownlee, *Authoritarianism in the Age of Democratization*, 10, 27.

25. Most often this office is the presidency. However, as Egypt shows, this can also be a body such as the Supreme Council of the Armed Forces.

26. Gerth and Mills, 296.

27. Linz, 255.

28. Brooker, 22.

29. In fairness to Weber, most social scientists acknowledge that he realized that hybrids of authorities mixed in practice. See Coser, 227.

30. Bratton and van de Walle, 62.
31. Weber, 49–70.
32. Sharabi, 3–4.
33. Ibid., 6.
34. Barakat, 26.
35. Ibid.
36. Levitsky and Way, 54–58.
37. Brumberg, "Authoritarian Legacies," 235.
38. Slater, *Ordering Power*; Smith; Gandhi and Przeworski, 1279–1301; Svolik, 477–94.
39. Lust-Okar.
40. Brownlee, *Authoritarianism in the Age of Democratization*, 42.
41. Slater, "Iron Cage in an Iron Fist," 81.
42. Ibid., 84.
43. Gandhi, 34.
44. Gerth and Mills, 334.
45. For an in-depth critique of the concept of modernity, see Mitchell, *Questions of Modernity*, 1–33.
46. North.
47. Huntington, *Political Order*, 8–9.
48. Ibid., 9.
49. Ibid., 412.
50. Collier and Collier; Haggard and Kaufman; Lieberman.
51. Fukuyama, "Political Order."
52. Brownlee, "Ruling Parties," 5.
53. Waldner, 37.
54. Ibid.
55. Interview, Kilo, September 30, 2003.
56. Corporatism differs from co-optation because it targets larger social groups, usually a socioeconomic class, by organizing people into structures such as unions or professional guilds. The use of corporatism is used as a channel and control mechanism in authoritarian states. See Brooker, 155.
57. Scott, 124–25.
58. Eisenstadt and Lemarchand, 15.
59. Brumberg, "Survival Strategies vs. Democratic Bargains," 77–78.
60. Cardoso, 43.
61. M. Kassem, *Guise of Democracy*, 83.
62. Arendt, 56.
63. Bellin, 143.

Chapter 2

1. Springborg, "Approaches," 137.

2. Interview, Hamidi, November 9, 2003.

3. Interview, 'Abd al-Hamid, December 1, 2003.

4. Perthes, *Political Economy of Syria*, 203.

5. Interview, Sadowski, March 16, 2004.

6. Brownlee, *Authoritarianism in the Age of Democratization*, 44.

7. Hinnebusch and Ehteshami, 141.

8. Quinlivin, 134.

9. Van Dam.

10. For an explanation of Egyptian nationalism emerging in relation to European colonialism, see Marsot; Beinin and Lockman; Fahmy.

11. B. Anderson.

12. Egypt's population is 90 pecent Sunni Muslim and 10 pecent Egyptian Coptic-Orthodox Christian. Although Egyptian Baha'is, Evangelicals, Catholics, and Jews exist, they constitute less than 1 pecent of the total population.

13. Hinnebusch and Ehteshami, 93–94.

14. Brown, "Egypt's Constitutional Ghosts."

15. These included the Liberation Rally (1953–56), National Union (1956–62), and the Arab Socialist Union (1962–76).

16. Syria was the "Northern Sector" and Egypt was the "South Sector" under Gamal 'Abd al-Nasser's leadership.

17. After the 1967 military defeat, Nasser's pan-Arab designs were dead. Subtle shifts toward an "Egypt First" project actually began before Nasser's death. Sadat accelerated the trend. See Baker, *Egypt's Uncertain Revolution*, 142.

18. Ibid., 124.

19. King, 83.

20. Interview, Shukar, April 30, 2004.

21. Waterbury, 349.

22. Ibid., 314.

23. According to an interview with 'Ali Wali, minister under Nasser and Sadat. From M. Kassem, *Egyptian Politics*, 21.

24. In addition to Sabri and Gum'a—Sharif, Fawzi, Mohamad Fayik (information minister), Hilmi Sa'id (electricity minister), and 'Adel 'Abd al-Nor (first secretary of the ASU Central Committee) were sentenced.

25. Waterbury, 367.

26. Ibid., 364.

27. El-Hennawy, 75.

28. M. Kassem, *Guise of Democracy*, 53.

29. Van Dam, 64.

30. Heydemann, *Authoritarianism in Syria.*

31. The B'ath was founded by Salah al-Din Bitar and Michel 'Aflaq in 1945. The fact that the B'ath was ideological and the ASU was a top-down creation based loosely on pan-Arabism, which was rapidly discarded in favor of the Egyptian nationalism after the 1967 War reveals a difference.

32. Hinnebusch, *Syria: Revolution from Above,* 65.

33. Asad created a subsidiary institutional base whereby the state could direct and control supporters and detractors through institutional co-optation. In 1971, he established the People's Assembly (Majlis al-Sh'ab). The legislative body assisted the regime in coordinating, legitimizing, and channeling regime supporters by providing them access to economic resources and power. Many urbanites, which Asad included to broaden the regime's base, were co-opted through parliament. The following year, Asad initiated the Progressive National Front (PNF, or Jubha Taqadim al-Wataniya) that gave the appearance of a "pluralist system" by including Nasserists, Communists, and Arab Socialist parties with the B'ath. However, unlike Sadat, Asad strengthened the party of state even while bringing in small formal opposition parties though the PNF. The Front's parties had consultative roles, were appointed to public offices, and held cabinet positions. As such, the opposition parties were neutralized by their incorporation into the Front. Another means of expanding power was the promulgation of the 1973 constitution that established the legal mechanism of Asad's rule. The 1973 constitution designated the B'ath Party as the country's "leading" party.

34. Hinnebusch, *Authoritarian Power,* 178.

35. Lobmeyer, 95.

36. Perthes, *Political Economy,* 154.

37. Hinnebusch, "Liberalization in Syria," in Kienle, *Contemporary Syria,* 109.

38. Sukkar, 33.

39. Perthes, *Political Economy,* 157.

40. Hinnebusch, "Civil Society in Syria."

41. Kienle, "Introduction," in *Contemporary Syria,* 4.

42. Kienle, "Return of Politics," in *Contemporary Syria,* 131.

43. Wilson.

44. Interview, Abbas, October 21, 2003.

45. Baker, 48–49.

46. Ouda, al-Borai, and Abu Saada, 24.

47. Baker, 55–56.

48. Aburish, 245.

49. Amir officially committed suicide in September 1967. Although conspiracies abound about Nasser's role in Amir's death, there is no smoking gun.

50. Hinnebusch, *Egyptian Politics Under Sadat,* 129.

51. Mubarak's participation in Sadat's Egypt is so inconsequential that Gamasi mentions him only once in his memoir.

52. Ayubi, 92.

53. Ouda, Borai, and Abu Saada, 24.

54. Hinnebusch, *Egyptian Politics Under Sadat*, 131.

55. For example, see Huntington, *Political Order*. For an in-depth article on the professionalization of the Egyptian military, see Harb, 269–90.

56. Quote from Seale, *Asad*, 150.

57. Hinnebusch, *Authoritarian Power*, 160–62. Such individuals included Rif'at al-Asad, Adnan al-Asad, Adnan Makhluf, Mohamad al-Khuly, 'Ali Haydir, Shafiq Fayad, and 'Ali Duba.

58. For example Mostapha Tlas, Naji Jamil, and 'Abd al-Rahman al-Khulafawi.

59. Longtime chief of staff Hikmat al-Shihabi is largely seen as representing the third circle.

60. Zisser, *Asad's Legacy*.

61. Hinnebusch, *Authoritarian Power*, 162.

62. Hinnebusch, *International Politics*, 138

63. An example of the autonomy of the security services can be seen in recent examples under Bashar al-Asad's presidency. Before Syrian interior minister General Ghazi Kan'an committed suicide October 2005, he oversaw the political security intelligence agency. Prior to that he oversaw Syria's security operations in Lebanon for eighteen years (1982–2000). His corruption and power from the two positions was so legendary that one Syrian journalist described Kan'an as "president of two states [Syria and Lebanon]." Interview, Syrian journalist, Damascus, April 2004.

64. Baker, 142.

65. Levinson.

66. Seale, *Asad*, 191.

67. Heikel, 43–45.

68. Shlaim, 321.

69. Kissinger, 459.

70. Ibid., 75.

71. Abdo, 54.

72. Heikel, 182.

73. Presidential-initiated legislation that reserved land reform came into force in 1997 while a law that liberalized the labor force was enacted in 2003.

74. Kissinger, 1249.

75. Tsebelis.

76. Hinnebusch, *Authoritarian Power*, 160–61, 165.

77. Fisk, 83.

78. Ibid.

79. Hinnebusch, *Authoritarian Power*, 293.

80. Ibid., 295.

81. Seale, *Asad*, 335.

82. Ibid., 333.

83. Hinnebusch, *Syria: Revolution from Above*, 101–2.

84. Seale, *Asad*, 327.

Chapter 3

1. Nongovernment actors are capable of producing policy change, but they are not political elites according to this standard. Examples of how opposition organizations or protests constrain a system's elites and their activities abound. One needs to look no further than the January 25 uprising. To see a variant of how protests challenge and change government policy; see Posusney. To consider an antielite approach to politics, see Singerman. Yet, the regime also maintains practices, such as corporatism and co-optation, that renegotiate power distribution disparities and make government agents more likely to introduce change as opposed to a protesting opposition.

2. All can sanction or criticize higher elite decisions publicly, but they are unable to independently introduce policy change. Businessmen with access to government decision-makers are also middle elites in regards to initiating political changes.

3. Harb, 269–90.

4. Prior to 2005, parliament nominated a single candidate for president. Then, the people chose "yes" or "no" in a popular referendum. Mubarak never garnered less than 93 percent in a national referendum. On February 26, 2005, Mubarak called on parliament to amend Article 76 of the constitution. Specifically, he wished to do away with the presidential referendum and replace it with direct, multicandidacy presidential election. The amendment, which was highly restrictive for independent and opposition party candidates was approved in parliament on May 10 and approved by 83 percent in a popular referendum. On September 7, 2005, Mubarak was elected for the first time by winning 89 percent of the national vote. While in theory Egypt's leader was selected by a competitive election, this change was designed to help guide succession. See Stacher, "Egypt: Anatomy of Succession," 301–14.

5. In constitutional amendments passed after the 2011 Egyptian uprising, Article 77 now stipulates that the next president will be subject to two four-year terms.

6. Stacher, "Democracy with Fangs and Claws," 83–99.

7. Stacher, "Parties Over," 12.

8. Kienle, "More Than a Response," 219; Kienle, *Grand Delusion.*

9. "My Word on History," broadcast on Egyptian State Television, April 24–26, 2005.

10. Interview, Kassem, February 12, 2004.

11. Interview, Hill, March 15, 2004.

12. Moustapha.

13. Springborg has developed this Mubarak-Abu Ghazala case study in his book *Mubarak's Egypt*, 98–104, 118–23.

14. At the March 20, 2003, protests in Cairo's Tahrir Square, protesters chanted, among others, anti-Mubarak chants, "Ya 'Ala [this is *qal*, or 'tell'] l-Abuak . . . al-milaynin biyakhrahu" [Hey 'Ala (the president's son), tell your father, millions hate him]. Kifaya held their first demonstration in December 2004.

15. Harb, 287.

16. Ibid., 289.

17. It is somewhat ironic that Field Marshall Mohamad Hussein Tantawi, who is the head of SCAF, was responsible for Mubarak's forced departure. US diplomatic cables, which were released by WikiLeaks, noted that in pre-2011 Egypt Tantawi was viewed as "Mubarak's Poodle." See Scobey, "Academics See the Military in Decline."

18. Perthes, *Political Economy*, 133.

19. Hinnebusch, *Syria: Revolution from Above*, 80–87.

20. Interview, Seale, October 10, 2003.

21. Perthes, *Syria Under Bashar al-Asad*, 5.

22. Interviews with academics, activists, journalists, and diplomats in Damascus, September–December 2003, and Beirut, March 2004.

23. Interview, Seale, October 10, 2003.

24. Interview, al-Taqi, December 29, 2003.

25. Interview, US diplomat, Damascus, November 1, 2003.

26. *al-Thawra* July 17, 2000.

27. International Crisis Group, "Syria Under Bashar II," 6.

28. Interview, former political consultant, Damascus, November 2003.

29. Interview,'Abd al-Nor, December 22, 2003.

30. Blanford, "As Reform Falters."

31. International Crisis Group, "Syria Under Bashar II," 12.

32. Interview, al-Taqi, December 2, 2003.

33. al-Dardari was appointed deputy prime minister for Economic Affairs of Syria in 2005.

34. Interview, al-'Azm, December 20, 2003.

35. Interview, Syrian political observer, November 3, 2003.

36. Interview, al-Taqi, December 2, 2003.

37. Khaddam was removed from all official capacities at the June 2005 B'ath Party congress. Some have speculated that the February 2005 assassination of Rafiq al-Hariri clipped Khaddam's base in Damascus. Since then, Khaddam has fled Syria and remains a dissenting voice in Paris. See "Majlis al-Sh'ab al-Suri Yutalib b-mahakma Khadam b-tihma al-kiana."

38. Landis, 4–6.

39. Interview, consultant to the president, Damascus, November 2003.

40. Interview, US embassy staff, Damascus, fall 2003.

41. The clearest argument Bolton made was in his testimony in front of the Middle East and Central Asia Subcommittee of the House International Relations Committee on September 16, 2003, when he advocated regime change in Syria. However, Bolton also argued such a position since December 2002. To read the transcript, see http://freelebanon .org/testimonies/t75.htm, accessed October 19, 2004.

42. Interview, former political consultant, Damascus, fall 2003.

43. Stogel.

44. Interview, 'Abd al-Hamid, October 8, 2003.

45. The constitution refers to the B'ath Party only in Article 8 of the constitution, which states that the B'ath "is the leading party in society." Syrian Constitution (1973).

46. Interview, Sukkar, October 22, 2003.

47. More than one power center can exist within a particular institution. The party, intelligence services, and military are not monolithic blocs and they do not act uniformly. Instead, institutions have degrees of autonomy and, therefore, provide a protective cover for elites inside them. Accordingly, elites have overlapping but separate patronage networks that articulate varying interests. These interinstitutional elite groupings, which are structurally engrained within the political system, constitute a power center within an institution.

48. Some could counterargue that Mosa's ten-year tenure was considerable and perhaps senior upper elites felt a need for change. Yet, considering that the particular actors had all been ministers or advisors for much longer than Mosa was FM, it is unconvincing.

49. "Egypt Refutes Israel's Claims."

50. Stacher, "Brothers and Wars," 2, 8.

51. "Profile: Amr Moussa."

52. Numerous conversations with Egyptian professors and analysts during 2000–2001, Cairo.

53. "Petition Calls for Elections."

54. Okasha.

55. Interview, Schemm, March 2004.

56. Conversation with Badr, April 2002.

57. Interview, former staff-intern in Mosa's office at the Arab League, Cairo, January 2003.

58. "Grounded for Greenbacks."

59. Along with Gamal Mubarak, members of his faction were included. This included all members of the NDP's Policies Secretariat, such as Ahmad 'Ezz, Mahmoud Mohy al-Din, Hosam Badrawy, Yousif Botros-Ghali, and Mohamad Kamal.

60. Al-Shazli was excluded from his position as parliamentary affairs minister and assistant secretary-general of the NDP in December 2005 and January 2006. He passed away in 2010.

61. al-Sharif has been considerably demoted despite continuing to serve the party as the head in the Shura Council, the political polities committee, and the Higher Press Council until the 2011 uprising.

62. M. Kassem, *Guise of Democracy*, 168–71.

63. Abdel-Razek.

64. H. Kassem, "2000 Elections" Lecture at the American University in Cairo.

65. Parliamentary elections under Mubarak had never produced less than a 78-percent majority (1987) prior to 2005. Its highest majority under Mubarak was 95 percent in 1995. The 2005 elections produced a 74 percent NDP majority. However, out of the party's 444 official candidates only won 145 seats (32 percent of the vote) in 2005. For a history of the party's electoral trajectory, see Brownlee, *Authoritarianism in the Age of Democratization*, 92–93, 124–28.

66. In the lead-up to those elections, NDP leadership claimed that independent party members that contested official NDP candidates and won would not be allowed to rejoin the party.

67. Interview, Kassem, February 12, 2004.

68. Hilal lost his youth ministry in part due to the 2010 World Cup bid scandal. Yet, Hilal continued to sit on the NDP's steering committee and was promoted inside the party. He became head of the NDP's Media Secretariat in January 2006. Since the 2011 uprising, Hilal has resigned from politics. Interview, Hilal, March 20, 2011.

69. Interview, Shams al-Din, February 25, 2004.

70. Brownlee, "Decline of Pluralism," 9–10.

71. Interview, Shams al-Din.

72. Ibid.

73. Schemm, "He Got the Job Done."

74. Khalil.

75. Interview, Sa'id, May 3, 2004.

76. Interview, al-Taroty, February 12, 2004. Also see Ouda.

77. Interview Shams al-Din. Shams al-Din also shared an anecdote of Gamal Mubarak giving a powerpoint presentation to a group of low-tech farmers from the Egyptian countryside at a sanctioned NDP event.

78. Ibid.

79. Interview, Wali, March 6, 2004.

80. Interview, Hilal, March 20, 2011.

81. After Wali's removal from the position of NDP secretary-general in 2002, high-profile corruption cases involving a number of Wali's key clients emerged. These cases opened public criticism of Wali's involvement. In March 2004 Wali was forced to testify in court regarding the long-term import of illegal pesticides by his ministry from 1982–2004. Wali agreed to testify only after a Cairo criminal court threatened to lift his parliamentary immunity. This was the first time an incumbent cabinet minister appeared in a

court case. See *al-Ahram Weekly* (March 4–10, 2004). These scandals subsequently made it easy for the president, in July 2004, to remove Wali from the ministry after serving for twenty-two years as Egypt's minister of agriculture.

82. In 2005, although Wali held no official position in any of the NDP's highest bodies, he was nominated to run in the parliamentary elections as the NDP candidate in al-Fayyoum governorate. He was defeated by a member of the Muslim Brothers and has retired from public life.

83. "Down with Duties."

84. Interview, Kitchen, October 22, 2004.

85. Egypt's labor force, however, has made its discontent known. Egypt has been experiencing its most sustained wave of protests since the 1952 revolution. See Beinin.

86. Schemm, "Egypt," 28.

87. Ibid., 29.

88. Hosam Badrawy, former MP (2000–2005) and NDP's Policies Secretariat Education Committee head, frequently described the change versus status quo dynamic in such terms. Also, interview, Kassem, February 12, 2004.

89. S. Shehata, "Political Succession"; and Brownlee, "New Generation."

90. In one of Hosni Mubarak's last denials about succession, he claimed, "only God knows who will be my successor," in "Egypt's President Sidesteps Question."

91. There were arguments that the amendment of constitutional Article 76 established the party as the institution from which Egypt's next president will come. The amendment states explicitly that the next president must be a senior member of a political party. Members of the Egyptian military were not allowed to be members in any of Egypt's twenty-one legal political parties during Mubarak's presidency. Hence, military officers appear to be legally excluded. For a more detailed version of this argument, see Stacher, "Egypt: Anatomy of Succession," 301–14.

92. Stacher, "Gamal Mubarak's Journey."

93. Stacher, "NDP Conference." Also, interview, Badrawy, January 2009.

94. Perthes, *Political Economy*, 182.

95. Ibid., 269.

96. "Bashar al-Assad: Eyeing the Future."

97. Zisser, "Will Bashshar al-Asad Rule?" 8–10.

98. Lesch; Leverett.

99. Stacher, "Re-interpreting Authoritarian Power."

100. Zisser, *Commanding Syria*, 1–10.

101. Interview, Stienen and Haider, December 6, 2003.

102. This included several prominent figures in the security services and military such as 'Ali Duba and Hikmat Shihabi as well as former B'athist prime minister such as Mahmoud Zo'bi.

103. The regime core consists of figures such as Tlas, al-Shara', Parliament Speaker

'Abd al-Qadar Qadora, Vice President 'Abd al-Halim Khadam, National Command head 'Abdullah Ahmar, and Vice President Zahayr Masharqa.

104. Quilty, 8.

105. The constitutional amendment's precision on the age of an eligible president is notable as Bashar's younger brother, Mahir, was thirty-three at the time. This excluded him from potentially challenging Bashar's succession. While Mahir made neither public claims to the presidency nor was visibly groomed, the elite's caution was linked to Mahir's position as a colonel in the elite republican guard. See Zisser, "Does Bashar al-Assad Rule Syria?"

106. The other two times Rif'at returned to Syria after being exiled, he had come by way of Lebanon. Jarrah, 6.

107. Ibid.

108. Ibid.

109. Ibid.

110. Hafiz al-Asad and Mahmoud Zo'bi died, and Rif'at al-Asad and former chief of staff Hikmat Shihabi were in exile. Shihabi resides in the United States.

111. Quilty, 9.

112. The remaining percentage represented spoiled ballots.

113. Correspondent, "Consolidating Bashar," 10.

114. Mostapha Tlas said, "Bashar is a young, promising leader, and he can rely on our support," in *al-Ahram* (July 15, 2000).

115. "Ibna' al-Nizam" is attributed to Salam al-Kawakbi, a civil society activist in Aleppo (interview, October 1, 2003).

116. Interview, Mostapha, February 26, 2004.

117. Interview, Wali, March 2004. Sharif Wali is the nephew of Yusif Wali but not in his patronage network.

118. Interview, Shams al-Din, February 25, 2004.

119. After being minister, Al-Ghamwari presided over the General Authority for Investment and Free Zones.

120. Interview, Sawi, February 15, 2004.

121. Ibid.

122. Interview, Wali.

123. Interview, Seale, October 10, 2003.

124. Interview, 'Abd al-Nor, November 2003.

125. Oft-repeated examples of the president's inability to protect his appointed people are the cases of 'Issam Z'aim or Ghassan al-Rifa'i. Interviews with journalists (Haider and Hamidi), diplomats (Steinen and others), consultants ('Abd al-Nor), and economists (Sukkar), in Damascus, fall 2003.

126. Interview, 'Abd al-Nor, November 2003.

127. Ibid.

Chapter 4

1. Nonelite co-optation describes how people—who may be part of a country's educated elite but not part of the political elite—go from being unaffiliated actors to being incorporated into the political field.

2. Interview, 'Ezz, September 11, 2005.

3. Interview, Mohy al-Din, December 12, 2005. After the LE lost close to half its value, the float was blamed on outgoing PM Atif 'Obayd.

4. Whitaker, "Egypt Scours Globe." Also interview, Badrawy, January 2009.

5. An example of this is the secretariat's call to abolish ordinary state-security courts in January 2003 while maintaining emergency state-security courts. Gamal Mubarak argued it was a significant reform. Yet, the measure eliminated the less draconian of state-security courts that operated in Mubarak's Egypt and left the more repressive court to be used. For example, the rulings from emergency state-security courts are final and cannot be appealed. Also, the bill enhanced the investigative powers of the public prosecutor's office. Despite these qualifications, when the measure was passed, the PS claimed their reform was akin to removing martial law, or emergency law, which had been in place in Egypt since 1981.

6. Essem El-Din, "Democratisation Debate." Al-Sharif's statement is false however. The idea of constituting a NCHR first emerged in May 2000 but was never realized. The NCHR initiative predated the PS's establishment. See Stacher, "Rhetorical Acrobatics and Reputations."

7. Stacher, "Gamal Mubarak's Journey."

8. Schemm, 28.

9. Whitaker, "Cairo Reformers."

10. El-Ghobashy, "Egypt Looks Ahead."

11. The subcommittees included Education, Economics, Foreign Affairs ("Egypt and the World"), Health and Housing, Youth, Women, and Transportation. The committees contained an additional three hundred members in addition to the Policies Secretariat's 123-person Higher Policies Council. Gamal Mubarak appointed its members.

12. Between 2006–11, the Higher Policies Council mushroomed. No list was ever made publicly available, but it was thought to contain around five hundred members.

13. Interview, Bishay, February 25, 2004.

14. Ibid.

15. Interview, Mostapha, February 2004.

16. Ibid.

17. Interview, Hilal, March 2, 2004.

18. Ibid.

19. Interview, Mostapha, March 2004.

20. Hinnebusch, *Authoritarian Power*, 197–219.

21. Interview, Landis, February 26, 2005.

22. Interview, Kilo, March 22, 2004.

23. No one left the subcommittee.

24. Interview, al-Taqi, March 2, 2005.

25. Ibid.

26. Interview, a Western diplomat who requested anonymity, Damascus, February 28, 2005.

27. Michel Kilo, however, was eventually imprisoned for his activism. He was arrested in May 2006 and held for three years after writing and circulating the Damascus-Beirut Declaration. Kilo's previous cooperation with the B'ath Party did not protect him.

28. Al-Mo'alim was made minister of foreign affairs in February 2006, replacing Farouk al-Shar'a, who was appointed vice president. Al-Shar'a was foreign minister between 1984–2006.

29. Interview, al-Taqi, March 2, 2005.

30. Heydemann, "Upgrading Authoritarianism," 5–10.

31. Bank, 167.

32. I thank *Middle East Report* for permitting me to recycle parts of my article in this book.

33. The NCHR was affiliated to parliament's upper house, rather than the presidency, because it was internationally illegal to affiliate a human rights council to the executive.

34. The NCHR was housed in the national headquarters of the NDP in downtown Cairo. To get to the council's offices, you had to tour the party's headquarters.

35. The NCHR was proposed to consist of twenty members. A parliamentary compromise increased it to twenty-seven members.

36. Essem El-Din, "More Than Window-Dressing?"

37. Ibid.

38. Background information on Abu Sa'ada's case can be found in Stacher, "Democracy with Fangs and Claws," 87–88. The al-Kosh incident (Sohag governorate) involved sectarian strife incited after the security services arrested and detained as many as one thousand villagers (primarily Christian) over the unsolved murder of a Christian man in 1998.

39. Howeidy, "Rights at a Crossroad." Of course, this press report invalidates that Gamal Mubarak's PS was the "brain child" of the NCHR.

40. Al-Bora'i was the head of the disbanded Group for Democratic Development, a NGO that specializes in educating people on democratic traditions.

41. Interview, Saif al-Dawla, December 2, 2004.

42. Interview, Saif al-Islam, February 16, 2004.

43. Interview, Saif al-Dawla, February 24, 2004.

44. Interview, Abu Sa'ada, February 18, 2004.

45. Interviews, Hassan, February 26, 2004, and December 16, 2004.

46. Interview, Boutros-Ghali, March 16, 2004.

47. Harb, a former member of the NDP's Policies Secretariat, resigned from the ruling party in March 2006 and launched a new party called the Justice and Democracy Party. He remained on the NCHR.

48. Badrawy lost his parliamentary reelection in Cairo's Kasr al-'Aini District in November 2005.

49. 'Abd al-Nor lost his parliamentary reelection in Cairo's al-Waily District in November 2005.

50. Zolfiqar, also a member of the National Council for Women, was a leading advocate of personal-status law in 2000, which nominally gave women the right to divorce.

51. Interview, Hassan, April 7, 2005.

52. Following the bombing of the Hilton in the Sinai resort of Taba that killed thirty-four people on October 7, 2004, the interior minister announced that nine Islamist radicals, led by a twenty-five-year-old microbus driver living in the northern Sinai town of al-'Arish, committed the atrocity. In keeping with the government's common practices of collective punishment and torture, al-'Arish and nearby al-Shaykh Zuwayd were subjected to flagrant repression. The reasoning seems to be that if the bombers resided there, the town's population had all the answers about the bombing. Cairo's human rights NGOs (including Abu Saada's EOHR) reported that more than twenty-five hundred people were indiscriminately detained and abused in late November. Human Rights Watch published a forty-eight-page report in February 2005, based on collaborative investigations with domestic Egyptian groups, detailing the targeting of women, children, and the elderly alongside accused "Islamists."

53. Interview, Hassan, April 7, 2005.

54. Interview, Abu Sa'ada, April 8, 2005.

55. SCS figures connected to Bashar al-Asad that became prominent are the Syrian ambassador to the US 'Imad Mostapha and Deputy Prime Minister 'Abdalah Daradari.

56. Bank, 170.

57. Interview, Tabler, March 9, 2005.

58. "Trying to Fit In," 6.

59. Interview, Moubayed, March 21, 2004.

60. "Trying to Fit In," 8.

61. Interview, Moubayed, March 21, 2004.

62. Ibid.

63. Interview, FIRDOS member who requested anonymity, Beirut, March 2004.

64. Interview, political analyst, Damascus, February 28, 2005.

65. Interview, Tabler, March 9, 2005.

66. NDP parliamentary majorities have been 87 pecent (1984), 79 percent (1987), 86

percent (1990), 94 percent (1995), 88 percent (2000), 72 percent (2005), and 93 percent (2010) under Mubarak's presidency.

67. Five MPs representing the Wafd were expelled from that party by its leadership after the 2000 elections.

68. This was reduced to fifteen because the government called for elections to be recontested, which resulted in two MB MPs losing in fraudulent reelections.

69. This number is misleading, however, as only 172 NDP-nominated candidates managed to win (39 percent of the vote). Another 181 "NDP independents" won seats and rejoined the party ranks. Another 35 actual independent candidates joined the NDP to give it an 88 percent majority in the 2000–2005 parliament.

70. *al-Ahram Weekly*, December 15–21, 2005.

71. Interview, Rabi'a, February 17, 2004.

72. Interview, Sabahy, March 1, 2004.

73. Perthes, *Political Economy*, 167.

74. Ibid., 166.

75. The B'ath receives 135 seats (54 percent) out of 167 allocated seats for the PNF in this managed system.

76. Perthes, *Political Economy*, 169.

77. "Elections Bring Little Hope," 25.

78. Ibid.

79. Interview, Akkad, December 11, 2003.

80. Ibid.

81. Ibid.

82. A recent example of the state apparatus attacking an independent MP is Tal'at al-Sadat in 2006. As a nephew of Egypt's previous president, he implied that the military and Mubarak may have had a hand in Sadat's death days before the twenty-fifth anniversary of his uncle's assassination. After the remarks the following occurred: on a national holiday and Friday, parliament stripped Sadat of his parliamentary immunity. His case was referred to a military court. On October 31, less than a month after his initial statement, Tal'at al-Sadat was convicted for disparaging the institution of the military and began serving a one-year prison term. There was no appeal possible because a military court handed down the sentence. Sadat's only legal recourse was for Mubarak himself to pardon him. He was released from prison in August 2007.

83. There are seven different branches of internal security in Syria.

84. Suleiman is credited with saving Mubarak's life during a 1995 assassination attempt in Addis Ababa. He is regarded as one of Mubarak's most trusted advisors. See Weaver, 7.

85. Hamalawy, "Powerful Egyptian Spy Chief."

86. "Kifaya" is Arabic for "Enough"—the slogan used to protest another presidential term for Mubarak or the Gamal's inheritance of power. See El-Mahdi, "Enough: Egypt's Quest for Democracy."

87. Interview, Saif al-Dawla, December 2, 2004.

88. Interview, Saif al-Islam, February 22, 2005.

89. M. Kassem, *Egyptian Politics*, 192.

90. Interview, Hossam al-Hamalawy, February 20, 2005.

91. Syria's security services are discussed as a single institutional bloc in this discussion. Nevertheless, the security services are divided into several agencies and include Military Intelligence (Mukhabarat al-'Askiraya), which oversees a Palestine Branch, Investigative Branch, Regional Branch, and Airforce Branch. Also Political Intelligence (Mukhabarat al-Siyasi) and General Intelligence (Mukhabarat al-'Ama), which controls an Investigative Branch, Domestic Branch, and a Foreign Branch also operate in Syria. Each agency and branch has its own director, and all maintain separate prisons and facilities. According to Alan George, there is one security service employee for every 153 Syrians, see George, 2.

92. Interview, 'Abd al-Hamid, March 2, 2005.

93. Ibid. 'Abd al-Hamid has since left Syria and resides in Silver Springs, MD.

94. Although at first glance one might be tempted to draw parallels with the public role of Egypt's intelligence chief, the comparison is not apt. Omar Suleiman's prominence derived from his role as the only Egyptian security figure that played a role politically by handling the Palestinian-Israeli and the Arab affairs dossiers on behalf of President Mubarak. Omar Suleiman, then, did not act independently on behalf of his agency. No other Egyptian security head or agencies were politically active. The Egyptian services played a more traditional role of disrupting and preventing unsanctioned politics before the 2011 uprising, while in Syria the services are politicized institutional political players.

95. Interview, al-'Azm, November 3, 2003.

96. Suleiman.

97. See Kilo; al-Zain.

98. Interview, al-'Azm, December 20, 2003.

99. For Background on al-Malih, see Abdel Salaam.

100. Kan'an served as head of Syrian intelligence in Lebanon for nearly twenty years. Following that, he was director of political security in Syria. He was appointed minister of interior in October 2004 and committed suicide in his Damascus office in October 2005.

101. Interview, al-Malih, December 6, 2003.

102. Interview, al-Malih, March 23, 2004

103. Interview, 'Abd al-Salam, March 1, 2005.

104. Bellin.

105. Blanford, *Killing Mr. Lebanon*, 70–127.

106. Perthes, "Syria: Difficult Inheritance," 87–114.

107. For Sa'id, see Chick. For al-Khatib, see "Tortured and Killed."

108. Shehata and Stacher, "Brotherhood Goes to Parliament"; "Boxing in the Brothers"; and Stacher, "Brothers and Wars."

109. El-Ghobashy, "Praxis," 12.

Chapter 5

1. Bureaucratic Authoritarianism (BA) was primarily practiced in Latin American states in the 1950s and 1960s. It relied on an alliance between military officers and existing landed and bourgeoisie elite in a narrow, exclusive ruling coalition in which economic development was paramount. In this form of authoritarianism, the population suffers the worst of the capitalist development project, which sharpens class distinction and invariably leads to class conflict and capitalism. According to Paul Brooker, ruling coalitions of the military and existing landed elite insulate themselves from economic policies. This, in turn, allows such states to achieve higher level of economic development. Also see D. Collier, "Overview of the Bureaucratic Authoritarian Model," in *New Authoritarianism*, 19–32. The difference between neoliberal authoritarianism and BA is the latter is an exclusionary system while the former is a middle ground between populism and BA.

2. For details on the ruling party's descent into the oblivion, see Brownlee and Stacher, 5–6.

3. Sallam.

4. Winegar.

5. Hanieh.

6. Stacher, "Blame the SCAF for Egypt's Problems."

7. Vitalis, "Democratization Industry."

8. Obama.

9. Slackman.

10. http://wikileaks.ch/tag/EG_0.html (accessed on December 14, 2010).

11. Schwedler, Stacher, and Philbrick Yadav.

12. Kienle, *Grand Delusion.*

13. Ehteshami and Murphy.

14. Heydemann, "Upgrading Authoritarianism."

15. Bank, 155–79.

16. Brumberg, "Authoritarian Legacies," 235.

17. For example, Vice Presidents Khaddam and Mushtariqa have resigned from their RC positions, as have Qaddora, Ahmar, Qaddah, Fayad, and Miro. Farok al-Shar'a has been elevated to the vice president position. Bashar loyalist Walid al-Mo'alim was appointed as foreign minister while other more Bashar-friendly B'athists will be ministers in the next cabinet reshuffle. Similarly, longtime heads of security were replaced in the lead up and aftermath to the 2005 conference. Names of those excluded include Hisham Ikhtiyar, Hasan al-Khalil, and Bahjat Sulayman. Names of the newly included

are Bashar's brother-in-law, Asif Shawqat in Military Intelligence, 'Ali Yunis with the Struggle Companies, 'Ali Mamlok in General Intelligence, Fuad Nassif Khairbik in Foreign Intelligence, and Mohamad Monsora in Political Intelligence. In short, the Syrian president is stronger now than when he assumed the presidency.

18. Zoepf and Shadid.

19. Shadid, "Syrian Elite to Fight Protests."

20. Carothers, 6.

21. I am indebted to Valerie Bunce for this advice, which is based off her presentation at the Project on Middle East Political Science conference at George Washington University in May 2011.

REFERENCES

Published Sources

Abdel-Razek, Sherine. "Swords Cross over Steel." *al-Ahram Weekly*. January 22–28, 2004.

Abdel Salaam, Hussein. "Al-Malih's Agenda." *Cairo Times*. April 15–21, 2004.

Abdo, Geneive. *No God but God: Egypt and the Triumph of Islam*. New York: Oxford University Press, 2000.

Aburish, Said. *Nasser: The Last Arab*. New York: Thomas Dunne Press, 2004.

Ambrust, Walter. "The Revolution Against Neoliberalism." February 23, 2011. http://jadaliyya.com/pages/index/717/the-revolution-against-neoliberalism-. Accessed on May 10, 2011.

"Amr Mosa Does not Rule out Nominating Himself for the Egyptian Presidency." Reuters Arabic. October 20, 2009.

Anderson, Benedict. *Imagined Communities: Reflections on the Origin and Spread of Nationalism*. New York: Verso, 1983.

Anderson, Lisa. "Demystifying the Arab Spring." *Foreign Affairs* 90, no. 3 (May/June 2011): 2–7.

Angrist, Michele Penner, ed. *Politics and Society in the Contemporary Middle East*. Boulder, CO: Lynne Rienner, 2010.

"Arab Human Development" Reports by the United Nations Development Program, Regional Bureau for Arab States: New York (2002, 2003, 2004, 2005, 2009). Published by the United Nations at www.undp.org/rbas and www.arab-hdr.org

Arendt, Hannah. *On Violence*. Orlando, FL: Harcourt Brace & Company, 1969.

al-Asad, Bashar. "Inaugural Presidential Speech." *al-Thawra*. July 17, 2000. An English translation of the address is available at http://www.albab.com/arab/countries/syria/basharooa.htm. Accessed on November 2, 2003.

Ayubi, Nazih. *Overstating the Arab State: Politics and Society in the Middle East*. London: I. B. Tauris, 1995.

———. *The State and Public Policies in Egypt Since Sadat*. Reading, NY: Ithaca Press, 1991.

Baker, Raymond. *Egypt's Uncertain Revolution*. Cambridge, MA: Harvard University Press, 1978.

Bank, Andre. "Rents, Co-optation, and Economized Discourse: Three Dimensions of Political Rule in Jordan, Morocco and Syria." *Journal of Mediterranean Studies* 14, nos. 1/2 (2004): 155–80.

Barakat, Halim. *The Arab World: Society, Culture and State.* Berkeley: University of California Press, 1993.

Barkey, Henri J., ed. *The Politics of Economic Reform in the Middle East.* New York: St. Martin's Press, 1992.

"Bashar al-Assad: Eyeing the Future." BBC World News. June 11, 2000. http://news.bbc .co.uk/1/hi/world/middle_east/785921.stm. Accessed on June 18, 2003.

"Bashar's Campaign." *Middle East International.* May 19, 2000.

Beinin, Joel. "The Struggle for Worker Rights in Egypt." Washington, DC: The Solidarity Center, 2010.

Beinin, Joel, and Hossam El-Hamalawy. "Strikes in Egypt Spread from Center of Gravity." *Middle East Report Online.* May 9, 2007. http://www.merip.org/mero/mero050907. Accessed on May 12, 2011.

Beinin, Joel, and Zachary Lockman. *Workers on the Nile: Nationalism, Communism, Islam, and the Egyptian Working Class, 1882–1954.* Princeton, NJ: Princeton University Press, 1987.

Bellin, Eva. "The Robustness of Authoritarianism in the Middle East." *Comparative Politics* 36, no. 2 (January 2004): 139–58.

Bianchi, Robert. *Unruly Corporatism: Associational Life in Twentieth-Century Egypt.* Oxford: Oxford University Press, 1989.

Bill, James, and Robert Springborg. *Politics of the Middle East.* 5th ed. New York: Longman Press, 2000.

Blanford, Nicholas. "As Reform Falters, Syrian Elite Tighten Grip." *Christian Science Monitor.* September 30, 2003.

———. *Killing Mr. Lebanon: The Assassination of Rafik Hariri and its Impact on the Middle East.* London: I. B. Tauris, 2006.

Bratton, Michael, and Nicolas van de Walle. *Democratic Experiments in Africa: Regime Transitions in Comparative Perspective.* Cambridge: Cambridge University Press, 1997.

Brinks, Daniel, and Michael Coppedge. "Diffusion Is no Illusion: Neighbor Emulation in the Third Wave of Democracy." *Comparative Political Studies* 39, no. 4 (May 2006): 463–89.

Brooker, Paul. *Non-Democratic Regimes: Theory, Government, and Politics.* New York: St. Martin's Press, 2000.

Brown, Nathan. "Egypt's Constitutional Ghost." *Foreignaffairs.com.* February 15, 2011. http://www.foreignaffairs.com/articles/67453/nathan-j-brown/egypts-constitutional -ghosts. Accessed on June 9, 2011.

Brownlee, Jason. "Authoritarianism After 1989: From Regime Types to Transnational Processes." *Harvard International Review* (winter 2010): 45–49.

———. *Authoritarianism in the Age of Democratization*. New York: Cambridge University Press, 2007.

———. "The Decline of Pluralism in Mubarak's Egypt." *Journal of Democracy* 13, no. 4 (October 2002): 6–14.

———. "The Heir Apparency of Gamal Mubarak." *Arab Studies Journal* (fall 2007–spring 2008): 36–56.

———. "A New Generation of Autocracy in Egypt." *The Brown Journal of World Affairs* XIV, no. I (fall/winter 2007): 73–85.

———. "Ruling Parties and Durable Authoritarianism." *CDDRL Working Papers*, no. 23. October 28, 2004.

———. "And Yet They Persist: Explaining Survival and Transition in Neopatrimonial Regimes." *Studies in Comparative International Development* 37, no. 3: 35–63.

Brownlee, Jason, and Joshua Stacher. "Change of Leader, Continuity of System: Nascent Liberalization in Post-Mubarak Egypt." *APSA Comparative Democratization Newsletter* 9, no. 2 (May 2011): 1, 4–9.

Brumberg, Daniel. "Authoritarian Legacies and Reform Strategies in the Arab World." In *Political Liberalization and Democratization in the Arab World*: volume 1, *Theoretical Perspectives*, ed. Brynen, Korany, and Noble. Boulder, CO: Lynne Rienner, 1995.

———. "Survival Strategies vs. Democratic Bargains: The Politics of Economic Reform in Contemporary Egypt." In *The Politics of Economic Reform in the Middle East*, ed. Henry J. Barkey. New York: St. Martin's Press, 1992.

Brynen, Rex, Bahgat Korany, and Paul Noble, eds. *Political Liberalization and Democratization in the Arab World*. Vol. 1. Boulder, CO: Lynne Rienner, 1995.

Bunce, Valerie. "Rethinking Recent Democratization: Lessons from the Postcommunist Experience." *World Politics* 55 (January 2003): 167–92.

Carapico, Sheila. "Foreign Aid for Promoting Democracy in the Arab World." *Middle East Journal* 56, no. 3 (summer 2002): 379–95.

———. "No Exit: Yemen's Existential Crisis." *Middle East Report Online*. May 3, 2011. http://www.merip.org/mero/mero050311-1. Accessed on May 12, 2011.

Cardoso, Fernando Henrique. "On the Characterization of Authoritarian Regimes in Latin America." In *The New Authoritarianism in Latin America*, ed. David Collier. Princeton, NJ: Princeton University Press, 1979.

Carothers, Thomas. "The End of the Transition Paradigm." *Journal of Democracy* 13, no. 1 (January 2002): 5–21.

Chehabi, Houchang E., and Juan Linz, eds. *Sultanistic Regimes*. Baltimore, MD: Johns Hopkins University Press, 1998.

Chick, Kristen. "Beating Death of Egyptian Businessman Khalid Said Spotlights Police Brutality." *Christian Science Monitor*. June 18, 2010. Available at http://www.csmonitor.com/World/Middle-East/2010/0618/Beating-death-of-Egyptian-businessman-Khalid-Said-spotlights-police-brutality. Accessed on November 18, 2010.

Chilcote, Ronald. *Theories of Comparative Politics.* Boulder, CO: Westview Press, 1994.

Collier, David, ed. *The New Authoritarianism in Latin America.* Princeton, NJ: Princeton University Press, 1979.

Collier, Ruth, and David Collier. *Shaping the Political Arena.* Princeton, NJ: Princeton University Press, 1991.

Cook, Steven A. "The Right Way to Promote Arab Reform." *Foreign Affairs* 84, no. 2 (March/April 2005): 91–102.

———. *Ruling but Not Governing: The Military and Political Development in Egypt, Algeria, and Turkey.* Baltimore, MD: Johns Hopkins University Press, 2007.

Cooley, Alexander, and Daniel H. Nexon. "Bahrain Base Politics." *Foreignaffairs.com.* April 5, 2011. http://www.foreignaffairs.com/atricles/67700/alexander-cooley-and-daniel-h-nexon/bahrains-base-politics?page+show. Accessed on May 10, 2011.

Correspondent. "Consolidating Bashar." *Middle East International.* July 14, 2000.

Coser, Lewis A. *Masters of Sociological Thought.* New York: Harcourt Brace Jovanovich, 1971.

"'Day of Rage' for Syrians Fails to Draw Protesters." *New York Times.* February 4, 2011. http://nytimes.com/2011/02/05/world/middleeast/05syria.html?_r=1&refsyria. Accessed on May 25, 2011.

Di Lampedusa, Giuseppe. *The Leopard.* Trans. Archibald Colquhoun. Milan: Feltrinelli Editore, 1958.

"Down with Duties." *al-Ahram Weekly.* September 9–15, 2004.

Dunne, Michele. "The Baby, the Bathwater, and the Freedom Agenda in the Middle East." *The Washington Quarterly* 32, no. 1 (January 2009): 129–41.

"Egypt Refutes Israel's Claims Regarding the Intifada." *Egyptian State Information.* March 12, 2001. http://www.sis.gov.eg/online/html3/0120321f.htm. Accessed on October 25, 2004.

"Egypt's Interior Minister Seeks Riot-control as Food Prices Spike." *World Tribune.com.* May 20, 2008. http://www.worltribune.com/worldtribune/wtarc/2008/me_egypt0154_05_20.asp. Accessed on May 12, 2011.

"Egypt's Military Plays Neutral Role in Protests." National Public Radio. January 31, 2011. http://www.npr.org/2011/01/31/133365418/Egypt-Analysis. Accessed on May 24, 2011.

"Egypt's President Sidesteps Question on Successor." *AFP.* May 19, 2010.

Ehteshami, Anoushiravan, and Emma Murphy. "The Transformation of the Corporatist State in the Middle East." *Third World Quarterly* 17 (1996): 753–72.

Eisenstadt, S. N., and Rene Lemarchand, eds. *Political Clientelism, Patronage, and Development.* London: Sage Publications, 1981.

"Elections Brings Little Hope of Change." *Middle East International.* April 4, 2003.

Essem El-Din, Gamal. "Democratisation Debate." *al-Ahram Weekly.* May 1–7, 2003.

———. "More Than Window-Dressing?" *al-Ahram Weekly.* June 19–25, 2003.

Fahmy, Khaled. *All the Pasha's Men: Mehmed Ali, His Army, and the Making of Modern Egypt.* New York: Cambridge University Press, 1997.

Fish, M. Steven. "Islam and Authoritarianism." *World Politics* 55, no. 1 (October 2002): 4–37.

Fisk, Robert. *Pity the Nation: Lebanon at War.* Oxford: Oxford University Press, 1990.

Fleron, Frederick. "System Attributes and Career Attributes: The Soviet Political Leadership System, 1952–1965." In *Comparative Communist Political Leadership,* ed. Carl Beck, 43–85. New York: McKay, 1973.

"Freedom in the World 2011: The Authoritarian Challenge to Democracy." Freedom House. Washington, DC, January 2011. http://www.freedomhouse.org/template.cfm?page=1310. Accessed on June 2, 2011.

Fukuyama, Francis. "Political Order in Egypt." *The American Interest* (May–June 2011). http://www.the-american-interest.com/article.cfm?piece=953. Accessed on June 6, 2011.

Gandhi, Jennifer. *Political Institutions Under Dictatorship.* New York: Cambridge University Press, 2008.

Gandhi, Jennifer, and Adam Przeworski. "Authoritarian Institutions and the Survival of Autocrats." *Comparative Political Studies* 40 (November 2007): 1279–1301.

Gause, F. Gregory, III. "Can Democracy Stop Terrorism?" *Foreign Affairs* 84, no. 5 (September/October 2005): 62–76.

———. "The Middle East Academic Community and the 'Winter of Arab Discontent': Why Did We Miss It?" In *Seismic Shift: Understanding Change in the Middle East,* ed. Ellen Laipson, 11–28. Washington, DC: Stimson Center 2011.

George, Alan. *Syria: Neither Bread nor Freedom.* London: Zed Books, 2003.

Gerges, Fawiz. *The Superpowers and the Middle East: Regional and International Politics, 1955–1967.* Boulder, CO: Westview Press, 1994.

Gerth H. H., and C. Wright Mills. *From Max Weber: Essays in Sociology.* London: Routledge, 1948.

El-Ghobashy, Mona. "Egypt Looks Ahead to Portentous Year." *Middle East Report Online.* February 2, 2005. http://www.merip.org/mero020205. Accessed on May 12, 2011.

———. "The Praxis of the Egyptian Revolution." *Middle East Report* 258 (spring 2011): 2–13.

Goldberg, Ellis. "Mubarakism Without Mubarak." *Foreignaffairs.com.* February 11, 2011. http://www.foreignaffairs.com/articles/67416/ellis-goldberg/mubarakism-without-mubarak. Accessed on May 11, 2011.

"Grounded for Greenbacks." *Cairo Times.* March 7–13, 2002.

Habib, Randa. "Syrian Regime Likely to Survive Uprising: Analysts." AFP. May 10, 2011. http://www.google.com/hostednews/afp/article/ALeqM5ilm4fDPB-lFCGFlsGgNQHFsd5s4g?docId=CNG.d9be2af4c7111ceebb9f06f4d37012ee.3f1. Accessed on May 25, 2011.

Haddad, Bassam. "Why Syria Is Not Next . . . So Far." *Jadaliyya.com.* March 9, 2011.

http://www.jadaliyya.com/pages/index/844/why-syria-is-not-next-.-.-.-so-far_with
-arabic-translation-. Accessed on May 24, 2011.

Haggard, Stephen, and Robert Kaufman. *The Political Economy of Democratic Transitions*. Princeton, NJ: Princeton University Press, 1995.

Hamalawy, Hossam. "The General's Budget." *3arabawy.net*. November 29, 2006. http://www.arabawy.org/2006/11/29/adlys-budget. Accessed on May 12, 2011.

———. "Powerful Egyptian Spy Chief No Longer Behind the Scenes." *Los Angeles Times*. February 8, 2005.

Hanieh, Adam. "Egypt's Orderly Transition?: International Aid and the Rush to Structural Adjustment." *Jadaliyya.com*. May 29, 2011. http://www.jadaliyya.com/pages/index/1711/egypt's-'orderly-transition'-international-aid-and. Accessed on June 23, 2011.

Harb, Imad. "The Egyptian Military in Politics: Disengagement or Accommodation?" *Middle East Journal* 57, no. 2 (spring 2003): 269–90.

Harik, Iliya. "Democracy, 'Arab Exceptionalism,' and Social Science." *Middle East Journal* 60, no. 4 (autumn 2006): 664–84.

Heikal, Mohamad Hassanein. *Autumn of Fury: The Assassination of Sadat*. London: Andre Deutsch, 1983.

El-Hennawy, Noha. "Pluralism at Death's Door?" *Egypt Today*. September 2004.

Henry, Clement Moore, and Robert Springborg. *Globalization and the Politics of Development in the Contemporary Middle East*. New York: Cambridge University Press, 2010.

———. "A Tunisian Solution for Egypt's Military." *Foreignaffairs.com*. February 21, 2011. http://www.foreignaffairs.com/articles/67475/clement-m-henry-and-robert-spring borg/ a-tunisian-solution-for-egypts-military. Accessed on May 11, 2011.

Herb, Michael. *All in the Family: Absolutism, Revolution, and Democracy in the Middle East*. Albany: State University of New York Press, 1999.

Heydemann, Steven. *Authoritarianism in Syria: Institutions and Social Conflict, 1946–1970*. Ithaca, NY: Cornell University Press, 1999.

———. "Defending the Discipline." *Journal of Democracy* 13, no. 3 (July 2002): 102–8.

———. "Tunisia and the Future of Democracy Promotion in the Arab World." *The Middle East Channel*. January 24, 2011. http://mideast.foreignpolicy.com/posts/2011/01/24/tunisia_and_the_future_of_democracy_promotion_in_the_arab_world. Accessed on May 10, 2011.

———. "Upgrading Authoritarianism in the Arab World." Analysis Paper, The Saban Center for Middle East Policy and the Brooking Institution, 13. Washington, DC: Brookings Institute, October 2007.

Hinnebusch, Raymond. *Authoritarian Power and State Formation in B'athist Syria*. Boulder, CO: Westview Press, 1990.

———. "Civil Society in Syria." In *Civil Society in the Middle East*, vol. 1, ed. Augusts Richard Norton, 214–42. Boston: E. J. Brill, 1995.

———. *Egyptian Politics Under Sadat: The Post-Populist Development of an Authoritarian-Modernizing State.* Cambridge: Cambridge University Press, 1985.

———. *The International Politics of the Middle East.* Manchester, England: Manchester University Press, 2003.

———. "Liberalization in Syria: The Struggle of Economic and Political Rationality." In *Contemporary Syria: Liberalization Between Cold War and Cold Peace,* ed. Eberhard Kienle, 97–113. London: British Academic Press, 1994.

———. "Liberalization Without Democratization in 'Post-Populist' Authoritarian States." In *Citizenship and the State in the Middle East,* ed. Davis, Butenschon, and Hassassian. Syracuse, NY: Syracuse University Press, 2000.

———. "The Politics of Economic Liberalization: Comparing Egypt and Syria." In *The State and Global Change: the Political Economy of Transition in the Middle East and North Africa,* ed. Hassan Hakimian and Ziba Moshaver, 111–34. Richmond, VA: Cruzon Press, 2001.

———. *Syria: Revolution from Above.* London: Routlege, 2002.

Hinnebusch, Raymond, and Anoushiravan Ehteshami, eds. *The Foreign Policies of Middle East States.* Boulder, CO: Lynne Rienner, 2002.

Howeidy, Amira. "Rights at a Crossroad." *al-Ahram Weekly.* May 18–24, 2000.

Huntington, Samuel P. *Political Order in Changing Societies.* New Haven, CT: Yale University Press, 1968.

———. *The Third Wave of Democratization.* Norman: Oklahoma University Press, 1991.

International Crisis Group. "Popular Protest in North Africa and the Middle East (I): Egypt Victorious?" *ICG Middle East Report,* no. 101. February 24, 2011.

———. "Reforming Egypt: In Search of a Strategy." *ICG Middle East Report,* no. 46. October 4, 2005.

———. "Syria Under Bashar II: Domestic Policy Challenges." *ICG Middle East Report,* no. 24. February 11, 2004.

International Monetary Fund Country Report, no. 10/94. April 2010. http://www.imf.org/external/pubs/ft/scr/2010/cr1094.pdf. Accessed on May 24, 2011.

"Interview with Syrian President Bashar al-Assad." *Wall Street Journal.* January 31, 2011. http://online.wsj.com/article/SB10001424052748703833204576114712441122894.html. Accessed on May 25, 2011.

Irby, Charles Leonard. *Travels in Egypt and Nubia, Syria and the Holy Land.* London: John Murray, 1845.

Issawi, Charles. "Social Structure and Ideology in Iraq, Lebanon, Syria, and the UAR." In *Modernization of the Arab World,* ed. Jack Howell Thompson, 141–49. Princeton, NJ: Van Nostrand, 1966.

Jackson, Robert, and Carl Rosberg. *Personal Rule in Black Africa: Prince, Autocrat, Prophet, Tyrant.* Berkeley: University of California Press, 1982.

Jarrah, Najm. "Changing of the Guard in Damascus." *Middle East International.* June 16, 2000.

Kassem, May. *In the Guise of Democracy: Governance in Contemporary Egypt.* London: Ithaca Press, 1999.

Kassem, Maye. *Egyptian Politics: The Dynamics of Authoritarian Rule.* Boulder, CO: Lynne Rienner, 2004.

Kerr, Malcolm. *The Arab Cold War: Gamal Abd al-Nasir and His Rivals, 1958–1970.* Oxford: Oxford University Press, 1971.

Khalidi, Rashid. "The Arab Spring." *The Nation.* March 3, 2011. http://www.thenation.com/article/158991/arab-spring. Accessed on May 10, 2011.

Khalil, Ashraf. "New Thinking, New Egypt." *Cairo Times.* September 19–25, 2002.

Kienle, Eberhard, ed. *Contemporary Syria: Liberalization Between Cold War and Cold Peace.* London: British Academic Press, 1994.

———. *A Grand Delusion: Democracy and Economic Reform in Egypt.* London: I. B. Tauris, 2001.

———. "More Than a Response to Islamism: The Political Deliberalization of Egypt in the 1990s." *Middle East Journal* 52, no. 2 (spring 1998): 219–35.

Kilo, Michel. "Syrian-American Relations: Discussing Bahjat Sulayman's Article." *An-Nahar.* May 21, 2003.

King, Stephen J. *The New Authoritarianism in the Middle East and North Africa.* Bloomington: Indiana University Press, 2010.

Kissinger, Henry. *Years of Upheaval.* Boston: Little, Brown, and Company, 1982.

Korany, Bahgat, Rex Brynen, and Paul Noble, eds. *Political Liberalization and Democratization in the Arab World,* vol. 2, *Comparative Experiences.* Boulder, CO: Westview Press, 1998.

Landis, Joshua. "The United States and Reform in Syria." *Syria Report,* no. 18 (May 2004): 4–6.

Lenczowski, George. "Radical Regimes in Egypt, Syria, and Iraq: Some Comparative Observations on Ideologies and Practices." *The Journal of Politics* 28, no. 1 (February 1966): 29–56.

Lesch, David. *The New Lion of Damascus: Bashar al-Asad and Modern Syria.* New Haven, CT: Yale University Press, 2005.

Leverett, Flynt. *Inheriting Syria: Bashar's Trial by Fire.* Washington, DC: Brookings Institution Press, 2005.

Levinson, Charles. "$50 Billion Later, Taking Stock of US Aid to Egypt." *Christian Science Monitor.* April 12, 2004.

Levinson, Charles, and Margaret Coker. "The Secret Rally that Sparked an Uprising." *Wall Street Journal.* February 11, 2011.

Levitsky, Steven, and Lucan Way. "The Rise of Competitive Authoritarianism." *Journal of Democracy* 13, no. 2 (April 2002): 51–65.

Lichbach, Mark, and Alan Zuckerman, eds. *Comparative Politics: Rationality, Culture, and Structure.* Cambridge: Cambridge University Press, 1997.

Lieberman, Robert C. "Ideas, Institutions, and Political Order: Explaining Political Change." *American Political Science Review* 96, no. 4 (2002): 697–712.

Lindsey, Ursula. "The Suddenly New Egypt." *Chronicle of Higher Education.* March 13, 2011.

Linz, Juan. "An Authoritarian Regime: The Case of Spain." In *Mass Politics: Studies in Political Sociology,* ed. Erik Allard and Stein Rokkan. New York: The Free Press, 1970.

Lobmeyer, Hans Gunter. "Al-Dimuqratiyya Hiyya al-Hal?" In *Contemporary Syria: Liberalization Between Cold War and Cold Peace,* ed. Eberhard Kienle, 81–96. London: British Academic Press, 1994.

Lucas, Russell E. "Monarchical Authoritarianism: Survival and Political Liberalization in a Middle Eastern Regime Type." *International Journal of Middle East Studies* 36 (2004): 103–19.

Lust-Okar, Ellen. *Structuring Conflict in the Arab World: Incumbents, Opponents, and Institutions.* Cambridge: Cambridge University Press, 2005.

El-Mahdi, Rabab. "Enough: Egypt's Quest for Democracy." *Comparative Political Studies* 42, no. 8 (2009): 1011–39.

"Majlis al-Sh'ab al-Suri Yutalib b-mahakma Khadam b-tihma al-kiana" [Syrian people's assembly request Khaddam is charged with high treason]. *al-Arabiaya.* December 31, 2005. http://www.alarabiya.net/articles/2005/12/31/19936.html.

"Map of Freedom 2011." Freedom House. http://www.freedomhouse.org/template. cfm?page=363&year=2011. Accessed on June 2, 2011.

Marsot, Alaf Lutfi Al-Sayyid. *A History of Egypt: From the Arab Conquest to the Present.* Cambridge: Cambridge University Press, 1985.

McFaul, Michael. "The Fourth Wave of Democracy and Dictatorship: Noncooperative Transition in the Postcommunist World." *World Politics* 54 (January 2002): 212–44.

Mitchell, Timothy. "The Middle East in the Past and Future of Social Science." In *the Politics of Knowledge: Area Studies and the Disciplines,* 9–12. Berkeley, CA: GAIA Books, 2003. http://escholarship.org/uc/item/3618c31x. Accessed on January 10, 2011.

———, ed. *Questions of Modernity.* Minneapolis: University of Minnesota Press, 2000.

Moustafa, Tamir. *The Struggle for Constitutional Power: Law, Politics, and Economic Development in Egypt.* New York: Cambridge University Press, 2007.

"Mubarak Mocks Opposition Proposed Shadow Parliament." *al-Masry al-Youm.* December 19, 2010. http://www.almasryalyoum.com/en/node/275490. Accessed on May 31, 2011.

"My Word on History." Broadcast on Egyptian State Television. April 24–26, 2005.

North, Douglass. *Institutions, Institutional Change, and Economic Performance.* New York: Cambridge University Press, 1990.

Norton, Augustus Richard, ed. *Civil Society in the Middle East.* Vols. 1 and 2. Boston: E. J. Brill, Academic Publishers, 1995 and 1998.

Obaid, Nawaf. "There Will Be no Upraising in Saudi Arabia." *The Middle East Channel*. March 10, 2011. http://www.foreignpolicy.com/articles/2011/03/10/there_will_be_ no_uprising_in_saudi_arabia. Accessed on May 10, 2011.

Obama, Barack. "The President's Speech in Cairo: A New Beginning." Cairo. June 4, 2009. http://www.whitehouse.gov/blog/NewBeginning/. Accessed on December 14, 2010.

O'Donnell, Guillermo, and Philippe Schmitter. *Transitions from Authoritarian Rule: Tentative Conclusions About Uncertain Democracies.* Vol. 4. Baltimore, MD: Johns Hopkins University Press, 1986.

Okasha, Saeed. "In with the New." *Cairo Times* 5, no. 12. May 24–30, 2001.

Ouda, Jihad. *Gamal Mubarak: Tajdid al-Libiraliyya al-Wataniyya.* Cairo: Dar al-Huriyya, 2004.

Ouda, Jihad, Negad al-Borai, and Hafiz Abu Saada. *A Door onto the Desert: Egyptian Legislative Elections of 2000.* Cairo: United Group and Fredich Nuemann Foundation, 2001.

Perthes, Volker. *The Political Economy of Syria Under Asad.* London: I. B. Tauris, 1995.

———. "Syria: Difficult Inheritance." In *Arab Elites: Negotiating the Politics of Change,* ed. Volker Perthes, 87–114. Boulder, CO: Lynne Rienner, 2004.

———. *Syria Under Bashar al-Asad: Modernisation and the Limits of Change.* New York: Routledge, 2004.

"Petition Calls for Elections, Nominates Amr Moussa." *Arabic News.* March 10, 2004. http://www.arabicnews.com/ansub/Daily/Day/040310/2004031002.html. Accessed on October 25, 2010.

Poliak, Abraham N. *Feudalism in Egypt, Syria, Palestine, and Lebanon, 1250–1900.* London: Royal Asiatic Society, 1939.

Pool, David. "The Links Between Economic and Political Liberalization." In *Economic and Political Liberalization in the Middle East,* ed. Tim Niblock and Emma Murphy. London: British Academic Press, 1993.

Posusney, Marsha Pripstein. *Labor and the State in Egypt.* New York: Columbia University Press, 1997.

Posusney, Marsha Pripstein, and Michele Angrist, eds. *Authoritarianism in the Middle East: Power and Resistance.* Boulder, CO: Lynne Rienner, 2005.

Pratt, Nicola. *Democracy and Authoritarianism in the Arab World.* Boulder, CO: Lynne Rienner, 2007.

"Profile: Amr Moussa." BBC News. July 23, 2002. http://news.bbc.co.uk/1/hi/world/middle _east/1766776.stm. Accessed on October 25, 2004.

Qandil, 'Abd al-Halim. *Did al-Ra'is Akhtar hamlat Maqalat didda hukm Al-ailah.* Cairo: Dar al-Merit, 2005.

Al-Qassemi, Sultan. "Twilight of the Arab Republics." *The Middle East Channel.* January 17, 2011. http://mideast.foreignpolicy.com/posts/2011/01/17/twilight_of_the_ arab_republics. Accessed on May 10, 2011.

Quilty, Jim. "The Politics of Mourning." *Middle East International.* June 30, 2000.

Quinlivin, James T. "Coup-Proofing: Its Practice and Consequences in the Middle East." *International Security* 24, no. 2 (1999): 131–65.

"Remarks by President George W. Bush at the 20th Anniversary of the National Endowment for Democracy." National Endowment for Democracy. Washington, DC: United States Chamber of Commerce, November 6, 2003. http://www.ned.org/george-w-bush/remarks-by-president-george-w-bush-at-the-20th-anniversary. Accessed on June 2, 2011.

Ricciardone, Frances. "Egypt Actions Louder than Words—Gamal Mubarak and the Presidency." *WikiLeaks.* April 3, 2006. http://www.wikileaks.ch/cable/2006/04/06CAIRO 2010.html. Accessed on May 11, 2011.

Richards, Alan, and John Waterbury. *A Political Economy of the Middle East.* 3d ed. Boulder, CO: Westview Press, 2007.

Rosen, Nir. "Syria: The Revolution Will be Weaponised." *al-Jazeera English.* September 23, 2011. http://english.aljazeera.net/indepth/features/2011/09/2011923115735281764.html.

Rutherford, Bruce. *Egypt After Mubarak: Liberalism, Islam and Democracy in the Arab World.* Princeton, NJ: Princeton University Press, 2008.

Sachs, Susan. "Transition in Syria: Syrians See in the Heir Possibility of Progress." *New York Times.* June 11, 2000. http://www.nytimes.com/2000/06/11/world/transition-in-syria-syrians-see-in-the-heir-possibility-of-progress.html?ref=basharalassad. Accessed on May 24, 2011.

Salame, Ghassan, ed. *Democracy Without Democrats: The Renewal of Politics in the Muslim World.* London: I. B. Tauris, 1994.

Sallam, Hesham. "Striking Back at Egyptian Workers." *Middle East Report* 259 (summer 2011).

Schemm, Paul. "Egypt: Economic Reform Only." *Middle East International* (October 8, 2004): 28.

———. "He Got the Job Done." *Cairo Times.* September 5–11, 2002.

Schlumberger, Oliver, ed. *Debating Arab Authoritarianism.* Stanford: Stanford University Press, 2007.

Schwedler, Jillian, Joshua Stacher, and Stacey Philbrick Yadav. "Three Powerfully Wrong— and Wrongly Powerfully—American Narratives about the Arab Spring." *Jadaliyya.com.* June 10, 2011. http://www.jadaliyya.com/pages/index/1826/three-powerfully-wrong_and-wrongly-powerful_americ. Accessed on June 24, 2011.

Scobey, Margaret. "Academics See the Military in Decline, But Retaining Strong Influence." *WikiLeaks.* September 23, 2009. http://www.wikileaks.ch/cable/2008/09/08CAIRO2091 .html. Accessed on June 14, 2011.

———. "Scenesetter for General Petraeus' Visit to Egypt." *WikiLeaks.* December 21, 2008. http://wikileaks.ch/cable/2008/12/08cairo2543.html. Accessed on May 11, 2011.

Scott, James C. "Patron-Client Politics and Political Change in Southeast Asia." In

Friends, Followers, and Factions: A Reader in Political Clientelism, ed. Schmidt, Guasti, Lande, and Scott. Berkeley: University of California Press, 1977.

Seale, Patrick. *Asad: The Struggle for the Middle East.* Berkeley: California University Press, 1988.

———. *The Struggle for Syria.* Oxford: Oxford University Press, 1965.

"Secretary Clinton Calls Egyptian Vice President Omar Soliman." *DipNote Blog.* February 2, 2011. http://blogs.state.gov/index.php/site/entry/clinton_calls_egyptian_vp_omar_soliman. Accessed on May 24, 2011.

Shadid, Anthony. "Syrian Businessman Becomes Magnet for Anger and Dissent." *New York Times.* April 30, 2011. http://www.nytimes.com/2011/05/01/world/asia/01makhlouf.html. Accessed on May 24, 2011.

———. "Syrian Elite to Fight Protests to 'the End.'" *New York Times.* May 10, 2011. http://www.nytimes.com/2011/05/11/world/middleeast/11makhlouf.html?ref=anthonyshadid. Accessed on June 27, 2011.

Sharabi, Hisham. *Neopatriarchy: A Theory of Distorted Change in Arab Society.* Oxford: Oxford University Press, 1992.

Shehata, Dina. *'Auda al-Siyasiysa: al-Harakat al-ihtijajat al-Jadida fi Masr.* Cairo: Center for Political and Strategic Studies, 2010.

———. "The Fall of the Pharaoh." *Foreign Affairs* 90, no. 3 (May/June 2010): 26–32.

Shehata, Samer. "Political Succession in Egypt." *Middle East Policy* IV, no. 3 (2002).

———. *Shop Floor Culture and Politics in Egypt.* Albany: State University of New York Press, 2009.

Shehata, Samer, and Joshua Stacher. "Boxing in the Brothers." *Middle East Report Online.* August 2007. http://www.merip.org/mero/mero080807. Accessed on January 26, 2012.

———. "The Brotherhood Goes to Parliament." *Middle East Report* 240 (fall 2006).

Shlaim, Avi. *The Iron Wall: Israel and the Arab World.* London: Penguin, 2000.

Singerman, Diane. *Avenues of Participation: Family, Politics, and Networks in Urban Quarters of Cairo.* Princeton, NJ: Princeton University Press, 1996.

Slackman, Michael. "Arab States Cool to Obama Pleas for Peace Gesture." *New York Times.* June 3, 2009.

Slater, Dan. "The Architecture of Authoritarianism: Southeast Asia and the Regeneration of Democratization Theory." *Taiwan Journal of Democracy* 2 (December 2006): 1–22.

———. "Iron Cage in an Iron Fist: Authoritarian Institutions and the Personalization of Power in Malaysia." *Comparative Politics* 36, no. 1 (October 2003): 81–101.

———. *Ordering Power: Contentious Politics and Authoritarian Leviathans in Southeast Asia.* New York: Cambridge University Press, 2010.

Smith, Benjamin. *Hard Times in the Land of Plenty: Oil Politics in Iran and Indonesia.* Ithaca, NY: Cornell University Press, 2007.

Soliman, Samer. *Al-Nizam al-Qawi wa al-Dawla al-Da'ifa: Al-Azma al-Maliyya wa al-Taghyir al-Syasi fil Mis 'Ahd Mubarak* [Strong regime, weak state: The fiscal crisis and political change in Egypt under Mubarak]. Cairo: al-Dar, 2006.

Springborg, Robert. "Approaches to the Understanding of Egypt." In *Ideology and Power in the Middle East,* ed. Peter Chelkowski and Robert Pranger. Durham, NC: Duke University Press, 1988.

———. *Family, Power, and Politics in Egypt.* Philadelphia: University of Pennsylvania Press, 1982.

———. *Mubarak's Egypt: Fragmentation of the Political Order.* Boulder, CO: Westview Press, 1989.

Stacher, Joshua. "Blame the SCAF for Egypt's Problems." *The Middle East Channel.* October 11, 2011. http://mideast.foreignpolicy.com/posts/2011/10/11/blame_the_scaf_for_egypts_problems

———. "The Brothers and the Wars." *Middle East Report* 250 (spring 2009): 2–8.

———. "A Democracy with Fangs and Claws and its Effect on Egyptian Political Culture." *Arab Studies Quarterly* 23, no. 3 (summer 2001): 83–99.

———. "Egypt: The Anatomy of Succession." *Review of African Political Economy* 35, no. 2 (2008): 301–14.

———. "Egypt Without Mubarak." *Middle East Report Online.* April 7, 2011. http://www.merip.org/mero/mero040711. Accessed on June 1, 2011.

———. "Gamal Mubarak's Journey to Power." *Daily Star.* November 3, 2004.

———. "NDP Conference: A Leap Forward or Succession?" *Arab Reform Bulletin.* October 18, 2006.

———. "Parties Over: The Demise of Egypt's Opposition Parties." *The British Journal of Middle Eastern Studies* 31, no. 2 (November 2004): 215–33.

———. "Reinterpreting Authoritarian Power: Syria's Hereditary Succession." *Middle East Journal* 65, no. 2 (spring 2011): 197–212.

———. "Rhetorical Acrobatics and Reputations: Egypt's National Council for Human Rights." *Middle East Report* 235 (summer 2005).

Stepan, Alfred, and Graeme Robertson. "An 'Arab' More Than a 'Muslim' Democracy Gap." *Journal of Democracy* 14, no. 3 (July 2003): 30–44.

Stogel, Stewart. "U.N.: Stumbling, Bumbling and Payola." *Newsmax.com.* May 23, 2003. http://www.newsmax.com/archives/articles/2003/5/23/152128.shtml. Accessed on May 11, 2010.

Sukkar, Nabil. "The Crisis of 1986 and Syria's Plan for Reform." In *Contemporary Syria: Liberalization between Cold War and Cold Peace,* ed. Eberhard Kienle, 26–41. London: British Academic Press, 1994.

Suleiman, Bahjat. *al-Safir.* May 15, 2003.

Svolik, Milan W. "Power Sharing and Leadership Dynamics in Authoritarian Regimes." *American Journal of Political Science* 53 (April 2009): 477–94.

Tilly, Charles. "Does Modernization Breed Revolution?" *Comparative Politics* 5, no. 3 (April 1973): 425–47.

"Tortured and Killed: Hamza al-Khateeb, Age 13." *al-Jazeera English.* May 31, 2011. http://english.aljazeera.net/indepth/features/2011/05/201153185927813389.html. Accessed on June 22, 2011.

"Trying to Fit In." *Syria Today* (winter 2004).

Tsebelis, George. *Veto Players: How Political Institutions Work.* Princeton, NJ: Princeton University Press, 2002.

Van Dam, Nikolaos. *The Struggle for Power in Syria.* London: I. B. Tauris, 1979.

Vitalis, Robert. "The Democratization Industry and the Limits of the New Interventionism." *Middle East Report* 187/188 (March–June 1994): 46–50.

———. *When Capitalist Collide: Business Conflict and the End of Empire in Egypt.* Berkeley: University of California Press, 1995.

Waldner, David. *State Building and Late Development.* Ithaca, NY: Cornell University Press, 1999.

Waterbury, John. *The Egypt of Nasser and Sadat: A Political Economy of Two Regimes.* Princeton, NJ: Princeton University Press, 1983.

Weaver, Mary-Anne. "Pharaohs-in-Waiting." *Atlantic Monthly.* October 2003.

Weber, Max. "Bureaucracy." In *The Anthropology of the State*, ed. Sharma and Gupta, 49–70. Oxford: Blackwell Publishing, 2006.

Wedeen, Lisa. *Ambiguities of Domination: Politics, Rhetoric, and Symbols in Contemporary Syria.* Chicago: University of Chicago Press, 1999.

———. *Peripheral Visions: Public, Power, and Performance in Yemen.* Chicago: University of Chicago Press, 2008.

"What Happens if Assad Goes? Government Opposed to Syria's Still Fear his Downfall." *The Economist.* May 19, 2011. http://www.economist.com/node/18713660?story_id=18713660&fsrc=rss. Accessed on May 25, 2011.

Whitaker, Brian. "Cairo Reformers Say Free Elections Is not on Agenda." *Guardian.* September 22, 2004.

———. "Egypt Scours Globe for Ideas on How to Update its Wobbling Infrastructure." *The Guardian.* September 21, 2004. http://wikileaks.ch/tag/EG_0.html. Accessed on December 14, 2010.

Wilson, Scott. "Syria's Baathist Under Siege." *Washington Post.* September 25, 2004.

Winegar, Jessica. "Taking out the Trash." *Middle East Report* 259 (summer 2011).

Wittes, Tamara Cofman. *Freedom's Unsteady March: America's Role in Building Arab Democracy.* Washington, DC: Brookings Institution Press, 2008.

Yacoubian, Mona. "Even if Bashar Wins, He Has Already Lost." *The Middle East Channel.* May 3, 2011. http://mideast.foreignpolicy.com/posts/2011/05/03/assad_loses_the_world_to_keep_his_throne. Accessed on May 25, 2011.

Al-Zain, Jihad. "A Lecture with Bahjat Sulayman." *An-Nahar.* May 2003.

Zisser, Eyal. *Asad's Legacy: Syria in Transition.* New York: New York University Press, 2001.

———. *Commanding Syria: Bashar al-Asad and the First Years in Power.* London: I. B. Tauris, 2007.

———. "Does Bashar al-Assad Rule Syria?" *Middle East Quarterly* 10, no. 1 (winter 2003): 15–23.

———. "Will Bashshar al-Asad Rule?" *Middle East Quarterly* 7, no. 3 (September 2000): 3–12.

Zoepf, Katherine, and Anthony Shadid. "Syrian Leader's Brother Seen as Enforcer of Crackdown." *New York Times.* June 7, 2011. http://www.nytimes.com/2011/06/08/world/middleeast/08syria.html?_r=1&ref=anthonyshadid. Accessed on June 27, 2011.

"1,100 Civilians Dead in Syrian Crackdown: Activists." *AFP.* May 25, 2011. http://www.abc.net/au/news/stories/2011/05/25/3226255.htm?section=justin. Accessed on May 25, 2011.

Author Interviews

'Abbas, Hassan. Political analyst. Damascus, October 21, 2003.

'Abd al-Hamid, 'Ammar. Writer and democracy activist. Damascus, October 8, 2003; December 1, 2003; March 2, 2005.

'Abd al-Nor, Ayman. Editor of *All 4 Syria* electronic newsletter. Damascus, November 2003; December 22, 2003.

'Abd al-Salam, M'an. Publisher and womens rights' activist. Damascus, March 1, 2005.

Abu Sa'ada, Hafiz. Director of the Egyptian Organization for Human Rights. Cairo, February 18, 2004; April 8, 2005.

Akkad, Hashim. Businessman and independent MP. Damascus, December 11, 2003.

Al-'Azm, Sadaq. Professor of philosophy at Damascus University. Damascus, November 3, 2003; December 20, 2003.

Badr, Hisham. Ambassador and former chief of staff to 'Amr Mosa. Cairo, April 2002.

Badrawy, Hosam. NDP Policies Secretariat member. Cairo, January 2009.

Bishay, 'Adil. HPC member, Shura Council Member, professor of economics at AUC. Cairo, February 25, 2004.

Boutros-Ghali, Boutros. Former UN secretary-general and National Council for Human Rights Chairman. Phone interview, Beirut to Paris, March 16, 2004.

Dardari, 'Abdallah. Head of the State Planning Commission. Damascus, March 2005.

'Ezz, Ahmad. Former NDP leader on Policies Secretariat. Cairo, September 11, 2005.

Haidr, Ziad. *al-Safir* journalist. Damascus, December 6, 2003; March 2004.

Hamalawy, Hossam. Journalist and blogger. Cairo, February 20, 2005.

Hamidi, Ibrahim. *al-Hayat* journalist. Damascus, November 9, 2003.

Hassan, Bahay al-Din. Director of the Cairo Institute for Human Rights Studies. Cairo, February 26, 2004; December 16 2004; April 7, 2005.

Hilal, 'Ali al-Din. Minister of youth (1999–2004) and former NDP member. Cairo, March 2, 2004; March 20, 2011.

Hill, Enid. Professor of political science. The American University in Cairo. Cairo, March 15, 2004.

Kamal, Mohamad. Former NDP member. Cairo, March 21, 2011.

Kassem, Hisham. Former manager of *al-Misri al-Yom*. Cairo, February 12, 2004.

al-Kawakbi, Salam. Civil society activist in Aleppo. Damascus, October 1, 2003.

Kilo, Michel. Civil society activist. Damascus, September 30, 2003; March 22, 2004.

Kitchen, Simon. Banker and economic consultant. Cairo, October 22, 2004.

Landis, Joshua. Historian at the Center for International Studies at the University of Oklahoma. Damascus, February 26, 2005.

al-Malih, Haytham. Head of the Human Rights Association in Syria. Damascus, December 6, 2003; March 23, 2004.

Mohy al-Din, Mahmoud. Minister of investment (2004–10) and NDP Policies Secretariat member. Cairo, December 12, 2005.

Mostapha, Hala. Analyst at the al-Ahram Center for Political and Strategic Studies. Cairo, February 26, 2004; March 2004.

Moubayed, Sami. Founder of the Syrian Young Entrepreneurs Association. Damascus, March 21, 2004.

Rabi'a, 'Amr Hashem. Parliament expert at the al-Ahram Center for Political and Strategic Studies. Cairo, February 17, 2004.

Sabahy, Hamdin. Independent MP. Cairo, March 1, 2004.

Sadowski, Yehya. Former professor of political science at American University of Beirut. Beirut, March 16, 2004.

Sa'id, 'Abd al-Men'im. Director of the al-Ahram Center for Political and Strategic Studies and member of the Policies Secretariat's Higher Policy Council. Cairo, May 3, 2004.

Saif al-Dawla, 'Aida. Human rights activist. Cairo, February 24, 2004; December 2, 2004.

Saif al-Islam, Ahmad. Director of the Hisham Mubarak Legal Center. Cairo, February 16, 2004; February 22, 2004.

Salah, Mohamad. Cairo bureau chief of *al-Hayat*. Cairo, February 9, 2004.

Sawi, 'Ali. Professor of political science at Cairo University. Cairo, February 15, 2004.

Schemm, Paul. Journalist. Cairo, March 2004; October 24, 2004.

Shams al-Din, 'Ali. Former NDP member. Cairo, February 25, 2004; March 2004.

Seale, Patrick. Journalist. Cairo, October 10, 2003.

Shab'an, Bothaina. Minister of expatriates (2000–2008). Damascus, March 24, 2004.

Shukar, 'Abd al-Gaffar. Political Bureau member of the Tugam'u Party and former head of Political Education in the ASU. Cairo, April 30, 2004.

Stienen, Petra. First secretary of the Netherlands embassy in Syria. Damascus, December 6, 2003.

Sukkar, Nabil. Economist and director of Syrian Consulting Bureau for Development and Investment (SCBI). Damascus, October 22, 2003.

Tabler, Andrew. Former consultant to *Syria Today*. Cairo, March 9, 2005.

al-Taqi, Samir. Member of the al-Faysil wing of the Communist Party. Damascus, December 2, 2003; December 29, 2003; March 2, 2005.

al-Taroty, Safinz. NDP youth member. Cairo, February 12, 2004.

Wali, Sharif. NDP Shura Council member. Cairo, March 6, 2004.

Additional Interviews

In the course of writing this book, I spoke with numerous people. Those most relevant to my research include:

In Syria
'Abdallah Dardari (head of State Planning Commission)
'Ali al-Atassi (*an-Nahar* journalist)
'Ali Salih (economist, Civil Society Movement member)
Anwar al-Bunni (lawyer and HRAS member)
Faris Tlas (CEO and businessman)
George Jabbour (MP, formal advisor to President Hafiz al-Asad)
Hisham Dajani (Civil Society Movement and democratic activist)
'Imad Shuebi (professor of philosophy, Damascus University)
Mohamad Sawwan (secretary-general of the Group for the Sake of United Democracy in Syria)
Osama al-Ansari (head of an NGO working with Expatriate Affairs)
Ratib Shallah (head of Syrian Chamber of Commerce)
Sarab al-Atassi (coordinator of Jamal al-Din al-Atassi Forum)
Zuhair Jannan (consultant to Syrian-Israeli peace negotiations during 1990s)

In Egypt
'Abd al-Halim Qandil (editor of *al-'Arabi* opposition newspaper)
'Abd al-Min'um Abu Futuh (member of the Muslim Brothers Guidance Council)
Abu 'Ala Madi (former member of the Muslim Brothers and Founder of al-Wasat Party)
'Assam al-Arian (member of the Muslim Brothers)
Ayman Nor (former MP)
Dia' al-Din Dawoud (president of Nasserist Party)
Gamal Essam al-Din (*al-Ahram Weekly* journalist)
Gasir 'Abd al-Razik (member of the Egyptian Organization for Human Rights)
Husayn 'Abd al-Razik (secretary-general of the Tugam'u Party)
Ibrahim Abaza (head of Economic Section of Wafd Party)
Mohamad Mahdi 'Akif (former general guide of the Muslim Brothers)

Mohamad Rageb (head of NDP in Shura Council)
Mohamad al-Sayid al-Sa'id (public intellectual)
Mohamad Sid Ahmad (journalist and liberal thinker)
Moheb Zaki (interim director of Ibn Khaldun Center)
Mostapha al-Sayid (professor of political science)
Mukhtar Nor (former member of the Muslim Brothers)
Nader Ferghany (coauthor of Arab Human Development Report and Director of al-
    Mishkat Research Center)
Nagla Mostapha (USAID Good Governance Section)
Negad al-Bora'i (director of the now-defunct Group for Democratic Development)
Rif'at Sa'id (president of the Tugam'u Party)
Sa'ad Eddin Ibrahim (sociologist and director of Ibn Khaldun Center)

Foreign Diplomats and Consultants
American: Michael Corbin; Ian McCary; Yael Lempert; Roger Kenna; Lisa Carle;
    William Roebuck; Steven O'Dowd
Canadian: Ulric Shannon; Aliya Mawani
Dutch: Peter Ellens; Petra Stienen
English: Claire Halperin; Mark Bell
Norwegian: Tor Kinsarvik Engen

INDEX

Stanford Studies in Middle Eastern and Islamic Societies and Cultures

Joel Beinin, *Stanford University*

Juan R. I. Cole, *University of Michigan*

Editorial Board

Asef Bayat, *University of Illinois at Urbana-Champaign*

Marilyn Booth, *University of Edinburgh*

Laurie Brand, *University of Southern California*

Saba Mahmood, *University of California, Berkeley*

Timothy Mitchell, *Columbia University*

Karen Pfeifer, *Smith College*

Rebecca L. Stein, *Duke University*

Bassam Haddad, *Business Networks in Syria: The Political Economy of Authoritarian Resilience*
2011

Noah Coburn, *Bazaar Politics: Power and Pottery in an Afghan Market Town*
2011

Laura Bier, *Revolutionary Womanhood: Feminisms, Modernity, and the State in Nasser's Egypt*
2011

Joel Beinin and Frédéric Vairel, editors, *Social Movements, Mobilization, and Contestation in the Middle East and North Africa*
2011

Samer Soliman, *The Autumn of Dictatorship: Fiscal Crisis and Political Change in Egypt under Mubarak*
2011

Rochelle A. Davis, *Palestinian Village Histories: Geographies of the Displaced*
2010

Haggai Ram, *Iranophobia: The Logic of an Israeli Obsession*
2009

John Chalcraft, *The Invisible Cage: Syrian Migrant Workers in Lebanon*
2008

Rhoda Kanaaneh, *Surrounded: Palestinian Soldiers in the Israeli Military*
2008

Asef Bayat, *Making Islam Democratic: Social Movements and the Post-Islamist Turn*
2007

Robert Vitalis, *America's Kingdom: Mythmaking on the Saudi Oil Frontier*
2006

Jessica Winegar, *Creative Reckonings: The Politics of Art and Culture in Contemporary Egypt*
2006

Joel Beinin and Rebecca L. Stein, editors, *The Struggle for Sovereignty: Palestine and Israel, 1993–2005*
2006